W9-BGW-089

Where the
Cherry Tree Grew

Also by Philip Levy

Fellow Travelers:
Indians and Europeans Contesting the Early American Trail

Where the Cherry Tree Grew

❧❧

The Story of Ferry Farm, George Washington's Boyhood Home

❧❧

Philip Levy

ST. MARTIN'S PRESS

NEW YORK

www.stmartins.com

Frontispiece drawing by Santosh Dhamat,
courtesy of the George Washington Foundation and Howard+Revis

LIBRARY OF CONGRESS CATALOGING-IN-PUBLICATION DATA

Levy, Philip, 1963–
    Where the cherry tree grew: the story of Ferry Farm, George
Washington's boyhood home / Philip Levy.
        pages   cm
    ISBN 978-0-312-64186-3 (hardcover)
    ISBN 978-1-250-02314-8 (e-book)
    1. Ferry Farm (Stafford County, Va.)—History.
2. Washington, George, 1732–1799—Homes and haunts—
Virginia—Stafford County.   3. Washington, George,
1732–1799—Childhood and youth.   4. Washington, George,
1732–1799—Family.   5. Historic preservation—Virginia—
Stafford County—Case studies.   I. Title.
    E312.5.L477 2013
    975.5'26—dc23

                                        2012040031

First Edition: February 2013

10 9 8 7 6 5 4 3 2 1

For Dave and Amy

Contents

❧❀❧

Where the Cherry Tree Grew

Introduction

❧❧

"Welcome to Ferry Farm"

Lights, Camera, Action. It's eastern Virginia in early July, so add to that some almost unbearable heat. Add, also, visitors—lots of them, all gathered for a well-promoted, high-profile public announcement of archaeological findings.

Curious locals and historically minded folks from far afield rubbed sweaty elbows with politicians including governors, a former senator, and a one-time presidential hopeful. Flags and bunting rustled in the occasional breeze, and in the hazy distance a man in eighteenth-century garb rode a brown horse back and forth for all to see. Closer in, a little boy dressed in similar, albeit smaller, costume, poked around and drew the lenses of the seemingly innumerable press photographers and TV cameramen.

The boy and the rider invoked two different sides of the long-gone man at the center of the day's festivities. On the one hand, we had the adult—a hero of the first order, a leader, a general, a president, an icon of the nation he helped found, and a face on its currency.[1]

On the other hand, there was the boy symbolizing the youth and optimism of a young nation and invoking a body of much-loved but never-theless questionable stories about the day's hero. These stories about throwing a coin over the nearby river, riding his mother's new horse to death and, most famously, killing a favorite imported cherry tree and then not lying about it, were all set on the land the governors and reporters now trod. Given the fame of the stories and their hero, one could argue that this was one of the most famous American places—even though most Americans had never heard of it before.

The place is best known as Ferry Farm—a nineteenth-century name it took from a nearby ferry crossing and its road that defined the north end of the property. Over the years, though, it has had many names.

The name Pine Grove spoke of the land's qualities as land just as the name Ferry Farm located it in the neighborhood right at the river cross-ing that linked the Rappahannock's north bank with its south one and the town of Fredericksburg. The name the "Cherry Tree Farm" recalled the most famous story of the place and showed it to be a possession of American storytelling. More forgotten names like Mercer's or Catlett's were titles that highlighted the land's sometime owners—names that used other names to show the place as owned property.

But the name of one owner overshadows that of all of the others. He did not own the place for all that long—just over one of his nearly seven decades—and he spent the bulk of that time living elsewhere. The land carries no visible remnant from his years here. Over the centuries, later residents have suggested that this building or that one had been the old owner's, but these claims were usually false, rooted more in desire than in evidence. The land produced stories as easily as it produced corn or wheat.

Its heralds have been varied. They have seen these acres as a perfect paradise, a place where the trees bent under the weight of their own fruit for a farm boy to learn of God's bounty. Others have called it a barren tract, a place with no agricultural merit to speak of—only the poor and sparse home of a shrewish, unlettered mother and not much more. Some saw in it a peaceful rustic retreat while others saw it only as war-torn battlefield. For some people, crossing the river away from slavery and to freedom, it was the place they dreamed of seeing all their lives. For others it was a perfect place for a large shopping mall and magnificent acres of well-lit parking.

So many possibilities for meaning, so many possible histories, and so many people. But, over the years, one name hung over the land no matter what the narrative. One name stood out, from all the many who had worked its acres or lived in and around its sequence of five farmsteads. One name topped the list of all of the others who walked the land, mapped and drew it, and profited from it (or sought to). Over and over, to many ends, in many voices, and in many contexts real and fictional, the land said Washington.

During his time at Ferry Farm, he and his family would have called it the "Home Farm." Once he left this land for good, he called it "My Mother's Farm." It would not bear his name until nearly a century after his 1799 death, when later generations of Americans saw value in commemoration. In those days it became "the "Washington Farm," or later" the "George Washington Farm," just in case there was any mistaking who was in focus.

Today it carries a rather long title that harkens back to early and mid-twentieth-century attempts to preserve the place. Ferry Farm, and sometimes Fredericksburg or even surrounding Stafford County, Virginia, itself, claim the title of "George Washington's Boyhood Home." That is a crafty little naming act. It is historically true—Washington certainly spent much of his youth here—but the title also recalls the most celebrated moment in that childhood, being "the boy who could not tell a lie." It is a perfect two for one.

Both sides of the place's name were there in the July heat. The rider in the distance and the little boy walking through the crowd served as twin stand-ins for the adult Washington of history, and the boy Washington of lore and storytelling. The crowd had gathered to connect with both versions of Ferry Farm's favorite son.

The day was the first official public look-see at the material remains of the Washington home—a grand unveiling of a collection of nearly a half a million artifacts, thousands of which dated to the Washingtons' years. It represented the culmination of decades of community-based efforts to remake the farm as a Washington historical site and to save it from development and destruction. It was also the culminating moment for nearly a decade of archaeology and research—work that had taken the old Washington home from rumor to reality. My longtime archaeology partner David Muraca and I began this project in 2001, and since then, with the extensive help of dozens of crew, staff, students, and volunteers, have opened a previously closed window into the world and setting of Washington's childhood.

The site was hard evidence, factual matter that could be tabulated and tied to other streams of Washington information such as letters, account books, surveys, court records, and so on—a brand new record, an unearthed archive of the least documented phase of Washington's celebrated and much-discussed life. This was a farm to which George's father Augustine brought his family in 1738. It was where Augustine died, and thus where his second wife Mary and her children had to carry on. At Ferry Farm, a young George Washington first faced life's challenges; it was the place that set him on the course that led first to the west, then to the army, and from there, to fateful providence. It was a unique place in the colony, sitting at the juncture of an estuarial river's farthest inland reach and a major road that snaked down the Northern Neck peninsula. That busy meeting place of river and road made the area a perfect town site, and from 1728 on, Fredericksburg slowly grew on the riverbank opposite Ferry Farm. Understanding this place, reading its land and buildings carefully, considering the options created and precluded by road and river, making sense of the many objects the family once owned, and coming to grips with what life was like here in the 1740s all promised new insights into the world that produced Washington. Seeing how these bits fit together, learning how they enlarged or changed the existing Washington story helped draw people to the site.

But at the same time, Ferry Farm's other George was never all that far away. The Cherry Tree Story made its first appearance in the pages of an 1806 book called *The Life of Washington* by a preacher, bookseller, and author named Mason Locke Weems—best known as Parson Weems. He credited a local elderly woman for the tale of the lad who hacked at his father's cherry tree and then confessed his misdeed. But despite many well-intended sleuths over the decades, no evidence has ever emerged to suggest there was much truth to it. The tale therefore remains presumptively an invention of Parson Weems alone.

No shame there, though. It is probably the best-known American eighteenth-century anecdote, and certainly the best-known moment in Washington's life (rivaled only by his crossing of the Delaware), albeit a made-up moment. Not a bad achievement for a writer. Weems and his moral parables all won a wide readership in their day. He powerfully shaped how Americans saw Washington, and remains a player in Washington literature—even if only as a constant, useful foil.

But nowhere has Weems's pen had more effect than on Ferry Farm itself. Before Weems's first mention of the place visitors had been coming by to see the home of the Great Washington. The parson only gave them more reason to stop by, and added a body of stories that defined the history of the land as well as its its ups and downs as a piece of property. Washington's name may have cast the largest shadow, but the name was often written in Weems's hand.

Being the Cherry Tree Farm has turned out to have been quite a burden for this landscape to bear. It has been both a curse and blessing for a place that has been over time farmland, a Civil War battlefield, a fledgling Washington "shrine," and a much-contested proposed Walmart site. At each turn in its story, Washington and the tree were there; each new storyteller or champion who took up the farm's cause or passed over its acres in some way wove their story with Weems's and Washington's.

Washington may have sold off this land in 1773 and never looked back. But it was Weems and a host of successors who kept the great name and the fabled Cherry Tree tied to the place. And as the latest Ferry Farm storyteller, I am doing it as well, as did all the media that came to see firsthand the place where Washington grew to manhood, and, as all the coverage noted, where he would have chopped at the Cherry Tree—if he had, that is.

Ferry Farm's story is an unintentional collaboration between the General and the Parson—a meeting of that boy dressed as Washington and the distant rider sweltering in the July sun.

But before there was an archaeological site and celebratory bunting, before developers dreamed of shopping plazas, before preservationists imagined shrines and tribute, before soldiers encamped and fought, before Weems saw a rural idyll, before Washington lived and left, before his father bought the land, before early planters first brought the British world here . . . there was a Native place, a stretch of land along the river and just below the rocky falls, which marked a line between upper and lower peoples.

1

❦

From Unburned Woods to
"Clear and Distinct" Views

George Washington never described the Rappahannock. He noted it as a busy place of ferries and roads in 1747. In 1772, when he sold off his old family home, he noted the land's "clear and distinct" overlook of "almost every house" in Fredericksburg on the opposite bank. From the rise by the road one could keep a harbor master's tally of "every vessel that passes to and from it."[1] He described the river only in terms of what mattered to a man weighing the value of the land as an object for sale.

Washington never mentioned what the river felt like when one jumped into its slow brown water on a hot day. He made no mention of the sound it made slapping on the bank or the smell it gave off when the shad were running. No ice to cut in winter, no stones skipping on the surface or splashing on the far side, no rising and falling of the tides.

No mention also of the home where he learned life's joys and its abiding fragility. No notice made of the places he walked, rode, ran, and jumped with his siblings. No reflection on the emotional struggles a young man had endured; only a crisp catalogue of the sellable attributes of a place upon which he was turning his back.

The river that passed by the Washingtons' doorstep was in reality two rivers—two impulses, each stemming from very different places and each functioning very differently amidst the world's waters. One was a creature of the western mountains—a clear rocky run made from countless collected mountain springs. The other was born of the ocean to the east—a slow-moving, muddy and salty wash pushed and pulled by the tides of the wide Chesapeake Bay and the great Atlantic beyond that. At Ferry Farm, the river's wild backcountry impulses soften into a more genteel and tamed run. The river becomes bridled and usable—a friend and ally to farmers and sailors.

As the river changes, so does the land itself. To the west, the dips and rises of the hills get steeper and become more frequent. The long views are blocked more and more by the terrain's ups and downs. Within a dozen or so miles of the river's bank one can make out the top of the Blue Ridge and see just why the mountains have that name. The dirt becomes redder in color than the brownish, silty, stoney soil at Ferry Farm, and the rocks in the dirt become bigger and flatter than the water-rolled, shattered stones of the Rappahannock.

To the east, though, and to the south as well, the land rolls more gently. The views are longer and the hazy sky is bigger. The rocks of Ferry Farm disappear from the soil. At the Falls they are everywhere, and have been built into local homes for as long as people have settled here. But just a bit downriver, the rocks are gone altogether and there is only sand and clay—covered of course with a rich loamy topsoil. The lapping and occasional flooding of the river makes this fertile, nutrient-rich land; its stone-free, sandy loamy mix has made it wonderful farmland for centuries.

Nature had made this a meeting place of landscapes—a transitional place between terrains. It was up to people, though, to give it meaning and what we like to call history.

In 1607, a group of former soldiers, Puritans, and well-connected dandies pooled their sovereigns, hired some ships, and sent a party of gentlemen and sundry laborers off to make a profit in America. Similar London-based ventures had tried and failed, first at North Carolina's Outer Banks, and then at a rocky Maine island called Sagadahoc, not to mention uncounted fishing camps and seasonal weigh stations. For more than a century Europeans had been wringing profits from America, and latecomer England was finally getting serious about getting in on the game.

The London Company's lot were to head over, find a nice spot in what folks around town ambitiously called "Virginia" (a tribute to the by-then dead queen who ruled the last time they tried settling at this latitude), and set about somehow to make a profit for the project backers. At a bend in a river they named after their current monarch, James, they set up a hasty trade fort and did the best that they could manage.[2]

The men were not the first Europeans to take a stab at settling on these rivers. That distinction went to a group of Spanish Jesuits who tried and failed in the 1570s. But Spain still saw this "Virginia" as, in fact, its own. Fear of the Spanish was uppermost on the fort dwellers' minds as they cowered and gradually died in their log and earth creation. As it happened, though, bad relations with the local Natives, internal bickering, diseases, famine, and foul water all proved to be far bigger and more immediate problems than were galleonloads of Catholic "Dons" looking to take back their colonial swamp from heretical Protestant interlopers. But in those earliest days, turning a profit and learning the land were paramount.

English colonization sent its ripples up every one of Virginia's rivers and into every Native town and hamlet. We don't know when the Natives living along the Rappahannock or near the Falls and Ferry Farm first learned of the new arrivals in the low country. They certainly learned in 1608, thanks to a reconnaissance party of young laborers and gentlemen in a heavy English shallow-draft boat led by Captain John Smith.

The adventurer did not spill much ink describing the Rappahannock River or the land that bounded it. What the short, stout, scruffy captain did make clear was that the Rappahannock tour was no pleasure cruise for the English would-be conquistadors. A few downriver Native towns welcomed them—Smith reported that the people of Pissassack, Nandtaughtacund, and Cuttatawomen, for example, "used us kindly."[3] But more often, conflict with the river's peoples marked their travels. Principal among these Native foes were the Rappahannock people themselves—the people for whom the river would hereafter be named.

They lived then in a large town in the heart of the river's tidal run—about fifty miles downriver from the Falls. The town's martial men devoted themselves fully to making clear to the invaders that this was their river and they were fully prepared and more than willing to defend it from all comers. Ultimately, they and almost all of Virginia's eastern Indians would lose that fight, but their actions that hot summer ensured that warfare would be imprinted on the river from its very first mention in English writing.

Along the way from the Chesapeake Bay to the Rappahannock's falls, Smith and his men were harassed by repeated flights of Rappahannock arrows fired by bowmen camouflaged by bushes or hiding behind trees. Where they could, English musket men fired at or pursued their attackers on shore, but the skilled Rappahannock warriors had every home turf advantage and simply disappeared at will, only to reappear later at another place of their own choosing. In one case the defenders mocked the boatmen by "dauncing and singing very merrily" in plain sight after dodging an ineffectual and unimpressive volley of musketry.[4]

The summer heat also took its toll. It probably was the cause of party member Richard Featherstone's death on August 16, about twenty miles or so downriver from Ferry Farm. Smith reported that the day after they buried poor Richard with a "volley of shot," and soon after the party "sayled so high" as their heavy boat "would float."[5]

This was the Falls, and the area around Ferry Farm—the first documented visit to the site. On seeing the rocks and the change in the river's character, the sailors knew they were at the end of this leg of their trip—

their bulky conveyance was of no use as the river changed character. In good explorer fashion, though, the English began "setting up crosses" and carving their names into the bark of trees near Ferry Farm.[6] They did not plan on staying, but such marks of possession were de rigueur for these "always leave a trace" campers. Souvenirs were nice, too. Eager to find reward for their efforts, the explorers poked around for valuable stones or, better yet, metals, and while searching looked for fiber-rich vegetables to eat and spring water to drink.

Soon, though, quartz-tipped Native arrows once again began to slam into the ground and tree cover. This time it was not the Rappahannocks, but war parties from communities above the Falls eager now to make their force and presence known and defend the edges of their homeland.

A party of men from the town of Hasinninga at the forks of the Rappahannock, about twenty miles distant, had gathered near Ferry Farm in a small hunting town called Mohaskahod and waited for the armed strangers to show up, as they knew they eventually would. These nearly one hundred Hasinninga bowmen infuriated the Englishmen who could not manage to get a bead on their nimble opponents "skipping from tree to tree, letting fly their arrows so fast as they could" while the explorers cowered behind the Native-made shields they earlier had lashed onto their boat.[7]

Despite this rough welcome, the Englishmen managed to take one of the Hasinninga bowmen captive. Through an interpreter, this man gave voice to a Native understanding of the river and the area around Ferry Farm.

The Falls area, he revealed, was a juncture in a vast landscape continuum. It began far to the west where the sun resided beyond the mountains. As one traveled downriver, south and eastward, one went lower and lower in altitude until at some unknown distance, a traveler would find himself finally going beneath the earth. To Native eyes, this underground alien place was where the English had themselves come. The informer was able to name the peoples along that continuum; the Monacan and Massawomeks lived high up, closer to the sun, while the Powhatan, the Rappahannock, and others lived lower down, nearer the earth's lowest point. The lands set back from the river's banks were harder to know, because, as he claimed, "the woods were not burnt," meaning they were thick, impassable, choked with untold ages of undergrowth—not a place for people.[8]

The visitors therefore had been traveling upward since they began their voyage, passing through worlds of increasing proximity to the sun. But the residents of the forks of the Rappahannock had decided these underworld dwellers had gone far enough. It was bad enough the strangers had floated through the river's lower miles—Native warriors were powerless to stop that advance—but the juncture of the upper and lower rivers would be as far as they would go.

With their advance stopped by Natives and their own boat's limitations, the English turned around and headed back downriver toward the earth's distant opening. Native archers hounded them all the way back to Richard Featherstone's grave site. Having made their point, the warriors from nearer the sun then set down their bows and made peace with the Underworlders. The latter finally drifted back downriver and for the time being, the world's order remained more or less as it had been.

But it would not be for long.

The change began at the lower reaches—far from the Falls. Along the broad rivers bearing new English names—James and York—English plans to use the land collided with Native plans to live as they always had. Through a series of singularly brutal wars against the low-country Algonquian-speaking Powhatan Indians and their allies, the new arrivals made clear that the new order had no place for members of the old one. Each war knocked back the number of Natives and pushed them farther and farther up country, away from the lowlands and the plague of Englishmen.

By the middle of the century, the once influential and powerful network of low-country Algonquians had been reduced to a few small camps of contained, subject peoples.

Distant low-country conflicts would nevertheless send shock waves to the towns near the Falls and the land that would become Ferry Farm. Travelers' stories would have brought the news to the Falls and everyone would have known the tragic tales of refugees heading westward looking to rebuild their lives in another Native community. For decades, the Falls served as a watch post from which Native peoples could look out nervously and see the growing pale of English settlement expanding acre by acre before them—a front row seat for the grandest drama anyone there would have known.

English colonization in Virginia was not a gradient—not a case of one color meeting another and the two gradually bleeding together until something new, neither one color nor the other, came into being. Instead, "English" was a dichotomous variable—a person, a place, a colony either was in or out. English Virginians had a plan, and Native peoples were not part of it: That is how these English played their colonial hand.

By the 1650s English colonial landowners began to claim the Falls areas as their own. By then it was already a completely different place from the one Smith had visited. The carved trees had healed or died, and Smith's crosses were long gone. Gone was the hunting town of Mohaskahod. Gone too were the Hasinninga and their bowmen to harass unwanted visitors.

It no longer mattered that the river ran from the sun on down to the earth's lower reaches. It no longer mattered that unburned woods bordered the Rappahannock. It no longer mattered that the Falls were a border between peoples—Siouxan speakers back toward the mountains, Algonquian speakers below. The old Native understandings of what made the place a transition between worlds were eclipsed by English ones. What mattered most now was that the Falls were the farthest reaches of English navigation. The rocks and shallows that stopped Smith's boat now trumped the other meanings people had long put on the land. What began to matter now was who had the court papers, surveys, maps, and properly sealed and signed legal documents to show to an English court's satisfaction that they were the rightful owner.

The area now became the deepest up-country reach of English settlements. It became a thin tendril in an Atlantic world that connected even the most remote colonial outpost to the varied commercial, governmental, and cultural pulses of Europe and other colonies. An English vessel fully loaded in London, or Plymouth, or Bristol could sail uninterrupted, if its captain wished and its supplies held out, all the way from English docks right to Ferry Farm's narrow wharf.

By the 1650s an ever-increasing number of Englishmen arriving in Virginia needed more and more land to turn to profit. At the same time the first colonists were taking up residence near Ferry Farm, a sailor named John Washington took up farming a small parcel of land on the far wider Potomac River near where it meets the Chesapeake Bay. But it would be nearly a century before the flow of his family's story ran into that of Ferry Farm's.

Long before the Washingtons arrived, though, low-country landowners were stocking up on Falls-area backcountry holdings for future use. The English had a cunning system in place for dividing up land and ensuring the growth of the Virginia colony all in one policy. It began with a 1618 law that granted fifty acres of land "for every person" which a planter "shall transport thither."[9] The system came to be called "headrights," referring to the right of land for every "head" brought to the colony, and by the 1650s it was working its special colonial magic in the area around Ferry Farm.

It worked this way. Virginia's flourishing was tied to agriculture, with tobacco quickly becoming its most important export. To grow the finicky crop, settlers needed, first, land to plant on, and second, labor to do the work. The headrights system brilliantly combined the twin demands of land and labor. Of course the colony would become infamous for its use of African labor, pilfered in one way or another and shipped to American plantations, there to serve for life. By the 1660s Virginia's most prosperous planters had well begun the momentous and deeply consequential shift to an enslaved African labor force. They leveraged commercial ties to the Caribbean's thriving trade in enslaved Africans and bought right in. But for much of the 1600s, the bulk of Virginia's working backs were shipped right from England and her immediate neighbors.[10]

The deal was that these workers would sign a contract—an "indenture"—obligating them to a term of service, usually seven years, though of course it could vary. At the end of that time (and if the worker lived), there would be a reward, most often in the form of a small piece of land. These sorts of contract-based labor terms were the norm in that day—no laborer in England would have attached any real stigma to serving a term as an indentured worker, any more than we today deride receiving a paycheck in exchange for one's labor.

In fact, there were far worse possibilities for workers. England was awash in harsh property laws. Dozens of seemingly mild crimes were punishable by death or dismemberment. Having one's labor sold to a Virginia master must have seemed a sweet reprieve compared to being executed for stealing a chicken or a loaf of bread to feed a family. While there were certainly hardened killers and cutpurses shipped to the colonies, most of the "convicts" were really just ordinary folks ground down between the twin stones of hard times and a brutal legal regime. And then there were the poorest of the landless poor. These people lived with the possibility of having their children rounded up and sold out by county courts to serve until the age of twenty-one, and only then perhaps move up to indentured servitude and a possible reward at the end of that negotiated term.

Thus, Virginia's landowners had a few ways to get the needed muscle to work their fields: poor folks sold into service, indentured servants, people convicted of one crime or another, and enslaved Africans as well.

On occasion Indian wars in the hinterlands or in other colonies could also provide Native captive laborers. But each laborer, however procured or whatever work regime he or she endured, had to be brought to the colony. And so long as they came across the ocean to their new colonial home, the headrights system came into play.

The Crown—the formal owner of all colonial holdings—through its representatives in the colony granted fifty new acres of Virginia land compensation per "head" to the person footing the bill for transporting new people across the Atlantic. Bring over 10 people, qualify for 500 acres; bring over 50, scoop up 2,500, and so on. Small fees applied here and there, and the headrights were themselves a commodity—like a sort of land-based promissory note—which could be traded around, saved up till needed, or used to pay off debts. But in all cases, it was a brilliant way to ensure the growth of the colony.

As better-off planters brought in new labor, they also acquired more land. That land could be granted as freedom payments to servants finishing their terms, or it could be consolidated into larger holdings—holdings which required more labor for its cultivation. Or, the land could be sold or exchanged for other parcels. More land, more labor, and more labor, more land thus created a snowballing policy which kept people arriving, and ensured that more and more land would fall under the plow and the hoe wielded by more and more Virginians.

From 1618 until, officially at least, as late as 1779, head by head, person by person, parcel by parcel the headrights system helped make Virginia Britain's largest and most populous mainland American colony.

The system landed at the Falls in 1655 when a woman named Margaret Brent claimed one thousand acres on the Rappahannock's south bank "about a quarter of a mile above the falls of the said river."[11] At least twenty new arrivals allowed her to make this claim. They were most likely farmhand servants: Walter Oliver, Richard Cherry, William Cooper, Thomas Allen, Giles Wright, and eleven otherwise forgotten men made the trip that became Margaret Brent's right to claim land. With them in the claim were a gentleman named John Underhill, two women named Sarah Loman and Mary Wagstaff, and one solitary "Negro woman" whose real name no one knew or wrote down. A small glimpse of the range of people becoming Virginians.

Smith's adventurers tried to change the land—or at least to put some claiming mark on it. They carved trees and named places. But these did not last. Smith himself recorded his adventure's findings on a stunningly accurate map. But these were acts for an English audience. What difference did it make to the people of Hasinninga that their town and the hamlet of Mohaskahod were memorialized and plotted on a piece of shredded wood pulp fussed over by people far away?

But the patenting of land? That was something of a different order altogether. The bounding of Native acres, the marking and recording of a landscape's various chosen features—here a large boulder, there a "marked oak"—the transcribing of thousands of tiny local details in hundreds of court documents, all invested with the weight and authority of government, and the rising tide of Englishmen clutching copies of those documents and claiming that the papers gave them, and only them, exclusive right to the land between the large boulder and the marked oak? Now that could not be ignored.[12]

This was how land became property—a totally different perspective on the same object. Certainly the original inhabitants owned the land. They used it daily. They saw it as theirs. They were prepared to fight for it when the uninvited visitors crashed in. But ownership as Natives understood it, and property as the English understood it, were not at all the same thing. The apparatus of law, writing, naming, mapping, and bounding were the complicated rituals that the English performed to change the ever-existing, ever-extending land into something more like a cup or hat—a thing that could be possessed, traded, sold, passed along. Property.[13]

Margaret Brent did just that at the Falls in 1655. Soon after that, others turned more transported people into Rappahannock patents. The arrival of Jonathan Boucher, Silvester Sparrow, Abram Stone, Elizabeth Tooth, "Tom—Negro" as well as ninety-one other British men, fourteen of their countrywomen, and sixteen unnamed Africans allowed two gentlemen named Lawrence Smith and Robert Taliaferro to claim well over six thousand acres just below the Falls—land that would eventually be part of the city of Fredericksburg. The arrival of Peter Plummer, Elizabeth Newhouse, Faith Edwards, and fourteen other fellow travelers let Captain Thomas Hawkins help himself to the land right at the Falls themselves.[14] People became the right to land, land became property, and gradually Virginia became British.

In 1666 Colonel John Catlett claimed the headrights for thirty-one men and nine women transported to the colony. These people netted him a two-hundred-acre chunk of land on the river's north side, a small way below the Falls and right opposite a parcel owned by Lawrence Smith. Catlett's acres sat right at a "bay" where the river widened just a bit, making it a fine landing. Behind that the land rose from the floodplain, first up to a broad plateau, and then gently sloping up even more to precipitous heights farther back. This land would become Ferry Farm.

New owners renamed their world. The banks of the river became known in documents as the North Side and South Side of the Rappahannock River. The Falls became a central point of reference as well, with properties listed as being "up the falls," as were the 9019 Mott family and associates' acres, "below the lowest fall" as in the case of Catlett's land, or "at the lowest fall," as with Hawkin's parcel.[15] Various creeks and streams or fields took on English names like "Smart's Creek," or "Tignor's Creek," titles which inscribed ownership into the land. Other names noted activities like "Mill Creek," while still others suggested meanings and personal experiences like the suggestively labeled "Omen Creek."[16] Some names like "Doegg's Clear Ground" and "Nusaponucks Creek" acknowledged the Indian presence that the patenting process itself was erasing.[17]

Above all, English Virginians described their land in relation to that of their neighbors. In June, 1666 Roger Richardson claimed a parcel that abutted one owned by Silvester Thatcher, while Jonathan Curtis's 250 acres bordered lands owned by Henry Corbin, William Copelin, and Robert Price.[18] Moreover, over time, people's names could morph with the land itself. One patent may refer to Lawrence Smith's land, but soon that same place became Smith's Field, before finally becoming Smithfield. Virginia places were fitting into the same mechanism that had shaped the place-names of old England for centuries.

Thus, page by page in the county court record book, a blanket of English names settled on the land, gradually creating a colonial patchwork which was both an enduring and transformative act of conquest, and simultaneously, a record of how that process took shape.

Every name was attached to a body, but where were those actual bodies? A casual reading of the rush of land claims in the 1650s and 1660s could leave the impression that English settlers were flooding the region like a storm-driven tidal rush from the lower counties. But that would be wrong.

As titles like colonel and captain suggest, these early landowners were well-connected, socially prominent Virginians—men well established in their low-country tobacco plantations. At the Falls the main players were not the wealthiest men in the colony, but were prominent local elites—big fish in sometimes small ponds, but with aspirations of getting bigger and bigger.

Most of these men were unlikely to abandon their Tidewater homes for residences at the still-somewhat-distant lands at the Falls. Instead, they could collect and trade parcels. They could rent them to tenants. They could use chunks of Falls holdings to pay off freedom dues to servants strong enough and lucky enough to live to claim their contract-granted acres. And of course, they could sell bits to other Virginians. They cut their parcels up, added them to new ones, sold them off, and left them to others with such dizzying frequency that to reconstruct the ownership history of even a single piece of land can be a daunting task. The game of land ownership was a way of life.

But move to the Falls? No, most did not. Take Ferry Farm's first English owner Colonel John Catlett, for example. Catlett came to the colony around 1655 with his wife, his brother-in-law Ralph Rousey, and a few other kin. Like many migrants in that moment, they were fleeing the fallout of English Civil War—a conflict which left supporters of the old king Charles I, like Catlett, on the losing side. Governor Sir William Berkeley made Virginia something of a haven for these so-called "Cavaliers" now that their parliamentarian enemies controlled the mother country. He invited many to come settle in the colony and made a few his confidantes and close associates. Catlett did not rise quite as high as that even though he was on very good terms with Sir William. Nevertheless, he did well along the Rappahannock and stayed loyal to his new governor—just as he had the king they both served—even while others questioned his rule.

Virginia had much to recommend to men like Catlett even without the added push of losing a war. Englishmen with land and titles in the old country rarely moved to the colonies. Why would they? So for the most part, England's upper social brackets were not to be found on colonial plantations. Instead, it was members of Britain's middling orders and the ambitious who made the journey over the ocean and became the upper crust in a society lacking a proper English gentry.

In England, these men were a middle strata in social layering that had the poor below them and nobility permanently above. But in Virginia, a well-off, well-set farmer found himself at the top of the heap—with few knights or barons to cast a shadow on the greatness granted by tobacco and land speculations, cattle raising, shipping, and other endeavors. These colonial gentryman—"Merchant Planters" they styled themselves— served their communities through church, government, and militia, gathering up local ranks and distinctions and building estates to pass along to their children. In this way, Virginia produced a colonial ruling class rooted in the values and aspirations of the British countryside, but playing the roles of noblemen ruling their communities.

Catlett and his little clan immediately cashed in their headrights for a tract on the river's south bank, about midway between the Falls and the Chesapeake—not far from the old site of the Rappahannock Native village. A 1670 map shows a little creek with his name at the end of it. Since the map lists very few settlers' names, that small "Catlet" written there speaks volumes about his family's prominence along that part of the river. The tidewater plantation at the end of the creek became the family's base of operations for the next twenty years as Colonel Catlett set about becoming great in the Virginia style.

Recalling his English Civil War experience, he quickly took the high rank of colonel in the Rappahannock County militia—a position that situated him right in the midst of conflict between the river's Native and British residents. That placement would ultimately cost him dearly.

He served as a justice of the peace, a lower-level office but an important one that inserted him into all manner of his neighbors' affairs.

He also sat on the governing body of the Anglican Church in his local Sittingbourne Parish. He even found himself in a doctrinal squabble with a minister named Doughty. Catlett and a few allies called the man out for being a less than loyal Anglican and his "scandalous liveing to the griefe of the whole parish." In return, the aggrieved good reverend denied his critics Easter communion and used his sermons for what Catlett called "pulpit cussings" lambasting his "Levityes and great Extravagances."[19] The great schism on the Rappahannock ended when Governor Berkeley himself told the combatants to settle down and play nice.

But perhaps most significantly, Catlett was also a surveyor. This vocation took him all along the upper Rappahannock and well beyond in search of new lands to claim and enfold in the English system of property. In fact, few Englishmen would have known the river and its banks as well as did the colonel. In all likelihood, he surveyed his Ferry Farm acres himself. He certainly spent as much time in the woods taking measurements as he did at home monitoring his tobacco plants.[20]

Surveying was hard work. It meant long trips far from home. It meant sleeping on the wet ground in the rain, or huddling near a campfire for warmth in the snow. It meant risking physical injury through accident or through a bad encounter with Natives who were learning more and more to resent surveying parties. It also required skill in mathematics, a steady hand with a pen, and good eye. Instructional books of the day like George Atwell's *The Faithful Surveyor* or Aaron Rathborne's *The Surveyor* were packed with equations, formulae, and pictures of triangles—it took a specially trained eye if one were to "mete his ground by my chaine," as Atwell told his readers. It also took specialized tools of the craft like quadrants, compasses, and preset lengths of measuring chains. These all worked in concert to create computations recorded in a notebook "well-bound with vellum" and filled with "good strong paper" to resist rain and wear in the field.[21]

Survey parties had hard work to do. First, they had to travel long miles to get to their destinations. Roads were few in the backcountry. Thus, travel meant walking narrow Native trails, or dodging branches on a horse's back as it gingerly picked its way down paths never intended for the beast.[22] Unexpectedly swollen rivers could block paths. Animal perils like rattlesnakes could strike at unprotected ankles or spook a nervous horse. The rain could pour in torrents, as well, as George Washington learned when an early surveying expedition to the mountains was temporarily shut down by rain "increasing very fast."[23]

But travel was only the first of a "faithfull surveyour's" ordeal. Once at the site, they still had to clear paths for the straight lines needed by those compasses and quadrants, and to run those specially measured lengths of chain. This required axes and saws to cut though tree limbs and slash away at view-obscuring underbrush. Once the cutting, clearing, and chopping was done, the mathematical calculations could be recorded.

For surveyors, it was blisters, shin splints, more blisters, and writer's cramp, experienced in that order.

It was hard work all around, but well worth the effort. To be able to map out a piece of land—to be the first to size it up through English eyes, taste its soil, feel if it were well-watered or dry, assess its timber stands, drink from its water sources—was the 1600s equivalent of getting in on a going concern's ground floor. Gather up good parcels, trade off or deed to freed servants the lesser ones, turn a profit from the lands under cultivation, put the profits into buying up more parcels or into bringing in more people whose headrights let one go back to the woods and claim new lands. This was the ongoing board game that the Virginia gentry knew, loved, and lived by. And in Catlett's day it was being played all along the upper reaches of every one of Virginia's rivers, from the Potomac to the Rappahannock's north, to the York and James to its south.

Landowning was a central value in Virginia life—perhaps more important and more significant even than the colony's celebrated tobacco crops. With a large landed nobility in England, centuries of property ownership, and a finite amount of island acres, it was very hard to buy land—even for those who otherwise had the resources.

But a place like Virginia offered a unique opportunity in the British world: the chance to own land. Of course, farming land required owning land. But it was more as well. A "free hold"—a parcel of land all one's own—gave a free man the right to vote and hold office. Landowning was a key to personal prosperity as well as a real and tangible stake in society itself. In a world so driven by the desire for land, the role of surveyor held a special pride of place.

There was a catch, though: Not all land was the same. For most of its colonial history Virginia's main prestige crop was tobacco. Sweet Scented was the most profitable, Orinoco, second best. Prices fluctuated across the century, but the sot weed remained a principal way to achieve a kind of landed gentility that mirrored that of the comfortable gentry of the old country. But the best tobacco stalks cared not about the dynamics of colonial landgrabbing. Tobacco wanted a certain balance in its soil—just the right mix of acidity, sand, loam, drainage, and as few rocks as possible. Those needs were perfectly met in the Tidewater's soft alluvial soils. The lower counties of James City, New Kent, York, Gloucester, and others rapidly filled with tobacco plantations, some of which made their owners quite wealthy. Decent estates had been made and dynasties established.

But these most desirable acres were finite. Virginians like Catlett could patent as many acres as daylight and determination would let them survey, but most of these would not sustain the kind of high-value tobacco production of the lower counties closest to the Chesapeake Bay.

By the 1650s and 1660s when Catlett and his compatriots were in the woods laying survey chains and taking measurements, almost all of the best tobacco lands were already owned and farmed by earlier arrivals. Even at this early date the colony was already developing local cultures of opportunity and in the west, and especially in the land between the Rappahannock and Potomac rivers, speculation was good business. Even though the most prized Sweet Scented tobacco crops were not going to grow in northern or western soils, there was still a growing market in new lands for a growing population along these northern rivers.

The Potomac was wide and inviting—it still is today. Ships could ply its waters easily and the river's snaking turns offer views, allow breezes, and let neighbors feel connected to the homes they could see from their doorsteps. When Catlett platted out his acres near the Falls, in 1666, Virginians already had filled up the Potomac's southern bank with their homes and fields. One of these Potomac settlers, as it happens, was George Washington's great-grandfather John Washington, who made his home on a well-placed spur between two creeks.

But the upper reaches of Catlett's Rappahannock was a very different place. Today, as then, it is narrow and linear. One can see the opposite side, but the Potomac's long views are not to be had. Catlett's downriver

home was a toehold in the wide tidewater world of the low-country tobacco growers. But it was also a springboard to the river's narrower upper reaches where an able and hardy surveyor could map out lands he
could sell at a good profit.

In August 1670 Catlett dropped by his Ferry Farm holdings during
what would prove to be his last trip into the western mountains. The trip
itself was pleasant enough—enchanting, even. A few days on horse passing through a "vast forest" of a "melancholy darkness" but whose "ver-
dure is wonderful pleasant to the eye," and then "into a clear open skie" to
"savanae" filled with "herds of red deer" nibbling on "luxurious herbage."
The travelers drank from the cool waters of the "first springs" that in
time became "the great rivers which run into the Atlantick Ocean, or
Cheseapeack Bay."[24]

After that, a ride up the mountainside and scamper "afoot" to a
surprisingly-chilly-for-the-season rocky summit.[25] In view of the next
range of peaks, he and his fellows "drank the king's health in brandy"
and named their cold mountain after their king Charles.[26] The men were
saddened a bit by not having found a passage through to the Pacific
Ocean which they had hoped would be spread out before them, but no
doubt the brandy helped. On the way back, the colonel took some measurements with the tools he had brought along and just missed getting a
nice bite from a poisonous "Mountain-spider," whatever genus that might
have been.

But the real danger was not in a spider or venomous snake's bite. For
while the mountains may have been blessed with a delicious "clear and
open skie," the lower land near the Falls was still draped with "a melancholy darkness," made less so by the thick forest canopy than by the
growing fight over who would own it.[27]

One of Catlett's party later described the Falls as sitting "in Indian
Mantapeuk," perhaps a mistaken reference to the down-country Matta-
poni or even a garbled version of the up-country Monacan.[28] In any case,
it was clearly still an unsettled place to English eyes. Roughly a day's

ride downriver from the Falls on the south bank was the home of Robert Taliaferro, a neighbor and associate of Catlett's and the last English home as one headed westward.

Yet even though there were still no English living as far upriver as the Falls, people like the Doeg Indians then living near Ferry Farm, and other western Indians just beyond, had seen sixty years of steady encroachment. They had the memory of how the Virginians had treated low-country Natives in the first decades of the century—some were even the children of refugees from those bloody wars. These western tribes had signed onto Governor Berkeley's 1646 peace treaty—but that peace was evermore uneasy as British property law enfolded more and more Native land. And with surveyors like Catlett chopping limbs and clanking chains with an infuriating determination, the pressure to strike back must have been unbearable.

Moreover, wherever English and Native Virginians lived close to each other they made poor neighbors. English cattle and pigs roved at will and sometimes wandered into Native farms, rooting up carefully tended gardens. Native hunters, in return, rarely hesitated to take down English livestock as if it was just so much more wild game. These may seem like trivial matters—rooted crops or skewered hogs—but they are exactly the kinds of daily conflicts that made men's blood boil. One result might be lawsuits—that is if English courts could find the Native hunters they sought to bring to trial. Another more common result, though, was violence—here a raid, there a sudden killing in the woods, each one leading to the next.

Affront by affront, Native and English alike concluded that life with the new neighbors was just impossible. And the dead mounted.

In 1666 Catlett had complained to Governor Berkeley that he and his up-river neighbors suffered from "Execrable murders" at the hands of "a combination of our Northern Indians" including a town of Doeg Indians then living hard by Ferry Farm.[29]

That same 1670 map that showed the "Catlet" home place, also showed the Doeg village at the center of the troubles. It was presented as a set of six curve-topped cabins sitting between two creeks on a bend in the river a few miles below the falls.

The map also showed lots of small boxlike English homes lining the banks of the river. No names near them, not even the suggestion that these were meant to be actual homes. Instead, these were symbols of a growing British presence along the river. The evenly spaced, regimented regularity of these little boxes contrasted ominously with the little cluster of Native homes at the bend—drawn intentionally twice the size of the little English boxes, and with "Doogs Indian" next to them in bold clear letters. A few of the English boxes sat between the Doegs and the Falls, but not a single box was at Ferry Farm or at the clearly marked rocks of the Rappahannock's falls.

Even more ominously, perhaps, Catlett singled out these "Doagge" people as being "particularly" a source of trouble, and sought his governor's blessing to "utterly destroy and eradicate" them once and for all. He was one of many "westerners" who worried daily about the risk of Native raid, but Catlett had rather a personal interest in this vendetta. Only twenty short days before his letter, he had legally laid claim to two thousand acres at Ferry Farm, upriver from the Doeg. No doubt he wanted to see that land secure its own cluster of little English boxes and make a profit along the way. But having a troublesome Native village between his new land and the lower settlements was not exactly a selling point. Catlett stood to gain if he and local militiamen were able to "utterly destroy and eradicate" the Doeg.[30] This was the dark side of land speculation.

It is unclear just how Berkeley responded to Catlett's grim request—no letter or record survives. But we do know a few things that fill in the gaps.

First off, soon after his return from drinking the king's health on the Blue Ridge, a raiding party of unnamed Indians killed Colonel Catlett near what is now Port Royal on the Rappahannock. As a militia officer,

planter, and surveyor—provocative vocations one and all—he was a perfect target for all that was enraging the up-country Natives, who were
pushed off their land survey by survey, English patent by English patent.
Given how face-to-face and personal these killings could be, there is every reason to suspect that the raiders knew just whom they were taking
out. Might Catlett's killers have been the selfsame Doeg whose murder
he plotted? We cannot know for sure, but it is a strong possibility.

Secondly, in July of 1675 a party of Doeg attacked the home of one of
Catlett's neighbors, a planter named Thomas Matthews. The immediate
cause of the raid was a disagreement over a debt, but everyone knew that
there was much more in the air than a few pounds sterling for some trade
goods. The killing of Matthews tipped the scale in a way that Catlett's
killing had not. Militiamen took to the marches and set about revenging
themselves—in their number was John Washington. When their fury
ended up killing Natives allied to Virginia as opposed to enemies, the
whole western edge of the colony exploded in violence.

When Governor Berkeley called for restraint, a host of long-lingering
grievances boiled over, and bands of rebels sought his head as well as
any Indian scalps they could lift. When it was all over, Virginia had
weathered its first civil war. Berkeley survived, but his capital, Jamestown, was burned, many of the colony's greatest homes were in ruins,
and a set of twenty-three gentry ringleaders met the hangman for their
insubordination.[31]

But, as in the first half of the century, it was the Natives that got the
worst of the 1670s fighting. The war opened to English settlement all
those great "savannae" acres Catlett had traversed just before his death,
thus a full generation of western expansion was secured by what in effect
began with Catlett's letter to Governor Berkeley. The colonel did not live
to see it, but his plans for the Doeg were met to the letter—and the Doeg
were not the only ones to feel that wrath.

The last echoes of the world the Hasinninga captive revealed to Captain Smith faded from the world. No longer did the earth slope down

from the sun to the sea. No longer were the Falls a border between peoples. The cool mountain water still would meet the sea at Ferry Farm, but from now on, the water, the land, and the "clear and distinct view" Washington would later describe would be for the benefit of the newcomers and their descendants. The once unburned banks of the river were, once and for all, property. And on that property began to cluster new little English boxes.

2

※※※

The Washingtons Make a Home at the Falls

T he first of those little boxes at Ferry Farm went up sometime in
1710. In that year, a recently freed servant named Maurice Clark
claimed a small part of the old Catlett patent. His deed gave him 150
acres of riverfront land—the same acres that would soon be the Washington family home lot.

Clark, his "servant man" Dennis Linsy, and some local craftsmen
built a modest but perfectly respectable two-room home just above the
Rappahannock's floodplain and a short walk from a drinkable, if a bit
smelly, stream of water. They framed up a house using hewed beams and
locally prepared boards all resting on posts set into the ground. A skin
of clapboard kept out the wind, and a roof of the same kept it dry. A
wood-framed, mud-covered chimney heated the home's main "hall,"
until it was replaced by something made more solidly of brick and stone.
A heavy door swung on iron hinges, and a window made of glass and
lead framing brought in a hazy light through its opaque green panes. It
was a type of house that was familiar to any contemporary Virginian.[1]

But these houses did not last long—often no more than a decade. And as it happens, Clark's time was short on the land as well. He was dead within a year of his deed and had willed his land and animals to his servant, his friends, and his neighbors.

The Falls had been a borderland of sorts in Catlett's day. Even in Clark's time, there was at least the possibility of an Indian raid, though none materialized. But what English eyes saw most was opportunity. Much of the river frontage had been cleared and planted in Orinoco tobacco. Wheat and corn also grew well and stalks of green and gold sprouted on the floodplains and the gentle slopes beyond them. There were other prospects as well. The ships that came and went made the area something of a trade hub, and native iron ore drew moneyed backers with an eye toward smelting out a new, profitable Virginia export.

These commercial promises granted the area something unusual in this colony of riverside plantations: a town. Being Britons, Virginians had seen towns as a natural and useful part of any rural landscape— places for trade and trades, the locus of local government—as logical a pairing to farms as was an ox to a plow.

To the recurring frustration of colonial legislators, few burgs developed along Virginia's waterways. Periodically, the House of Burgesses would pass another bill calling for the founding of such and such a town, but these usually failed to develop. Instead, the plantation stayed the central unit in this riverfront agricultural way of life.

But after its 1728 founding, a town on the Rappahannock's south bank took root where the land rose up from the river more gently than at Ferry Farm. It was named for King George II's son and the Prince of Wales, Frederick, and although it would never become a Falls-line answer to Philadelphia or Barbados's Bridgetown, it was significant by Virginia standards. Its small collection of buildings clustered near a muddy wharf where ships carried in all the goods of the empire and carted out local produce. A steady run of smaller river and coastal crafts gave the new town a rare feeling of bustle.[2]

Fredericksburg was a local magnet. Spotsylvania County government made its home there and a local market served both business and social needs. A growing network of roads led to the wharves from farms all over the Rappahannock's southern bank. At the wharf there was a ferry to take people, wagons, and horses over to the river's steeper northern bank. The ferry crossed to the small ravine cut by the stream where Clark and Strother took their water. That cut eased the steepness of the bank and made for a perfect connector road up to the main thoroughfare, which in turn wended its way down the Northern Neck.

That road—King's Highway—took its name from the peninsula's most prominent resident, Robert "King" Carter. It linked his tidewater plantation, Corotoman, to the Falls area and all that lay between them. The road ran right through the heart of the Northern Neck Proprietary—a sort of colony within a colony governed by the Fairfax family in England. As far back as Maurice Clark's day, Thomas Lord Fairfax and his kin owned all the land between the Rappahannock and the Potomac as a gift from the Crown. All of the peninsula's residents essentially had two governors; one was the Royal Governor of the Virginia Colony, and the other was the Fairfax family. But being in England, the governors relied on local administrators to keep affairs in order, and King Carter was the Fairfaxes' man on the ground. He profited from that role immensely and there was nothing witty or ironic about his local nickname—his wealth, influence, and connections made him as close to a Virginia king as one could imagine.

But King's Highway was more than his own personal administrative pathway. What the river was for ships, the highway was for wagons and horse travelers: the artery that connected plantations along the northern Potomac to those on the peninsula's Rappahannock-fronted south bank.

One of those plantations near the road was a patch of land between Pope's and Bridge's creeks, sitting just east of a large and quite scenic bend in the broad Potomac. In the troubled years in the middle of the seventeenth century, John Washington laid claim to land here and set about building a plantation and a dynasty. He made good, serving in the

House of Burgesses, acquiring more lands, and leading men in the 1670s
Indian war that permanently changed life at the river's upper reaches. His
son Lawrence carried on when John passed, not loving the acquisition of
land perhaps as much as did others of his line, but certainly taking an active interest in politics both in the county and in the House of Burgesses.
And after Lawrence's 1698 death, his son Augustine carried the name
into the dawn of the eighteenth century.

These men shared a few defining traits. They were utterly characteristic colonial Virginians. They held the common gentry values of land,
office holding, and title. They did well at these endeavors, even though
they could only look with envy at the far larger holdings of the great
tobacco barons on the lower rivers. They nevertheless were well set up
men of local influence and prominence, models for their neighbors, and
good loyal subjects of their king.[3]

Augustine Washington, George's father, spent long stints in England
for schooling as a boy, and for business as an adult. But for most of his
life he lived at the place of his birth, the Potomac River estate first settled
by his grandfather John. Augustine had inherited the full one-thousand-
acre family holding when he reached his majority age. He took a wife
around the same time—a woman named Jane Butler who, like him, came
from short-lived parents. The couple set about laying the groundwork
for the next generation of Washingtons. In their short time together, they
had four children, but only two survived to adulthood. Their eldest son,
Lawrence, was born in 1718 and another, Augustine Jr. (called Austin)
arrived two years later.

Around 1726, Augustine built himself a new sturdy gentry home
near a point of land on Pope's Creek. Made of locally fired brick, it had
one large main floor, with a finished loft story above that. Dormers and
windows brought light into those upper sleeping rooms, and a full brick-
lined cellar made for a well set up, fully stocked home.

Augustine tried to live in the fashionable style of the colonial gentry.
He attired himself and his family with the right buckles and cuff links

that one expected to see gracing the sleeves and collars of the better sort. He bedecked his table with fancy cutlery—in those days, mostly elegant, though soon to be outdated, twin-pronged forks with expensive metal adornments and carved bone or horn handles. Diners at Augustine's home could poke, stab, and skewer their food with abandon while quaffing sweet wine poured from bottles bearing specially pressed "A.W." seals, and then wipe their mouths on fine English tablecloths like real lords and ladies.

By local standards Augustine was a wealthy and well-connected man. At the end of his life he had title to over ten thousand acres and owned forty-nine enslaved Africans. Through their labor he grew Orinoco tobacco and turned a profit from his crops. Like the others of his line he added property to property, held offices like captain in the militia and sheriff—one of many remunerative offices open to the gentry. He sat on the Washington Parish Vestry of the Anglican Church as well.[4] He sought out other profitable ventures, and kept close ties with friends and partners across the Atlantic. He even had the resources to send his sons to England to receive the kind of proper English education that was unavailable in Virginia. Colonial society prized this mother-country tutelage as a vital mark of refinement, and Augustine had received his polishing at Derbyshire's Appleby School. Despite going there as young boy just after the death of his father (or perhaps for just that reason), Augustine maintained a long connection to the place and even sent his and Jane's sons to the same Tudor-era brick school building.

After three generations in Virginia, the Washingtons ranked in the top ten percent on the colonial wealth index. But even though nine in ten of his neighbors could only look in envy at Augustine Washington, with his solid home and profitable lands, men like King Carter lived almost as if in another world at the top of the colonial heap. Carter died in possession of over 300,000 Virginia acres and over 1,000 enslaved people. The Washingtons were junior members of the fraternity of Virginia's wealthiest families.

Had Lawrence and Augustine Jr. remained their father's only sons, he would have had an easy time handing his properties over to these two proper British Virginians. But things were about to change quite a bit for the little family.

In 1729, Augustine sailed over the ocean to draft up papers for a new venture and enroll his sons in the Appleby School. Colonial mining activities had been legally restricted for years, but that was changing ever since the beginning of the century. Rather than go it on his own, Augustine planned to make his mines work by partnering with the Principio Company, an English firm that had just begun to turn ore to cash in neighboring Maryland. Augustine's 1729 English trip was his chance to meet some of his new partners and make sure he was happy with the terms of their agreements. Augustine was a controlling and circumspect sort of businessman and took great pains to make sure that each detail of the new partnership was just to his liking.

But while he was overseas dotting every possible "i," Jane Butler Washington succumbed to an unknown ailment and, like her parents before her, died young. When he returned to Virginia, the new widower Augustine set about restoring order to his life. He worked to turn his stake in the Principio mine company to some value, but also set about finding a new wife with whom he could make more Washingtons. The two activities—mining and courting—may not have been totally unrelated.

Virginia families often grew through complicated webs of alliances and associations that are better understood through the calculating lens of business deals than through the hazy lens of romance. To be sure, there were many love matches in colonial homes—indeed, there is reason to believe that Augustine was genuinely saddened by the loss of his Jane. More usually, though, marriages (and particularly those of elite families) were collective decisions made by all of the interested parties for their own individual and shared interests.

The Washington men had a talent for advantageous marriages. John had come to Virginia in 1657 with not much more than a sea trunk to his name, and with shocking speed married Anne Pope, the daughter of a well-off landowner. His sons and grandsons would also have a nose for the ladies—but in their case that meant the ability to sniff out the ladies who had property in their apron strings and well-connected kinsmen behind them.

One such woman was Mary Ball, who since the age of twelve had lived in the care of Jane Washington's brother, Colonel George Eskridge. Part of his guidance entailed managing the over one thousand acres in Mary's name and ensuring that she would find a fitting husband. A wife's lands would fold into a husband's land at the words "I do," so it was of great importance that good marriages be carefully arranged.

So it seems that Colonel Eskridge suggested his then twenty-three-year-old propertied ward to his brother-in-law Augustine as a suitable successor to his sister Jane. The move made perfect sense. It kept all the properties in the family and had an added bonus: Mary owned a large tract adjacent to the land at the center of Augustine's Principio mining company project. A marriage would bring the two parcels under the same domain.

And so it was that in 1731 the couple took their nuptials at Yeocomico Church in Augustine's native Westmoreland County, and Mary Ball Washington took up housewifery at the Washington estate at Pope's Creek. Within a year she was pregnant with the couple's first child.

It was a boy, and they christened him George—presumably in honor of Colonel Eskridge. He was born on February 11, 1732. Twenty years later when Britain switched from the Julian to the Gregorian calendar the date would become February 22. Later, when George Washington had become great, folks remembered (or fabricated) portents of this retrospectively momentous birth. Some even claimed to know in exactly what room of the house the Great Man had breathed his first. The place became a shrine in a secular American religion. But in reality, there were other things capturing people's attention that year and the world hardly noticed that Washington had arrived.

That same year British merchants won the right to claim a Virginia planter's land and even his enslaved property for the nonpayment of debts. It was called the Debt Recovery Act and it made frequently indebted planters furious. On top of that, Northern Neck tobacco planters in particular were suffering. The year before had been a hard one. Poor weather had led to an even poorer crop of the "bewitching vegetable," and no group of people is more on edge than a community of farmers facing possible ruination. The poor crops ran smack into Governor William Gooch's newly instituted tobacco inspection policies designed to pull the colony out of a long economic slump.[5] It rested on the policy that lower-quality leaves would be burned rather than brought to market. Fair enough—every tobacco planter could understand the very simple marketing principal of keeping the "brand" valuable.

But the Northern Neck had always been a second-best place for sot weed. As planters there came to realize that it was in fact their tobacco that was the object of the Tobacco Inspection Act of 1730, anger at the law bubbled up. All over the area and near the Falls, planters rioted. They burned inspection barns, set fire to crops in the field, and generally brawled. Their discontent failed to end the inspection regime that they so hated. But it was an early sign that tobacco would not always be king at the upper reaches of the Rappahannock. Clever planters would need to think more creatively as any possibility of becoming a great tobacco baron at places like Ferry Farm receded like the tide.

On August 4, 1732, Virginia lost Robert "King" Carter. He had risen as high as a Virginian could and was a man with few peers. But despite acres and acres of high-value tobacco stalks, a significant part of his fortune rested on his relationship with the Fairfax family. For the last decade of his life, Carter oversaw the deeding of land, collection of taxes and customs duties, and maintenance of the borders—a position that made him the great family's main Virginia representative and very rich and very powerful.

When Carter died the office became vacant. Lord Fairfax arranged to have his cousin William take over the profitable business of running their proprietary colony, and soon after that, the lord himself became a Northern Neck resident.

They ultimately settled on a piece of Potomac front land very near a parcel at Little Hunting Creek owned by Augustine Washington. That accident of proximity would make the Washington boys well known to the hugely powerful Fairfax family—first Lawrence, who married a daughter of the clan, and later, George, who, like King Carter, would become very wealthy indeed, thanks to Lord Fairfax's favor.

In 1735 Augustine made a somewhat unusual decision. In his forty-first year, he packed up his things and clan and moved the whole lot to Little Hunting Creek. The move was curious. The Pope's Creek homestead had been the epicenter of the Washington empire for three generations. The family had done well there and made themselves mainstays of local government, Church, and militia. At a time in their lives when most great planters were settling in, Augustine left behind the world that had made him in favor of some place distant and new.

Moving to the upper Potomac, though, let Augustine set Austin up at Pope's Creek while getting the new place set for Lawrence. He and his two wives together had already produced more Washingtons than had his parents and grandparents combined—a total of seven, by 1735, with three more still to come. Augustine faced a challenge none of his immediate ancestors had experienced: how to set up a large number of sons. And in 1735 he was forty-one. Washington men never had had long lives; he must have known that his clock was ticking.

So the family headed upriver to their home and acres at Little Hunting Creek. Here the Potomac bends and is far narrower than at Pope's Creek, even though it seems vast when compared to the Rappahannock about fifty miles to the south. Their new home there was part way up the creek that ran inland from the river and a fair bit from the road that led down to Fredericksburg. The land was fine—better than fine, even—but the home was small and somewhat isolated. The trip to the Accokeek mines was still a long one, about thirty miles southward, and the ride down entailed using poor roads and fording streams. But the Washingtons stayed at Little Hunting Creek for over two years, adding two new sons—John Augustine and Charles—to the growing brood.

Soon, though, Augustine was thinking about another move.

We don't know whether he himself saw the April 21, 1738, *Virginia Gazette* advertisement for a home on the Rappahannock overlooking Fredericksburg, or if one of his associates directed him to it. The ad heralded the auction and sale of a "very handsome Dwelling house, three store houses, several other convenient out houses, and a Ferry belonging to it."[6] This last claim was a bit of an oversell. The previous owner—a member of the House of Burgesses named William Strother—had sought permission to run a ferry at his landing, but the one then there was not in his control. He got to hear the ringing bell or the horn blast every time a traveler called the flat ferry to the other side, but the enterprise's profits went elsewhere.

But the ad's claims, the prospect of living closer to Accokeek, and the possibility of using the growing town of Fredericksburg as a new base of commercial operations clearly appealed to Augustine. Strother had died and left the land and wood-framed gentry-quality home to his wife. She was now selling and moving on. On the appointed date Augustine was at the old Strother place, walking the grounds and giving the buildings a good looking over. And in the end, he placed the winning bid. The stone-seated frame home and its attendant structures, as well as close to four hundred surrounding acres, became the new Washington home place.

For then six-year-old George, it was the second major move of his young life. The consequences of it would be great even if they were hidden from view at the time. Likewise, the consequences of this new family of owners would be great for the land itself. George would be the first of the Virginia branch of his line to not be raised at the ancestral acres between Pope's and Bridge's creeks. There, generations of relationships and partnerships had created a nice comfortable web of extended kin and allies that would in all ways have smoothed a young gentry man's entry into elite Virginia society. Rather than come of age in sight of the graves of his ancestors, he would set his initial roots elsewhere—on land chosen for its commercial value, as opposed to that steeped in family lore. True, during his childhood he would return again and again to the old family estate to see his uncle and cousins. But he was always a visitor there—welcomed no doubt, kin to be sure—but this was land he would never—could never—own for himself. There was a large and significant piece of being a Washington that he could never really possess. Instead, he would come to manhood at a place new to his family, chosen for simple, practical reasons, and in important ways rather unique in the colony.

This was to be a Washington home place quite unlike the others that either Augustine or George had known. The homes at Pope's Creek and Little Hunting Creek were both set within neighborhoods on different parts of the wide Potomac. The local community at those homes was made of the other planters living in the immediate area. "Strangers" there meant neighbors, who in time were not that strange at all. Ships passed on the wider river, but there was not much traffic on the creeks that sat at the homes' doorsteps. On the occasions when a ship made its way up the narrower runs, it was certainly there on Washington-related business. These plantations were contained worlds, intimate ones, small villages really, composed of the master's family, the people they owned, and the various buildings in which they lived and worked, and all surrounded by the fields that made them comfortable or miserable, depending on their status.

The celebrated planter William Byrd II likened his life as the master to that of a biblical patriarch. Even a smaller planter could feel great and patriarchal as he looked out at his property knowing that what he saw was his. But Ferry Farm was a very different sort of place. Certainly, its fields and buildings made it a familiar home to any of Virginia's Abrahams, Isaacs, and Jacobs. But its proximity to neighbors, to a town, to a fairly active wharf, to the area's main road, and to a ferry virtually at its front door all made this a rather odd place in this colony filled with plantation-fiefdom villages.

For people accustomed to a regular plantation's comparative isolation, this new home place seemed unnervingly crowded and public. From the front door one could see the curling smoke of other people's hearth fires and see ships conducting other peoples' commerce. Other peoples' roofs and painted outer walls, all there for an easy scan, allowed a regular tally of who was doing well and who was letting their property go just a bit. The sounds of ships' loading and unloading—even the chatting of the sailors and workers loading and unloading—would all drift into earshot. So, too, would the sounds of other peoples' lives, the lowing of their cows, the barking of their dogs, even their scolding of their servants and their songs in happy times. The blast of the ferry's horn, the rattle of wagons rolling onto the boat's flat wooden pallet, and the rumble of carts on King's Highway all added their unscheduled din to regular sounds of daily rural life.

Today, we would consider all of this quaint or charming—the river, the view, the ferry, the little cluster of buildings on the sloping floodplain. But in the eighteenth century when a Washington contemporary like Daniel Boone could allegedly seek out more "elbow room" because someone else had the gumption to move as close as twenty miles away, Ferry Farm was positively bustling.[7]

The location of the home between road and river placed it quite literally at the crossroads of local life and commerce. The farm sat right across the Rappahannock from the south bank's finest wharf site making it, in navigational terms, the head of the river. As if that was not good enough, King's Highway took a sharp turn nearby and connected to a ferry lane that led right to the river crossing. That meeting of road and river offered its own opportunities, but it came at the cost of a life lived to the soundtrack of creek water lapping on the bank. Clearly, Augustine saw this as a price worth paying. He became a trustee for Fredericksburg, purchased in-town property, and devoted himself to the Accokeek operations. Meanwhile, his wife and children settled into the home he had moved them all to.

The *Virginia Gazette* called it a "very handsome dwelling house." This was more than realtors' sales talk. Strother had the resources to build well, and he used them skillfully. To be sure, there were grander homes. King Carter's Corotoman, his son John's seat called Shirley, and the Custis Family's Arlington, to name just a few contemporaries, were all two- and three-story giants surrounded by rows of outbuildings, some of which were themselves larger than the actual homes of many a well-off Virginian. Homes like that could virtually swallow whole Augustine's new "handsome dwelling house."

But those homes were the very tip of the gentry iceberg. In its context—the residences of the lower levels of Virginia's wealthiest families of the 1730s—the Strother home was right in line. And from what we can glean from contemporary homes in the area (none of which have survived) Strother's was probably one of the nicer ones. It was roughly fifty feet long and thirty feet wide. It had at one time been built as an L-shaped structure, one room deep on the south side and two on the north. But by the time it became Washington property, its floor plan had been filled out to a full rectangle. This gave the home's first floor a total of four rooms, each about fifteen feet wide, with a large hallway running right across its waistline.

Above that were three smaller rooms built into a finished loft space. A fine stone cellar sat right beneath the central passage hallway, and smaller earthen cellars were in other parts of the house near the main fireplaces.

Seven rooms with a cellar and central passageway was altogether not a bad home at all. But while these rooms were numerous enough and well suited to the needs of a large family and their enslaved attendants, they were also the regular run, as rooms went. A "hall," a "parlour," a "back room," and a "hall back room" graced the first floor while three "chambers" filled out the loft spaces. Plastered to keep out the wind, dry and warm in the winter, these were better accommodations than most Virginians could hope for. It was also a sign of gentle living that all of the work and food preparation spaces had been relegated to other nearby buildings. But at the same time, the home lacked the fancy specialized spaces that adorned the colony's highest-style fashionable homes. No library, no study, no office or closet pressed in amidst the large family rooms and smaller, more private ones. Augustine's new home was very much the right one for a man of his place in the great colonial chain of being.

On the outside, the home broadcast the station of its owners. There was no such thing as hiding one's wealth in Augustine's day. The tight connection between money and influence ensured that anyone who had them wanted to show them. From clothing to horse furnishings to home decor, how a man presented himself was a solid indicator of where he and his family stood in society. To look ragged was to be taken to be ragged— a condition that could jeopardize one's opportunities, chances for good marriage, and social advancement. In our day of credit ratings and computerized bank records, we can look as we choose and let the numbers do the talking. Even people in tee shirts can get home loans. But in Augustine's day, threadbare clothes were the equivalent of a bad credit score. Appearances mattered immensely, and few appearances were as apparent as a family's home's façade.

Virginia's elite planters had long honed "curb appeal" to a fine art. The styles might have changed over time—a taste for the ornate brick-work of John Page's 1660s Jacobean cruciform house at Williamsburg, for example, might yield to the more delicate lines of Thomas Jefferson's octagonal Monticello—but in both cases, the message was quite similar: Here resides a man of substance.

Since this residential message was meant to be seen, the view mattered. For so many planters living along the colony's waterways within easy reach of ships to carry out their crops, that meant a great home sitting majestically atop a river's bluff. Some of the wealthiest Virginians could set their laborers to sculpting their front yards to enhance the view for new arrivals as they floated into sight of the home. Terraced plateaus and manicured, cleared yards offered views from and to the front doors of the rich and powerful. All that was needed was a labor force, some shovels, and time—commodities all in the hands of Virginia's grandees. Others tried to select bends in rivers or creeks that set off the home as well as possible for those getting their first impression of a place and its family's worth from the ship's deck.

The next concern was the home itself. Simple visible things we take for granted today carried considerable clout for the Strothers and the Washingtons. Windows and paint all revealed resources to be used and fashionable judgment to make the right choices. The shape of the home as well as its size and the number and quality of its surrounding outbuildings all told a visitor right away about the station of the residing family. Virginians counted on this unambiguous material barometer of social standing, and used it well.

William Strother had built his dwelling a few dozen yards to the south of where the Clark home once stood. Perhaps the ground still showed residue from the older, far less fashionable home that once stood there. Perhaps Strother, with his enslaved Africans, was less worried about the somewhat longer walk down to the water source—a walk he would never have to make carrying a full bucket. What is clear, though, is that he set his home just at the curve of the bay in the river below—a situation that not only gave it a great view, but also moved it a bit farther away from the ferry lane.

Placing the house atop the Rappahannock's steep bluff forced riverborne arrivals to crane their necks up a bit to fully take in the home. The view also hid the various outbuildings behind the home from immediate view. Strother knew well what he was doing. He could build big—his home would be a full fifty feet by thirty feet, against a regional norm of forty feet by twenty. Nevertheless, he could not build on the grandest scale. But he could use his land's topography to make what he could build appear taller and more dominant on the landscape than its story and a half in fact were. It was a crafty and clever move.[8]

Paint also helped in the illusion. The home's clapboards were painted in the brick-red color that was quite popular on gentry homes. The trim, with its beaded edges and crenulations, was probably painted in the same color, in keeping with a contemporary taste for wooden adornments outside and paneling inside all larded over with dark-colored paint. The effect of all of this red paint was to give the wooden frame home the appearance of being built in more expensive brick when viewed from a distance. It was a good and cunning, if somewhat overdone, trick.

And lest a visitor be disappointed to see that this imposing brick structure was just an illusion made of paint and wood, the dwelling had new treats close-up to distract away that thought. For one thing, the whole façade was punctuated by fully glazed windows, each flanked by its own protective shutter coated in the same brick-red paint. The steeply pitched roof was clad in wooden shingles, and windowed dormers jutted out and brought light into the upper chambers. These windows were expensive and impressive imports—an undeniably costly adornment.

On top of that, or beneath that more accurately, was also a special local feature. Augustine's iron ore were not the only rocks locals had been digging for. Near Aquia Creek, a bit north of Fredericksburg, stonecutters had been carving out a vein of very malleable grayish tan sandstone dotted with primeval shells and riven with reddish stripes. Quarrying began in the 1690s and soon the stone had become a distinctive part of local building—it even gained national fame for its presence in the White House and the Capitol.

Augustine's new home sat atop a foundation made up of well cut, finished, and fully faced Aquia stone. It also boasted a nearly twenty-foot-by-ten-foot cellar built to the stonemason's highest standard. On top of that, the thick lower layers of the home's three chimneys were also in Aquia, before bricks took over for the more delicate upper work. In muddy, sandy Virginia, stone was an impressive thing indeed. In another generation, settlers in the more mountainous west would make stone a more regular constituent of Virginia housing. But in the 1730s and in a world still Tidewater-dominated, these blocks, chimney bases, and cellar were impressive indeed.

Vista, positioning, paint, glass, internal plastering, and stone beneath it all fairly earned the home the praise of "handsome." But in addition to being a thing to be seen, a home was the stage on which family life was enacted. Ferry Farm's home was a fitting theatre for the Washingtons to play out their daily dramas, comedies, and tragedies. And like all stages, it had its main areas and its wings, its places revealed and hidden, and its cues and props dictating the movements of its various actors.

The home and its surrounding landscape worked in concert to create plantation life. Like the rings of a tree radiating outward, the different partitions of place surrounded the core—the home—sitting at the social and economic center. And within the home, hierarchies of rooms and access cut up the inside space. In each partition, large or small, differing rules and logics held sway. This way of living rested on each human part of the puzzle—understanding its place, following the rules, playing its role, and living properly in its allotted space. Of course it did not always work perfectly, and coercions were built into the system, but the whole plantation landscape sought to attain an ideal, and so the home, its surrounding outbuildings, and fields all were an argument—a plea—for a particular vision of an ordered world.

A crucial part of this order was a fundamental difference between the many occupants of the Washington farmstead—some were free and some were enslaved and they consequently experienced their shared world very differently. The Washingtons of Ferry Farm were a mixed lot. The master's family was the product of two different marriages and all the varied genetic streams that led into them. Jane's sons Augustine and Lawrence never lived at Ferry Farm, although there seems to have been at one time a plan for Lawrence to come to Fredericksburg to take on a role in the Accokeek project; but Mary's babies all were there.

George was about six and the eldest of Mary's children when they moved to Ferry Farm. His sister Betty was a year younger, and Samuel was the next down the line and four years old at the time of the 1738 move. John Augustine and Charles were both born after the family had left Pope's Creek and made the move in toddler's togs, while little Mildred would be born once the family had settled into its new Rappahannock digs—a full complement of six newly minted Washingtons who also had Ball genes twisted up in the strands of their mitochondrial inheritance.

The enslaved Washingtons were an even more complicated group, drawn from several farmsteads, and from places beyond memory before that. Some lived far from the master's gaze in quarters near the outlying fields they tended. They worked hard, but at least slept in their pallets at night, away from the master's snoring and passed their days out of sight of his watchful eye. Others lived amidst their owning family, sharing their fires' warmth, living by the same daily schedules, dressing in approximations of the family's clothing, and even eating what remained of the meals they had prepared for the people who kept them as property. These differences in labor, housing, and time management defined a large part of their identities and the lives they lived.[9]

Three or four different communities of the enslaved combined at Ferry Farm. Some would have been people Augustine had brought down from Pope's Creek to Little Hunting Creek, and finally on to Ferry Farm. Jack, Bob, Ned, and Lucy, for example, all probably made each of the relocation trips with their owners. Others, though, were people whose ownership changed when their home place changed hands. Phillis, Jemmy, Hannah, and London had all lived at Ferry Farm when it was still in Strother's hands, but now found themselves owned by the Washingtons and welcoming into their own small quarters people from other plantations. In addition to those two communities, there were individuals purchased along the way—new to both groups—and probably a few people who had originally belonged to Mary who made the trips as well, or maybe came over from her other nearby land down the Rappahannock.

All told, this extended free and enslaved Washington family resulted from a very widely cast net. They all gathered together in Ferry Farm's outlying quarters—a half-dozen or so outbuildings—and the eight-room dwelling house. The home lot's buildings had a fixed number of rooms, but locked doors and blocked ways created sets of distinct overlapping geographies. How different members of the household navigated these spaces depended on who they were and the role they played in the domestic system.

There were two interrelated yet distinct worlds. One was the home—a tightly connected group of rooms, each with its own rules, purposes, and equipage, all tied together under one roof. Outward-facing windows surrounded these rooms and brought in light; expensive mirrors helped bounce that light around, as well. But there also was considerable darkness, because the sun's rays drifted unequally, blocked here by a door, there by an interior partition wall. Moving between these rooms was simply a question of opening these doors, but metal locks could keep them closed, and people inside the room could lock themselves in and thus bar all access at will. There also were social locks—rules, protocols, and habits—blocking some rooms to some people. Not every hand could open every door; not every person could walk at will through the home. One must know the rules and be granted entrance.

The second space was the lot behind the home and a north-to-south-running line of outbuildings. Here there also were distinctive rooms with jobs to do. But these were spread out, scattered—like a home turned inside out. To get from one place to another meant going outside; if it rained, it meant getting wet; in heat one sweated. Locks did not work here as they did in the home; here they were only on the outside of doors. They could lock people or loose animals out, but those inside had no ability to lock themselves in. Life in these spaces was always open to intrusion.

In the home, the names of the rooms bespoke their purpose, but did so in a genteel code. The Hall had pride of place in the home's front side, on the north. Here, the windows looked out onto the river and the manicured clean yard that greeted the world. In this room, with its large table and nearly a dozen fine chairs, the family formally dined and visitors chatted long into the night while watching the glow of Fredericksburg in the near distance.

Opposing the Hall, to the south, was the Parlour, an intimate family room with beds, chairs, leather-topped trunks, and other accoutrements for family living. Here the master and his family reposed informally, enjoyed light meals, played with the children. The mistress and her daughters practiced the gentle arts of fine needlework and board games. Only the closest of friends and other kin passed time here.

These were the two finest spaces on the plantation, and fashionable paneling and plastering adorned their walls. Crafted cupboards held delicate plates, and carved mantle pieces were berths for delicate figurines recalling Chaucer and other proud English references.

Behind these front rooms, with windows facing rearward into the yard, onto the outbuildings, and to King's Highway behind them, were more rooms with other coded names. The Hall Back Room served as the master's sleeping quarters while the Back Room behind the Parlour served as a sometime office, sometime sleeping accommodation. Above these were three more rooms where the children and perhaps some trusted enslaved maids and nannies slept.

Despite every attempt to enclose and button up life, there was little that was hidden in these rooms. The sounds of life were easily heard by one and all, and it was a rare moment when one was in a room all alone. The master may have been the only one who could secure some time all on his own in his chamber or office. But even so, the activities outside the windows were almost constant, and the sounds of family life in the home equally unrelenting. The grand view and open fields created prospects of the countryside, but the home lot was a small crowded village.

The living artery of the home was the Central Passage Way that ran athwart the center, linking the front and back. Dark, narrow, and sparsely furnished, it was an indistinct place, neither in the home nor outside of it. Yet, it was where visitors first entered the home. For some, it was a momentary pause before entering the more select rooms. For others it was as far as they got, waiting, cap in hand, for the master. The passage granted or blocked access and one could know a person's status and position from how the Passage Way treated them. It was also the main link to the rear yard; it was where the cooked food entered the home, and where the dirty linens left. It was a place of coming and going. It was a place to which the people of this little village could all lay a claim to belonging.

The rooms and spaces behind the house had names as well. But these were direct unambiguous reflections of the place's main purpose in daily life. A Kitchen sat about twenty-five or thirty feet behind and to the north of the home. It was a frame structure with a large stone-lined cellar beneath it. As its name suggests, this was where the bulk of the cooking took place. The painstaking work of preparing joints on rotating spits, baking bread in brick ovens, or keeping stews on the boil in the coals all went on, overseen, probably, by cooks named Sue or Nan. It was always hot here, no matter what the outside temperature, as the fires were going all day and all night. But this was also a home for the cook and her immediate family and staff. They slept in the loft or on impromptu pallets on the floor.

Next to the Kitchen sat a dairy—an immaculate and well-plastered structure where cream was skimmed and milk kept clean and fly-free. South of that were storehouses, perhaps a smokehouse, and a quarter to the north for the men who worked the near fields.

Families socialized in these spaces just as they did in the Hall and Parlour inside. But here, private activities were governed by the scheduling and needs of the people inside the main house. Everything here was open and observable—witnessed and watched—by the family inside and the people they employed to oversee work. Life here was lived on call.

Day in and day out, the routines of plantation life flowed over the house and yard. Food came and went; discussions between master and supervisor, supervisor and labor all echoed in the Passage Way or in the Yard. Children played in and around the home, the enslaved ones near the spaces of their parents' work, the free ones in their special rooms and elsewhere, supervised by parents, siblings, and enslaved nannies. The activities at Accokeek took up dinner discussions, as did the overall planning for the farm, talk of local affairs, and Imperial matters. Letters from Lawrence, in his Majesty's service, made fights in faraway ports seem very close and personal.

For a young child like George, whose day to day was in and around his family home, the Passage Way, the Hall, and the Yard were his classroom in the rules of Virginia society. Seeing who made it through the Passage and who did not, watching how people of lower standing acted before the gentry, and seeing how his father spoke to the ordinary sort were formative lessons in how hierarchies functioned. He saw the comings and goings of enslaved Africans, movements so frequent that these people became like the skirting boards or the couch—all but invisible for their ubiquity. This made their presence and their peculiar condition seem simply a natural state of affairs—part of the large order, ordained, as it must be.

Ferry Farm's twin spaces of house and yard were the center of young George's world from the time he arrived in 1738. The lessons learned in these rooms and lots were amongst the most deeply ingrained of his life. Soon life-altering events beyond a little boy's control would add new lessons and introduce unforeseen questions.

3

George Washington,
Master of Ferry Farm

Augustine Washington was a man who liked things planned out. But no amount of careful planning can avoid certain realities. There was a small walled-in cemetery just south of the home standing as a silent reminder of the limits of plans.

Ferry Farm's new family had their own lesson in these limits in 1740. Mildred Washington had been born sixteen months earlier—the only member of the family born at Ferry Farm. In October this little girl became the only one of her line to lie buried at Ferry Farm. She was the last of Mary's babies, and the only one of her six that she lost in childhood. The family gathered in the small enclosed yard in the fall chill, and set a lovingly washed and wrapped Mildred in a small hole in the rocky soil.

Sometime around then there was another fearful brush with fate. The southern side of the home was heated by a large chimney that divided into two hearths—one in the corner of the Parlour family room and the other in the Rear Room where some of the family slept. It might be that the burning wood spilled out onto the wooden floor, or that sooty buildup caught flame, but whatever the cause, the rear rooms filled with smoke as a slow-moving fire gnawed away at the trim and plaster.

Some sort of impromptu bucket brigade must have been able to douse the flames early on, since they failed to engulf the whole house. But the damage was severe. Parts of the ceiling, walls, and perhaps a section of the roof itself all had to be replaced. Workers dumped some of the charred remains into a hole under the home, and life continued on as before. Nevertheless, this near calamity was an unwelcome reminder of the perils of eighteenth-century living. Late in life, George mentioned in passing to a would-be biographer that his "father's house burned."[1]

Then, in April 1743, Augustine himself lay dying. No one recalled specifically what ailment laid Augustine low. Later chroniclers called it a stomach illness, others claimed a fever of some kind, some blamed gout. All are perfectly plausible, and all are equally immaterial—Washington men did not have the habit of living long.

On the eleventh of April in the company of family members and neighbors such as William Strother's brother Anthony, Augustine dictated his last will and testament. His hand gripped life's tiller as tightly as possible one final time. From his bed in the Hall Rear Room, or perhaps from a more public repose in the Parlour, he laid out plans to control from beyond the grave a lifetime of arranging and acquiring.

Each piece of his land he allocated to his various children. Each interest and project received a designated custodian. Each enslaved African he assigned a new master. He designed contingency plans so that, should Mary die or remarry his will would still be the one directing his property's fate.

On the twelfth, two somewhat different veils of sorrow fell on the homestead—one over the free Washingtons and the other on the enslaved. The free Washingtons set about cleaning the corpse, getting possessions in order for the legal counting that would soon follow. They nursed their sadness and contemplated what the division of Augustine's over ten thousand acres would mean for their aspirations and how they would live their lives. He had three full gentry homesteads, mine interests, and seats on sundry boards. He had business contacts on both sides of the ocean, crops going into the ground, orders awaiting fulfillment in the commercial houses of British merchants, and piles of signed legal obligations.

He and his enterprises were the great unifying link for his family—a father's sheltering shadow covering and providing for his wives and their children. They were the harvests of a lifetime's labors and the seedbeds for the next generation's planting. His death broke that link. It disrupted the pattern of acquisition. It was a reckoning in the form of reversal: where there had been in-gathering, now there would be division.

The enslaved Washingtons would also have been keeping a close eye on the rapid deterioration of their master. They could not have read the will he had dictated, but it is easy to imagine that curious ears heard the discussions as their chores kept them at the edge of the scene. In whispered voices, or hidden discussions, all would have been inquiring about what was said of their name or those of their loved ones. Who would go where? Who would remain together and who would have to leave? Word would have spread as each member of the community eagerly inquired about to whom they would now belong and what that change of ownership might portend. The death of a master was every bit as great a tragedy in the yard as in the home—perhaps even a greater one.

As Augustine lay stiffened and cold, washed, wrapped and readied for the tomb, his empire devolved to its new owners guided by the terms he had laid out on April 12.

Lawrence had already been settling into his new life as a Virginia gentleman. Augustine had set him up perfectly with connections and an English schooling. On his death, Augustine left his eldest the Little Hunting Creek acres and control over Accokeek. Soon he renamed the place Mount Vernon and married into the Fairfax family. Austin went back to the place of his and his father's birth and became the master of the Pope's Creek estate. He had wanted a career in the law—he may even have hoped to build a life in England rather than on the Northern Neck. But it was not to be. With his schooling cut short and his inheritance located on the Potomac he was soon back on the ancient family acres.

The old Strother home and its surrounding near four hundred acres would now all belong to son number three—eleven-year-old George Washington. The land was divided into northern and southern detached parcels sandwiching a few hundred acres still owned by Anthony Strother. The northern tract was about 160 acres, then rented out to Mathew Tiffy, who paid an annual fee for the rights to farm the landlocked fields. The southern tract was a similarly sized long narrow strip holding the home and yard at the waterside and fields in full production.[2] The rest of the plot stretching back from the river and up the rise of land was covered with trees—the same unburned woods dating back to Smith's day.

In addition to the two Ferry Farm plots, George got just over two thousand as yet unused acres at Deep Run nearer the Falls. The acreage was well positioned, but was not yet making money. The plan was that Mary would have a cash annuity from Austin's lands at Pope's Creek to supplement income and help cover costs of getting Deep Run into production. Then, if all went well, when George came of age, he, and little brother Samuel, who also had Deep Run acres, would come into a nice little business. All young George had to do was steer clear of disease and disaster, not drown in the Rappahannock's riptides, make it to twenty-one, take claim of his properties, and then live the life of a moderately well-off planter. Many Virginians would have been thrilled to have such a deal drop in their laps.

But just after inking the document, a dying Augustine changed his mind. Anthony Strother had had his eye on Ferry Farm's northern tract. It sat like a wedge against his own land, and buying it only made good sense. On his deathbed Augustine suddenly agreed with Strother—who was sitting there at the bedside. The clerk took up the quill once more, and Augustine added a spontaneous postscript to a rather carefully thought-out will. He granted Lawrence the right to sell the acres to Strother and hand the earnings over to George if Lawrence thought it was a good idea. As compensation for this change, George would get two additional parcels in Fredericksburg.

The change in the will was a time bomb. It confused control of Ferry Farm. Were the two parcels George's with Mary as his regent until his maturity, or did Lawrence have the last say? After all of Augustine's careful planning, this last minute change sowed confusion and tension.

The rest of the boys received parts of distant parcels and sister Betty received something from Lawrence's hand to ensure a good dowry. At any rate, Mary's children were still far too young to take care of themselves and their new possessions. She would act as their agent as well as manage her own lands that she retained throughout her fourteen years of marriage.

The enslaved Washingtons in the Yard did not receive bequests, although on occasion masters might offer something after their deaths—even freedom—to their human property. Instead, they changed owners, but were not scattered to the winds.

An enslaved man named Frank, who may have hailed from Ferry Farm, went to Austin—and logically would have followed his new master to Pope's Creek. Ownership of Ned, Jack, Bob, Sue, and Lucy went to Mary, meaning that these folks probably stayed home at Ferry Farm. To Betty, Augustine left two little girls; one was Sue's daughter—a fact that may mean that Mary's bequeathed people stayed at Ferry Farm. The other was Judy's daughter. The girls also had rather curious names—Betty and Mary. Why did these two little girls have the same names as members of the family? Who made these name choices? What might have enslaved women (had they chosen the names) been saying about their lives at Ferry Farm, or even the girls' lineages, by naming their babies after the master's wife and daughter? Was it tribute, a rebuke, or something very much else? We can only guess. But the fate of these little girls was more certainly redirected by this change of owners. Daughter Betty would in time marry and leave for a husband's home, but for the next several years Ferry Farm had two pairs of Mary and Betty—one free and one enslaved.

In his share of the estate, George also received ten people, about a third of all of the enslaved then living at the Ferry Farm. The will did not list them, but they were presumably people already living in the yard or at the quarter. Their number may have included field hands like Tim, Ralph, or Dublin. He may also have gotten skilled domestics and cooks like Sue or Nan. He may even have received one young man named George, whom the inventory valued at twenty pounds.

So, at the age of eleven, the free George became both a landowner and a slaveholder. For so many Virginians, attaining these cherished titles was the culmination of years of work. Before he even needed to shave, George had far more land and human property than poor Maurice Clark had even after a decade's toiling away on other people's acres. He now had an estate comparable to William Strother's—and he had been a member of the House of Burgesses. Augustine's bequest could hardly be called stingy—it alone set his son up for life.

But it is hard to imagine that the little boy would have felt much beyond sorrow that spring. And there was still more.

Augustine's wealth and connections had provided the older sons with English educations at the Appleby School. This sort of schooling was a curious vanity for wealthy colonists. These folks considered themselves Britons living in Virginia, and while the colony was a fine place to make money and build estates, it nevertheless lacked certain elite amenities. The difference was that there was a certain panache and finishing that came with English schooling. Little of practical planter use was acquired in the hallowed Public School halls of Eton, Wakefield, and Appleby. Latin, Greek, and some history and philosophy were all wonderful refinements, but they did nothing to help tobacco grow in difficult soils or to survey new acres. But this training did serve as a sort of entry into a club—the fellowship of genteel Britons overseas who could be assured of each others' character based on intangibles like manners and airs.

An English schooling at Appleby may well have been in the works for George as well, but if it was, it was rather slow in coming. Lawrence and Austin had traveled to England with their father in 1729 to begin school at ages eleven and nine respectively. George was already eleven and yet there was no indication that he had been packing his bags by the time his father died. In fact, the trip to England Augustine took just before his death might have been the perfect time to set George up at school. But that chance came and went with the tide. And once Augustine was dead, that particular door closed for good. Like most well-off Virginian children, he had been learning the basics in local schools, and working at home or with his cousins and with tutors.

Augustine's death also denied his third son the advantages of a well-connected father to open doors, secure offices, and push a well-polished child to the front of the right lines. This was a world of patrons and networks. Ability, strength of character, and sheer determination were all wonderful attributes for a young man to have. But all doors were locked from the other side—it always took a better-positioned patron to open them. So the loss of a well-connected father left a child without a patron of first resort.

As spring turned to summer in 1743, the new youthful master of Ferry Farm found himself rather well set up with investments but now lacking a father's connections and a chance at an English schooling. The road ahead looked comfortable in the provincial style. It might have been lacking flash and fashionability, but it had the promise of local prominence and status—a merchant planter with acres and warehouse, community offices, seats on local boards—a plump and well-set member of the local gentry. George had every reason to believe that one day his name might rise to the status of a Lewis or a Strother—but no higher.

From the age of eleven until 1752, the year when he would come into his own, the fates of George, his siblings, and Ferry Farm itself all came down to how well Mary was able to manage the farm, her own lands, her children's bequests and educations. It was not a light load.

English and Virginia property law envisioned male heads of households. While there certainly were women of property, they were often seen essentially as custodial owners—place savers until an inheriting son or a new husband was able to take the reins of real proper male ownership. Augustine's will protected the children's inheritances should Mary remarry and left Lawrence as a sort of back-up leading man. But much of the weight fell on Mary's shoulders—and as a woman, management of estates was a challenge.

One way many a widow might solve this problem was to take a new husband. At thirty-five when Augustine died, Mary was not beyond her marrying years and more than a few gentry women collected two, three, or even four last names like lineage-revealing bridal trains showing their paths through the marriage market. Witness George's future betrothed, Martha Dandridge Custis Washington, or Lawrence's too-early widowed Anne Fairfax Washington Lee. But George's mother, for reasons she kept to herself, was to remain Mary Ball Washington until the end. That choice ensured that her fortunes would hereafter be tightly entwined with those of her children—particularly her two eldest, George and Betty. By accident or by design, Mary now absolutely needed to do everything she possibly could to ensure that they would be ready for good gentry lives.

It was not going to be easy. The decade had begun poorly for the Washingtons amidst deaths and fire. On top of that, the colony was hitting hard economic times. In the 1730s and 40s Virginia's population nearly doubled—by the 1760s it would double yet again. Meanwhile, English and European markets were flooded with Virginia tobacco—much of it substandard—and the effects of a poor market were most strongly felt where the soil never yielded the best output in the first place. Ferry Farm was just that sort of place.

The family had to live on the income gleaned from Ferry Farm's southern tract, earnings from the rented northern lot, five years of the annuity from Pope's Creek, and planting at Mary's lands at Little Falls, a few miles below Fredericksburg. In time the Deep Run acres would, ideally, add some income as well. Mary and her family were what we would call today house rich, but cash poor. The family had the trappings and values of the gentry, but did not have the cash-in-hand buying power that they had only the year before. Time, careful land management, alliance building, and luck could fix all that.

Betty would quickly need to become the most gentile and fashionable bride-on-a-budget she possibly could be. Getting her trained was Mary's corollary to the four-hundred-pound dowry that Augustine had left. Land management and matchmaking were well within Mary's experience and abilities. She also needed to ensure that George would be ready and able to take over the properties' management as soon as he was of legal age. Some of that training she could cover. His reading and writing abilities, basic farming knowledge, managing a home and yard filled with free and enslaved people, and ensuring that he was properly mannered and presentable were all skills she could impart.

Connections, though, were harder for a widowed woman to manage. In that venture, Mary had to rely on influential men in and close to the family—her stepsons Lawrence and Austin primarily; her brother Joseph, then living in London, might play a caring uncle's role; while local friends and allies could be tapped when needed. She could get George cleaned, literate, and mannered, but beyond that would prove tricky— but, ideally, not impossible.

Mary's was a complicated plan, one with many moving parts and eggs in many baskets. It would also mean some privation now in the hope of future rewards of position, marriages, and property. Indeed, the 1740s would turn out to be some of the farm's hardest years—Washington himself later recalled them as some of the poorest years of his life. Mary was used to these slowly unfolding schemes of advancement. This sort of careful slow growth was almost a Ball family trait. In fact, Joseph himself reminded her that she must teach George to be Aesop's tortoise. "He must not be too hasty to be rich," Ball cautioned his younger sister; he must instead "go on Gently and with Patience, as things will naturally go."[3]

But the Ball tortoise had wed a Washington hare. Not long for this world and filled with a healthy dose of Virginia gentry ambitions, the Washington way was to move quickly and dramatically, leap while there was the chance, live fast, die young. It had been a trait of each of the generations. Time would prove that George had more Washington blood in his veins than the more cautious Ball stuff. But as his mother's ward in the 1740s, he had, for the time being, little choice but to live the Ferry Farm way and go on gently as things will naturally go.

By the 1740s, the twenty-year-old house was also beginning to age. This would be a decade of deferred maintenance as resources went elsewhere. Tastes were changing and some members of Virginia's elite were building homes that were far greater. But even so, Ferry Farm had what would still have been a very respectable substantive gentry home for the area, even though the red walls might be fading a bit and the plaster cracked as the frame settled.

Inside the home, Mary and her children enjoyed a somewhat austere gentility. The family still had the plate and furnishings Augustine had left them. High-style trinkets like molded ceramic figurines adorned the fireplace mantle and the imported mirrors hung on the walls and English stone firebacks warmed in the hearths. But many of the dressings were just a touch behind the curve. There was not much silver or pewter in the cupboard. Instead, the plates—a major expenditure for an eighteenth-century family—were of a recently fashionable white stoneware ceramic embossed with little patterns along its edges. Instead of ivory or even jeweled fork handles, Mary's table setting boasted more affordable bone. She cut corners in the home, but everything was in place for fashionable entertaining in a perfectly respectable style.

Mary spent more liberally, though, when it came to outward appearances. She and her children would have to be seen in town looking the part as best they could manage. Silvered buckles helped give shoes a sparkle, shiny royal tribute buttons were on coat fronts and cuffs, and even wigs were kept in fine order—even when the maintenance took place on the farm as opposed to in a craftsman's shop. Teach the children the ways of elite society and ensure that their manners and appearances were always up to snuff. That way the boys would be seen as clean, proper, and respectable, and Betty, trained in the delicate arts of housewifery, would be well positioned for a fine gentry marriage. This was a Ball plan, slow and steady to win the race.

But Mary was not the only one who could make plans.

Lawrence was busy moving along at a brisk Washington pace at his Potomac estate. Well connected and ambitious, Lawrence acted as if he actually knew that his life would be short. He remade Little Hunting Creek as Mount Vernon, his home and a center of his schemes and activities; a place where George could visit to touch his Washington roots and visit the Fairfaxes' nearby Belvoir.

Lawrence was active. After his Appleby years, he sought out colonial military office and played a small role in the disastrous British Siege of Cartagena, a venture that would incubate within him the lung disease that would later take his life. In Virginia, he helped establish a major land speculation company in the western Ohio country, a venture that would help bring on the Seven Years' War. In 1743 he married Anne Fairfax, the daughter of William Fairfax, his friend, neighbor, and business associate—as advantageous a marriage as could be had in the colony.

Lawrence could also be a force to be reckoned with, though, and could be destructively single-minded in pursuing his aims.

In 1745, he accused Mount Vernon's local Anglican minister, Charles Green—a friend of his father's and a longtime associate of his powerful father-in-law—of being a negligent minister; but what was worse, Lawrence accused him of serial pedophilia and attempted rape. The alleged victim had been none other than Lawrence's new wife, Anne Fairfax.

The family had wisely worked to silence these accusations many years before to protect Ann, her reputation, and her marriage prospects.

But Lawrence undid that and brought it all out into the open. The case became an instant sensation, and his poor wife never fully recovered from the public humiliation of her chastity becoming a topic of Virginia court testimony and tavern jokers from Williamsburg to Philadelphia.[4] The gentry dived on the case, and finally Governor Gooch (Lawrence's former commander) called an end to the proceedings. Lawrence won on the small claims of mismanagement, but Green kept his job and the matter was to be dropped. But Lawrence had shown himself ready to burn to the ground anything that set itself between himself and his goal. Such men change the world. Such men also wreak havoc along the way.

Five months after the humiliating case ended, Lawrence next turned his attention to his brother George, then settling into the slow and steady plans of his mother.

If Mary thought about the future, Lawrence thought about the now. What Mary might have described as a slow start, Lawrence might have described as a problem that needed fixing. In the fall of 1746, Lawrence came up with a way to jump-start George's life. At the age of fourteen, this third Washington son would undo what three generations before him had become, and instead, harken back to the life led by his great grandfather John. George was to become a sailor. Aided by his father-in-law and former navy man Colonel Fairfax, Lawrence sought a berth on a merchant or military ship for his brother. If the scheme was meant to be a way to advance George in the world then its fulfillment would have been nothing short of disastrous. It did, however, place George, Mary's plans, and Ferry Farm itself at the center of a tug-of-war.[5]

In early September 1746, Fairfax was in Fredericksburg bearing two letters about the plan—one for George and the other for Mary, who opposed the idea right away. The influential Fairfax enlisted allies to persuade Mary "to think better" of the plan to rob her of her eldest son and undermine her own plans to advance him.[6] But entreaties and emissaries could not silence what the cabal called Mary's "trifling objection" of the type "fond and unthinking mothers naturally suggest."[7]

Joseph Ball summed up these "trifling" objections with the insightful and direct prose of one who knew his topic. Ball made clear that the navy was not in the cards for George. No matter how confident of obtaining a midshipman's commission his advocates in faraway Virginia might feel, Ball assured his sister that England was awash with young men "always gaping" for the "preferment in the navy," all with the right connections, whereas George, he felt, "has none." As for a berth on a merchantman—Ball wrote that as a "common sailor before the mast" George would get poor pay and limited control over his life while running the risk of naval impressment where cruel boatswains would "Cut and Slash him and use him like a negro, or rather a dog." And if George "should get to be a master of a Virginia ship," which Ball asserted would "be very difficult to do," even then, a better life was to be had by a planter with "three or four hundred acres of land, and three or four slaves" who could with work and time "leave his family in better bread than such a master of a ship can."[8]

It was no coincidence that this was almost exactly the situation faced by George with his rights to four hundred Ferry Farm acres and ten on-site enslaved Africans. Ball knew exactly what he was saying and was no doubt fully aware of whatever were Mary's plans. Slow and steady, "without aiming at being a fine Gentleman before his time," and being careful with his level of debt, he advised his nephew—through Mary—would "carry a man" well and would lead him "comfortably and surely through the world."[9]

Hidden within the back and forth between Lawrence and his mother's schemes for him was also the beginning of the end of Washington's relationship with Ferry Farm, his first property. From then on it was something of a fait accompli that part of George's path would entail work—a career of some sort—in any case, something else other than just growing up in place and following Uncle Joseph's advice for slow and steady advancement. Mary voiced no objections to subsequent career paths—so long as they were sufficiently gentry.

The flaw lay in Ferry Farm itself—or more specifically, in the land's division and Lawrence's control over its distribution. Its two separate tracts of about two hundred acres each was itself a legacy of the way that Strother had gathered smaller parcels owned by men like Maurice Clark. Since the northern parcel had no river access, whatever came onto or off of those landlocked fields had to pass over Anthony Strother's acres. Renting out the 165 acres half solved the problem by handing the day-to-day logistical problems off to some poorer planter in exchange for annual payments. But as properties went, a small isolated tract was not ideal.

In the 1740s, Mary's family was not in the financial feather to buy Strother's land and make the farm bigger that way. But for his part, Strother never stopped considering adding Ferry Farm's northern acres to his own. Small wonder Mary was nervous about her situation at Ferry Farm. She had even asked her brother for help with relocating to Little Falls. So much was against her to begin with. Many small and distant parcels to juggle and get under production and the children to raise and train were challenging enough. She lived on subpar tobacco lands, and progress was slow in getting better prospects into the game. But on top of that, she also was partly dependent on the earnings from a portion of Austin's lands, and all the while Lawrence had his executor rights, which added more unpredictability into the mix. Even in a world where women could only partially control their fates, this fragile arrangement was singularly precarious.

Then in July 1748, Anthony Strother got what he had wanted. As per his rights in his father's will, Lawrence sold Ferry Farm's northern tract for "one hundred and ten pounds sterling money of England"—close to twenty thousand U.S. dollars in today's money.[10] The will stipulated in that ambiguous last-minute codicil that the sale could only go forth if the "Executors shall think it for the benefit" of George, though.[11] Presumably that meant that the proceeds were his although there is no evidence to suggest that whatever payments were forthcoming made it to George.

The loss of the northern tract doomed Ferry Farm as a viable platform upon which George could build his future. The income off of the twin parcels was slender enough already, but then halving them turned slender to scrawny. It was a devastating strike against Mary—and if Lawrence meant to exact revenge against his stepmother for thwarting his sea plan he could hardly have done better.

The sale cut the already cramped and busy farm in half. As George looked out over the view he saw from the farm, his longing for advancement must have been trodden on—not so much by the 1740s rough economics, but rather by the feeling of being a small fish in a very crowded pond stocked with bigger fishes. The Strothers, the Lewises (distant kin to the Washingtons), the Spotswoods, the Taliaferros, and others were all enjoying their successes and exercising their local prominence and power. From Ferry Farm George could see their homes and fields, he could see their warehouses near the river and the masts of their ships bringing their crops and goods to and fro. He could take in the commanding view, and realize with full clarity that none of this could be his, that there was no room for him to spread his wings here, and that staying at Ferry Farm meant living on in the shadows of others already successfully managing a world of which he had but a small part.

But the sale of the northern tract also happened right as George had landed on a promising remunerative scheme that located his future away from Ferry Farm. Like Catlett before him, his immediate future and fortune were in the westward woods, laying chains, recording measurements in one of those large leather-bound ledgers, and turning land into property. With the help and support of the Fairfaxes, George took to surveying—a trade that had both gentry respectability and an almost guaranteed chance at making money, especially when one's patron was

the colony's largest landholder and one's brother was a founding partner
in the largest land speculation venture to date.

Augustine had left behind a small set of surveying instruments which
he kept with sundry other dry goods. Later, a legend would emerge that
as a boy George eyed these tools with longing and anticipation. True or
not, George certainly did set off toward the northern end of the Blue
Ridge in March 1748, just before the final sale of Ferry Farm's northern
tract. Surveying linked George to Lawrence and the Fairfaxes, while the
land sale made Ferry Farm untenable. The way forward was set.

At the age of sixteen he was a large and sturdy young man, fit and ready
for a surveyor's days of riding, chopping at brush and running chains. He
took obvious delight in the travails of the woods. After a night in one particularly vermin-infested bed George chose instead "rather to sleep in ye
open air before a fire." He was "agreeably surprised" at meeting a party of
"thirty-odd Indians coming from war with only one scalp" and took great
joy in shooting at turkeys, swimming his horse through swollen rivers, and
roasting meat over an open fire.[12]

On top of that, the job entailed prolonged travel in the company and
in the service of prominent Virginia grandees. Add to that the chance to
meet and visit all manner of people along the way, and one thing becomes clear: George Washington of Ferry Farm had found his first true
calling. He returned from that first surveying trip saddle worn, scratched
by branches, and bitten by lice, but more important, he had been bitten
by the surveying bug—and he was hooked. He honed in on his studies of
the craft, received a hasty credentialing at the College of William and
Mary and, with the help of the patronage and influence powerhouse of
Fairfax, Fairfax, and Fairfax, secured the office of surveyor for the newly
formed Culpepper County. A brand new county, a brand new office, a
brand new Washington.

In October 1750, Lord Fairfax granted his young protégé a 453-acre
tract in western Frederick County and the next month, George surveyed
and purchased for himself an adjoining tract.[13] And the parcels piled up,

so much so that he soon had close to two thousand acres in western lands to his name. At the age of eighteen he had more acres acquired by his own hand and through his connections than he stood to gain when he came of age three long years in the distant future. How small and irrelevant Ferry Farm must have seemed to a young man who was already a budding western land baron before he even came of full legal age. He barely looked back again.

From the moment he had arrived at Ferry Farm as a child, the land had offered George three vistas—three views into what his life there might be—the river and the sea beyond, the land itself, and the road. The sea was not to be. The land stuck with him, but not as one might have expected. Although he long professed (even demonstrated) a love for farming, he was never the dutiful cultivator, tied to the soil, monitoring its wetness and quality day to day. He had been brought at a young age from a place rich in family history to one chosen for its proximity and its use as property. It was always what it had been since Smith's day: property. Useful? Valuable? Desirable even? Yes, on all counts. But even so, no sentimentality attached. It was a holding, not much more.

Back at the little tract on the Rappahannock, though, the price of Lawrence's sale and the toll of the hard decade was hitting home. On one trip home in May 1749, George wrote that he could not join Lawrence in Williamsburg, since he could not scare up the corn "sufficient to support" a horse already "in very poor order." On top of that, George's mind seemed preoccupied with just how crowded, small, and claimed the whole area was. He lamented plans to locate a new ferry near Mary's other holdings and complained "I think we suffer enough" from the noise and bother of the ferry and its road. Too many neighbors with too many schemes.[14] Ferry Farm and Fredericksburg must have seemed to be yesterday's news: a great place to be from, perhaps, but no place for him to build a future. From then on, George became a less and less frequent visitor to his nominal home.

But even though Mary's Ball family plan sputtered for George, her efforts paid off well for sister Betty. She was not a great beauty—or at least that is how she comes off in her only surviving portrait. She stares out with a bemused grin and thick roseate cheeks—the body under her face may well have been a stock one from the painter's repertoire, as that was how most painters plied their trade. Instead of beauty, Betty's success on the marriage market rested largely on her abilities. She had been promised an impressive dowry of four hundred pounds in Augustine's will. Her desirability rested less on the blush in her cheeks than on her skill at serving tea—a practice she mastered early with her own tea set complete with monogramed spoons. Her allure stemmed from her skill at embroidering delicate lacy adornments crafted with special hooked needles.[15]

In the fall of 1750 Catherine, the wife of prominent Fredericksburg merchant planter Fielding Lewis, took ill after a troublesome birth and the loss of the infant. Both Lewises were Washington cousins, so it was logical that the sixteen-year-old Washington daughter at Ferry Farm come over to the Lewis home on a terraced slope just south of town and help take care of the two toddlers left behind by their mother's death. Four months later, Betty became the second Mrs. Lewis. Like her mother before her, she had wedded an older widower, and had taken up the reins of a household that had recently been the domain of another woman.

Rather than marrying, George spent much of April and August of 1750 making surveys out west. The rest of the time he was back at Ferry Farm or sometimes visiting at the Fairfaxes' Belvoir, Mount Vernon, and Pope's Creek as well. As he acquired money of his own, he spent it on the trappings of gentility. Dancing and fencing lessons and joining the Freemasons kept Fredericksburg a useful place for him. On one visit home, probably in July 1750, he went down to the river for a short bath. While he waded into the Rappahannock, two servant women from town, Ann Carrol and Mary McDaniel, used the moment to rifle through the clothes he left by the bank. The two might have hoped to find monies or valuables hidden somewhere in the garments, or they may even have planned to steal and sell them outright. Whatever their intentions were, though, their plan did not get too far beyond the offing.

George either caught them in the act or they were later located in town in possession of some telltale item they should not have had. In any case, both were incarcerated "on Suspicion of Felony" but in the end, Carrol turned on her confederate, leaving only McDaniel convicted for their "petty larceny."[16] For the crime, McDaniel was tied to a public whipping post and given "fifteen lashes on her bare back."[17] She would carry the resulting mass of scars the rest of her life.

For George, this small, irritating affront was another reminder that this place at the Falls was full of all manner of problems. But then another, far more chilling crime touched on even deeper tensions and anxieties.

Sometime in early September, or perhaps late August while George was still in the woods surveying western lands for clients, something terrible flared up in Ferry Farm's community of enslaved Africans.

Harry had been a field hand working at Ferry Farm's quarter from the time when Augustine was still his master. This quarter was not some far-flung outlier. After Lawrence's sale of the northern tract, Ferry Farm's usable acres were set near the house and along the river. The back acres were still forested. At post-land-sale Ferry Farm, everyone was close to everyone else. And the goings-on at the quarter were known in the big house.

The field hands' lives consisted of working the outer fields and supplying the muscle that kept things moving. Their immediate community was one another. They worked, ate, and slept alongside each other, living in a framed home set on the ground near the place of their labor. They knew the people working in the yard and in the main house and many would also have very close intimate relationships with these other Washington-owned Africans.

They all had English names. Harry was only one of a score of folks with names like Ralph, Adam, Tim, Dick, Ned, London, Steven, and Jack. But sometime after Augustine's death Mary acquired a new man.

Unlike the others, he had a West African name—Tame, an Anglophied version of Tameah or Ahtame, or maybe Tamesah.[18] Someone living at the farm owned a hand-carved carnelian jewel bead—a personal adornment popular in Africa and associated there with power. Some believed that these stones had the power to grant wishes, others saw it as a symbol of kingship. Some enslaved Africans valued these glittering amber-colored beads enough to be buried with them.[19] This gem may well have come to the site with the man with the African name.

Other people were using objects in curious ways. Someone or some people in the household were so troubled by what they saw in the tough 1740s that they turned to magical acts to try to control events. They stashed small bundles in the stone cellar and carefully set enclosed oyster shells in each of the corners near the door leading in and out. Each person passing, therefore, walked through a form of spiritual porthole formed by specially set charms. Someone, no one can know whom, and no one can say if African or European, was appealing to spiritual forces to make the world a better place or grant them some long forgotten private wish.

On top of their day-to-day stresses, some grudge or strife developed between Harry and Tame. The members of the King George County Court, in the fall of 1750, learned the whole story, even though they did not feel it was worth recording. George himself may have known the whole story as well—he may even have been at Ferry Farm when the conflict turned violent as Harry killed Tame.

Whatever its cause, however it was done, this killing was a huge trauma for the enslaved Washingtons. There had to have been partisans for each of the men, not to mention friends and even family left in deep grief. For the owners, as well, acts of slave violence were discomfiting in the extreme. No one who owned human beings ever wanted to consider the possibility that their possessions might actually kill. The speed and ferocity of colonial law made that much clear and ensured that Harry's killing would also effectively be a suicide.

On September 7, a bound Harry was brought out of jail and made his appearance before the King George County court. He protested his innocence in terms and arguments that never made it into his trial's short and stark written record. Whatever his defense, the court quickly found him guilty and he was returned to his cell.

On October 10, Harry was brought to "the place of execution" somewhere near the courthouse. "Then and there" a designated official fulfilled the court's order that he "hang" Harry "by the neck untill he be dead."[20] All that remained was for Mary to receive "the sum of thirty five pounds current money" as a legally mandated repayment for the value of an enslaved man executed by the state.[21] The enslaved Washingtons lost two members of their community. Mary lost two of her people, but she only lost money on one of them.

Seven days after the hanging, George was back in the woods surveying 265 and one-quarter acres along Long Marsh Run for Thomas Loftin.[22] On the twentieth of that October, George received his first land grant from Proprietor Fairfax—the first of many tracts that made him rich and took him far from his old home.

Right after George came into his first independently owned parcel, a trio of King George County officials convened at Ferry Farm. They met on October 31, All Hallows' Eve, under the authority laid out in Augustine's will, with an eye set on redistributing the Washington's enslaved property. In one of Ferry Farm's more formal rooms, Mary and officials rearranged the placement of all of the Africans she had in her charge. The same people who had just endured the killing of Tame and the execution of Harry were now to be shuffled.

The plan may have been to reorganize these communities in the wake of the killings. It also may be that Mary was trying to secure her bequeathed human property lest Lawrence interfere there as he had with the land itself. On the other hand, this may have been Lawrence—or even George himself—using the will's provisions as a way to chastise

Mary for perceived mismanagement in the lead-up to Tame's murder. Whatever the reason, as George was beginning a career in land owning, Ferry Farm was little more than a headache.[23]

He continued to be George Washington of King George County in legal documents as late as 1754. But he had long since turned his eyes and his heart to other places and turned his back on Ferry Farm, that crowded, busy, trouble-filled place of limited options, petty harassments, and a slave owner's deepest fears. It became in his mind his "mother's home," a place he visited still, conducting business there and staying involved in its affairs—but more and more as an absent partner.

As he became rich he helped pull the old place back from the troubled times to the 1740s. He acquired a few of the small parcels on the home place's southern boundary, gradually building the farm up to close to six hundred acres. But this was all for his mother so that she would have lands enough from which to draw a good living. He bought plates and other objects for the home, and life on the farm became a bit more delicate. With a son beginning to fill in the gaps and a daughter living well across the river, Mary became less interested in her other lands and settled into the place that had been a bit of a worry for her. She could now confidently concentrate on raising up the remaining three of her and Augustine's babies.

Ferry Farm became their home now. George was elsewhere.

4

✣

Washington's Parting Survey and the Parson's Pen

In the spring of 1749, George wrote to Lawrence, "I hope your cough is much mended since I saw you last."[1] That fall he wrote of his joy on learning of Lawrence's "safe arrival in health in England."[2] The cough and the illness it portended, though, became an increasing concern. Despite trips to fairer climes, the cough did not mend. The mountains did not help. Nor did Barbados—although the trip with Lawrence gave George smallpox and probably sterility as well. "The unhappy state of health which I labor under," Lawrence wrote from a sickbed in Bermuda, "makes me uncertain as to my return. If I grow worse I shall hurry home to my grave."[3]

Without hurry, he returned to both: home in mid-June, and the grave on July 26, 1752. Augustine's then-still-remembered will stated that George would receive Lawrence's inheritance should he "die without heirs of his body lawfully begotten."[4] But Lawrence had both a wife and a child at the time of his death. The terms of the old will were no longer relevant. So, Mount Vernon became the property of another Widow Washington and her small orphaned daughter, Anne. Unlike the more senior widow, Anne Fairfax Washington added another name to her list of male heads of households when she married George Lee of Westmoreland County and moved to his lands.

Lawrence left his properties in Fredericksburg to George, a logical bequest as Ferry Farm was still the only proper estate George could call his own, even if he was away from it nearly as often as he was there. He was in Fredericksburg in November of 1752 when he joined the Freemasons at the local lodge. He was there again the following August when he received a new rank in the society.

But the matter of permanent address resolved itself once and for all when George and Anne Lee leased Lawrence's estate to a tellingly named "George Washington of the County of King George" on December 17, 1754. Every Christmas he would pay the Lees fifteen one-thousand-pound barrels of tobacco, or less should an enslaved African die that particular year.[5]

The lease document, therefore, was the last one in which anyone would claim that George Washington was "of" King George County—the home county of Ferry Farm and of his childhood. From here on in, all mail needed to be addressed to that same "GW," but now of Fairfax County. How fitting for both the home and its protégé owner that both should be known as "of" Fairfax. Within a short time though he bought Mount Vernon outright from the Lees. In future, their Christmas gifts from George would be a bit more modest.

So in 1754, Washington once and for all ended his tenure at Ferry Farm. He had done so in stages, really, ever since he first arrived in 1738. Each trip to one of his brothers' estates weakened the bond between him and his four hundred-some-odd acres on the Rappahannock. His gradually being pushed toward a career rather than a future of stewardship of this land only further loosened an already wiggly tooth. Finding that career in surveying western land, and then Lawrence's halving the old place, opened the gap past the point where it could close again. So

George's final move to Mount Vernon was really just the paper on what was an already finished wall.

On top of that, George became rich and famous. He ended his career as a for-pay surveyor once he had Mount Vernon. He kept his chain and quadrant skills up by making plats of his own eastern properties, but his days measuring lands for a fee were over. He stayed in the western land game, but now as a moneyed speculator as opposed to a woodsman. He took up his brother's role in Virginia's defense, donning the red coat of His Majesty's colonial forces. In the same woods he knew as a surveyor, he carved out a reputation as an officer of great personal bravery, even if not always of the best judgment or deferential disposition toward his superiors. Nevertheless, the war with France and its network of Native allies that flared in the 1750s allowed him to rise in the ranks and in the esteem of his imperial overlords and his fellow Virginians. He used that reputation to settle himself even more firmly in the running of his native country. He went to the House of Burgesses in 1759. That same year he married a widow, Martha Dandridge Custis, a woman of lineage, connections, and land. He maintained his useful ties to the Fairfaxes and built others with local gentry families. He even built an enduring friendship with none other than Charles Green, the man so hated by Lawrence. What would his long-dead brother have thought if he could have seen Washingtons, Fairfaxes, and Lawrence's execrable Green all dining together in Mount Vernon's dining room? Perhaps George knew just what he was doing.

But while George may have been gone, there still were other Washingtons living in the plastered walls of Ferry Farm's old home. George's newfound wealth and increasing colonial stature lifted the clouds of the 1740s. New goods made it into the household and the standard of living for Mary and her remaining three children improved somewhat. With a well-off son now the land's full and legal owner on whom she could lean a bit, and Betty well established just over the river, Mary had achieved a rather secure widowhood. She never fully dropped the idea of heading

down to her Little Falls land, but as she entered her fourth and fifth decades of life, she more and more considered Ferry Farm her true home.

Washington was up to his three-cornered hat in the affairs of the colony and busy building his own empire. But he stayed involved in the
place he had left. He expanded the acreage of the core holding by buying
up the smaller strips of land south of the farm as they went on the market. Most of these were still wooded, or at least not ready for crops. But
even so, the combination of well-situated, well-established children and
a bit more land on hand only made Mary's life there that much easier.
Mary could sit in the parlour, drink tea or sip punch from a pricy cherry-
motif-adorned punch bowl while entertaining guests feeling secure in
her future.

Yet the land still caused him trouble. There had been an ongoing
land dispute with Anthony Strother over some lingering confusion
about that very parcel Lawrence had sold back in 1748. In 1760 the issue
came to a head. Strother had recently sold his entire estate (including the
northern tract) to Colonel Henry Fitzhugh. But for reasons long lost, the
actual ownership of that portion was unclear—perhaps a result of flawed
surveying or a bill never paid in full.

In any case, in 1760 Strother conceded that he had made an error in
the sale and owned up to owing Washington money. In a pained letter,
Strother, a man who had attended the death of George's own father,
pleaded to little George that it would take some time to scare up the
needed funds. "However," he wrote to his younger and far more powerful former neighbor, "as your right seems to be very clear, I only desire
youl let it lye" until he could see his distant nieces and beg them to return the monies he had just handed over.[6]

But four years later the whole thing had reversed itself, and now it
was Washington who was in the wrong. Whereas Strother accepted his
fate with the deference so prized in colonial society, Washington was not
a bit pleased to be so disadvantaged over Ferry Farm.

He begrudgingly accepted the debt upon which he "was adjudged to make good."[7] But at the same time, he professed an astonished ignorance of the details of the "whole transaction."[8] "Now Sir," he wrote to his new creditor, "the favor I have to ask is, that you that you would be so good" as to explain "the full state of the case."[9] He went on, "I really know little or nothing of the matter," the dusty details of which happened "so long ago" at a time when George, by his own account, "had very little leisure to attend" to his own "private affairs."[10]

With palpable frustration Washington wrote to Strother that "common sense and equity tells me, That if I was answerable to you for lands sold by my Fathers Exrs that your Brothers Estate should be liable to me for the same Lands, sold by his Executrix."[11] Here was a man made rich and powerful through the acquisition of land. He had married into a wealthy landed family, he ruled a vast estate beset with its own maintenance issues, and had recently served his king in a war designed almost exclusively to secure even more western lands for himself and men just like him. And what was he doing? Squabbling with an aging crony of his father's over a small tract that he had long ago left behind and forgotten about. It was as if all the confusions and unfinished transactions from the deals and agreements of the dead were reaching out from the grave and intruding in on George's life.

Then, on September 10 and 11 of 1771, George made the overland trip from Mount Vernon to Fredericksburg. He dined that night at Ferry Farm and the next morning he saddled his horse and rode over the lands of his childhood. His circuit took him along the waterfront and along the fields and home lot in the shadow of the land's gentle rise. He kicked up dust along the road that connected the farm to King's Highway and tracked the length of the fence just before it. When he had completed that ride, he then led his horse inland to trace the outline of the outlying quarter and its surrounding fields.[12]

He passed much of the day in the saddle wandering the cleared and farmed acres he had inherited and bought. Fields of harvest-ready corn, or just cleared stalks waiting to be knocked down, and low green waves of recently planted winter wheat—a few hundred acres rolling back from the river and up the rise of land. Cut with private and public roads, marked with fences, and backed by well-watered forest. He scouted out the land's edges and corners. He sought out its best and most memorable markers. And then, he went back to the house by the bluff and the ferry road which he tellingly called "my mother's."[13] After dinner, he crossed the river and passed the night in town with his brother Charles and Fielding Lewis.

The next morning he was back. He had breakfast with Mary, and then went back out on the land. Armed now with tools of his old trade— the chain, the compass, and the leather binder—George Washington began to perform the first ritual in the sale of land: the recording of a place's metes and bounds. Ferry Farm was to be measured, and George would do this survey himself.

Washington could easily have contracted out the job to a local artisan. He had been with his colleague William Crawford only two days before. Here was a man as skilled in the art as was Washington and the two already had a long association based on land acquisition. Why not ask Crawford? There had to have been local men skilled in the craft as well—surveying was hardly a rare skill. Indeed, 1771 was a rather busy year. Washington's time was absorbed with expanding his holdings and managing what he had already acquired. On top of that, the previous decade had been full of war and the Imperial crisis that followed it. A new king who knew not George had come to the throne in 1760 and begun to rethink how to govern his empire. There had been boycotts and riots in response to a host of new rules, restrictions, and taxes. The worst was yet to come, but in these tense and busy times, one might imagine that Washington had better things to do than take up the chains and the binder and once more tramp over the acres of his old bequest. But that is just what he did.

Perhaps he wanted the best and clearest possible survey so that he never had to deal with this place again. Leaving the job in local hands could mean problems or shoddy work—after all, it was errors and confusion in the earlier records that led to his dispute with Strother. But in this last survey Washington only cast his eye over the riverfront fields—the lower part of the land—and he made no effort to measure the far larger wooded stretch behind the farmed acres. If an accurate dispute-proof measurement was the goal, Washington would have hacked his way through the scrub just like he used to in the Blue Ridge shadows. Perhaps he planned to just sell off the lower fields and hold on to the rest? Perhaps, he planned to return at a later date to complete the work and just found no time? Possibly, but his records suggest instead that he finished what he set out to do.

We cannot know his reasons, but we can know the outcome of Washington's last ramble in 1771. More was at work here than a clear handle on the old homeland's metes and bounds.

The surveyor was a unique poet. It was his art to take the land and its contours, its rises and falls, its turns and trees, and render them in a simple practical terse prose—the poetics of property. The map is of course the most celebrated of the surveyor's creations, but the main art is a text version—something akin to a set of directions, or the document a maritime navigator would call a rudder. It is a description in words and numbers rather than a drawing. It is an itinerary of how the artist walked over the land, what he saw along the way, which bits of it seemed most important and defined, and of course, what compass point to head to and how far to follow it.

In surveying Ferry Farm that fall, George did not need to cut any trees, clear any brush, or open any closed views. Instead, all he had to do was go back over this working farm, pick the visible features he thought stood out best, and record the distances and directions between them. As surveying went, it was a pretty easy job—a pretty routine description, a walk in the fall air. But this was no western tract platted out on a contract for a new owner. This was this particular surveyor's old home, his mother's home, a place filled with his own personal memories and those of his family. It was a place of personal loss and trials, a place of feelings and thoughts that he kept hidden from posterity. Thus, each choice of landmark, each marker, each describing word for what he called the "fields where my mother lives," was more than practical measurement.

The principal features were roads. This was a busy little crossroads cut through with avenues and paths, each of which had strangers and neighbors opening and closing the family's gates to go onto and off of the farm's acres. Washington caught the King's Highway running right through the heart of the land. George called it the "Great Road" and he recorded where it split in two. Half turned off through a farm gate and became what he called the "Road to Stafford Court" as it cut back through one of the farm's cornfields and connected to a "path leading to Fitzhugh's quarter." The other half of the "Great Road" fork became a "country road" wending its way to "the lane," which in turn ran the edge of the "gulley leading to the ferry landing" and then flowed into the "ferry lane."

He recorded the fences surrounding the upper cornfield and noted "some pretty good land," watered by a nearby creek, though the acres were still wooded and awaiting clearing. He showed a long "slipe of woods" running parallel to "the low grounds on the river," an echo of a time George could not have known, when the man from Hasinninga told Virginia's original soldier Captain John Smith that the sides of the river were covered in trees.

But in all of this observation and recording, he never found a need to note where the home itself actually was.

Had she cared to, Mary could have sat by the Rear Room's windows and watched her son practice the trade, which, more than any other, took him from this land. She could have sipped tea and watched her son and his assistants take the measure of the land she had called home for half her life. For much of the day, George saw the red home in the near distance, anchoring the land and setting a depth of field for Fredericksburg beyond. It was far and away the most obvious marker of the land.

And yet, he did not record it in this survey of fields. He noted the rough location of the "hen yard," the "garden pales," and even where his path crossed the "end of the garden" as he skirted the home lot. But apart from that, nothing.

But Washington chose a rather singular place to be an end to this last survey. His path was a circuit—he ended at the same point from where he set out. That means he could have picked any landmark as the anchor for the survey. Out of all the fences, gates, and marked trees, he rooted his work at "the little gate by the tombstone" which sat a few dozen yards south of the home yard.

This was the lot where his sister Mildred lay—the only Washington to be buried at this homestead. It was probably her very tombstone he noted, the only one the family left behind. The home lot had gates as well—it also had fences and buildings, any of which would have provided a fine marker for a survey. Yet instead of these, he chose to memorialize the enclosure that was the last resting place of his baby sister, noting the "little gate" and the "tombstone" in what was his most sustained treatise on his childhood home place.[14]

The survey was an almost private document, noted in his diary but not added to the land's official record. It was as if it was a secret act. Even when he sold the land to Fredericksburg physician and drug maker Hugh Mercer a few years later, he neglected to mention how he had passed September 13, 1771. Mercer wrote to Washington on March 21, 1774, that he "had an inclination to purchase" Ferry Farm at the asking price of three pounds an acre and that he had "heard that the tract contains about 600 acres."[15] Washington concurred on the price and terms, although he noted that old parcels first surveyed and mapped back in Catlett's day were "generally over measure" in their acreage, making their assumed size a bit unreliable by the more scrupulous standards of the 1770s.[16]

Most curious, though, Washington wrote back to Mercer on March 28 that, whether his mother's farm "measures more or less" a full six

hundred acres "I really know not, as it never was survey'd to my knowledge."[17] "Never was survey'd"? That was rather a remarkable claim and
on its face that was a lie. Washington was well aware of the land's original surveys—he had even mentioned them disparagingly to Mercer. He
can be forgiven there though, as his comment "never was survey'd" was
certainly referring to more recent and reliable activity than the century-
old patents. But what about his own survey of the farm's core—surely his
own work might have been worth a mention? Forgiven here as well, since
he clearly meant that the holding had not been measured in full.

Perhaps he might have said never "fully survey'd" just in the name of
accuracy. But this was just a simple land deal between friends—it was
fair to assume some understanding. Nevertheless, George's silence on
the September 13 survey right at the moment of disposing of the land
makes even clearer that this survey was a private affair, something he
had done for himself and therefore was not really relevant to the task at
hand. Had George been a painter he might have rendered the farm on
canvas. Had he been a scribbler of odes or plays, perhaps he might have
set a story on the land or maybe recalled its verdant fine pastures, lit
bright with the sun's shine.

But he was none of these things. He was a surveyor. And it was as a
surveyor with a surveyor's terse yet deeply symbolic pen that he said
good-bye to the land where he had come of age, the land he had long ago
outgrown.

In 1772 he took out an ad in the *Virginia Gazette* to rent, sell, or trade
his paternal bequest "for back land in any of the Northern counties of
this colony."[18] In the ad, he recited the one and only description of Ferry
Farm he ever penned—the one that noted the "clear and distinct view of
almost every house" in Fredericksburg.[19]

That same year, George purchased a modest wooden-frame home
sitting just below the site of a magnificent new house Fielding Lewis was
building. Soon, Mary and her belongings were ensconced in her own
in-town residence. She lived there for her remaining sixteen years, close

Benson Lossing's Washington home
This is one of many reprints of the rendering Lossing claimed to have based on Gadsby Chapman's notes. This vision of the house matches Weems's portrayal of a humble rustic Washington home and for over a hundred years was widely accepted as being a true-to-life, accurate impression.

Federal Troops cross the Rappahannock in 1864
This is at least the third pontoon bridge soldiers set up to tie Ferry Farm (on the far side) to the Fredericksburg wharfs (in the foreground). In the farthest distance is Stafford Heights—barely discernable just below that is the line of the plateau where the Washington home stood. The tents below that sit on the flood plain made high here because of low tide. The growth of trees on the left shows where the stream and the old Ferry Lane ran.

Ferry Farm and Fredericksburg from Stafford Heights
Artists and photographers loved this view of town in the distance. This shot from
the early 1880s shows the new Corson Family Farm on the land. The small white
Surveying Office is in plain view on the left. It was this farm that J. B. Colbert bought
in 1909.

J. B. COLBERT

at Ferry Farm

*James Beverly
Colbert, circa 1920*
Colbert sitting proud
on a fine mount amid
the chaos and indus-
trial architecture of his
ever-busy Ferry Farm.
More than any other,
this image portrays
the contrast between
the day-to-day and
grand airs that defined
both Colbert and
Ferry Farm during his
tenure.

The Surveying Office, circa 1920
Here is the contradiction that was the Surveying Office as it came to fame. At once a utilitarian part of a farm-scape—attached here to the old Corson house moved to the spot—and a venerated object covered by its own special extra roof. Note the carefully maintained decay, giving it the feel of antiquity.

Cherry tree and cheery lad, circa 1950
The old tree has suffered some-what—it is a sliver of its former self and here is held up by wires. But the commemorative plaque at the base and this boy's Sunday-best keepsake show that its aura still outgrew the actual trunk.

Bartlett's Washington bust and the Surveying Office, circa 1965
The bronze sits outside, open to the elements, just in front of the recently renovated Surveying Office as space-age tourists take in the sights. The pillar that the bust sat upon will soon become the assumed marker of Mildred Washington's grave site.

Ferry Farm in the early 1990s
The Surveying Office is again showing its less than considerable age while a plastic tent shows where excavation teams are digging down to the bottom of Colbert's ice house shaft, hoping to prove it a Washington relic. They did not. Colbert's big farmhouse sits corroding as well. In a few years it would be consumed by fire—the only farmhouse at Ferry Farm to have that dubious honor.

Student excavator digs into Maurice Clark's cellar
Here the cellar has been cut in half so that we could see its full outline and get a sense of the date from the artifacts the fill contained. It was these finds as well as the actual form of the building that revealed that it was far too early to belong to the Washingtons. *(Photo courtesy of Philip Levy)*

Excavation in progress at the Washington home site
It took considerable time to expose this much area, but even at this early stage elements of the Washington home are already showing. The line of stones on the lower right will prove to be the base of a chimney, and the ladder is there to photograph what we were then realizing was a cellar of some consequence. Note the Surveying Office in the background. *(Photo courtesy of Philip Levy)*

The Colbert ice house shaft cutting through the Bray House cellar
This shot captures the complexity of Ferry Farm's excavations. The grass and stones and dirt all sit inside the deep footprint of Colbert's ice house. His workers dug right through the 1850s Bray House cellar in making their hole. Visible at the bottom are the cellar stairs that showed us that "Daddy's Little Disappointment" was not Washington-era. Many of these stones, however, had once been part of the Washington House foundations.

Dawn over the Washington home late in its excavation
The main elements are all in place. The two cellars (partly excavated here)—the lower one being the earlier, better-made one, the upper one being the later addition. The Civil War trench (also only partly excavated) runs across from left to right while the 1920s waste water pipe (mostly removed here) runs from the bottom of the image to its stone-lined sump terminus in the Washington home.

One of the surviving sections of the Washington House cellar wall—one of the oldest parts of the site. Note the fine stone finishing and the careful—even artistic—arrangement. George himself would certainly have known this place, even if he was not perhaps responsible for stashing magic totems in the wall's cracks and corners.

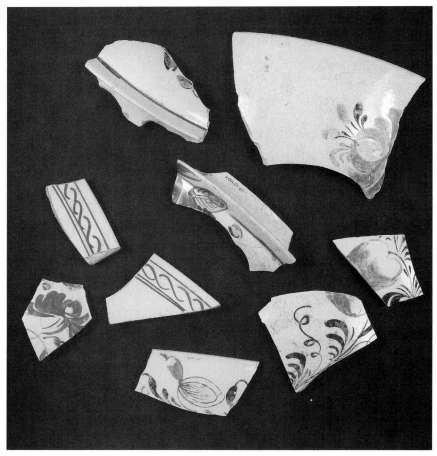

Our excavations unearthed more than a half million artifacts; here is a small sample. These were all tablewares owned by Mary Washington, dating to the 1760s. On the right are fragments of the cherry-adorned punch bowl.

by Betty and her children and on the edge of Fredericksburg. Not far from that home the land dropped and there was a large rock outcropping. Later, a story would emerge that Mary had a special love for this place. They said that she used to stroll there to take the breezes, read her bible, and pray for the health and success of her son George during all of his trials and travails.

In 1774 he signed the papers with Hugh Mercer, and like that, it was over. Thirty-six years of Washington family ownership quietly ended when Mercer agreed to a "round sum of two thousand pounds" for the whole parcel "as it stands."[20] Parts of the fields were rented out to neighbors Hunter and Fitzhugh, but sometime after April of 1774, Washington received the first of Mercer's payments. The last Washington stake in the land had been pulled up.

Hunter and Fitzhugh might have seen Ferry Farm as a place to rent for corn and winter wheat but Mercer had a different plan. In their sales discussion Washington had said that he had always thought the land's main value was "on accont of it situation and contiguity to Fredericksburg."[21] Mercer and family members in on the deal could not have said it better. It was not the corn they wanted. It was that bend in the road and the path down to the ferry. Their idea was to set a new town right where Washington had lived.

"Mercertown" would be a north-bank answer to Fredericksburg. Local farmers could save the river crossing and bring their crops to a new wharf just below Ferry Farm's aging home—conveniently set below the growing sandbar by the old wharf. It was an ambitious plan that made logical use of the activity that George had always found so annoying.

But it was a short-lived scheme. Hugh Mercer was killed by the British in the Battle of Princeton in 1777, and even though his son William carried on the flame, the idea itself never got much further than a sheet of paper marked up with speculative lots to be laid out on Ferry Farm's acres. That map was quite a statement, though. It showed ranks of carefully drawn two-acre-square lots set in a grid of roads, each an ample sixty-six feet wide, and all covering roughly seventy-one acres of land—the bulk of the area of Mary's old fields.

In a veiled way, Mercertown's shape was a commentary on Fredericksburg, with its narrow urban roads and tightly packed lots. Mercertown was an odd, ahead-of-its-time vision of suburbia: a single farm cut up into a place of spacious parcels and wide side lanes. But this was a drafter's dream—not a builder's. The map showed the lots going right down to the river without any regard for the fact that there was a large sweeping hill and a pretty steep graded drop down to a flood-prone plain where all those new homes and avenues would have to be. For that matter, the plan erased King's Highway—apparently the road would have to be rerouted even though the ferry road would remain in place.[22]

The whole idea may have been nothing more than a scheme to push up the land's price by making it seem like the next big thing, or it may have been a very reasonable response to a growing town. In either case, it would be another two centuries before suburbia came to Ferry Farm.

Meanwhile, life went on. The Mercers continued to rent out the land, and the old house became the residence of tenants or enslaved Africans working the immediate fields. Once Mary was gone, though, the building suffered. Already long shown up by the next generation of gentry riverfront homes, it decayed further as a rental property. Its whole logic changed. The front became the back and the old yard area, while its road access became the new front. New residents pulled away the old stone platform that had welcomed visitors and dug out the whole area to make it a second cellar made of river cobbles held together with mud and clay. A doorway connected the old fine cut-stone one to the leaky, musty new one. The cellars filled with mud and rubbish, the expanded roof leaked and sagged, the walls bent under their own weight and age. It was all but forgotten. As events made Washington famous, his old home became less and less a Washington place in anything other than memory.

In the summer of 1777 a Philadelphia bookseller named Ebenezer Hazard was making his way along the Eastern seaboard when he rode into the Fredericksburg environs amidst a "drizzling rain."[23] The place impressed him not. He thought the Falls worth mentioning only to claim them "so trifling as not be worth mentioning."[24] He was unimpressed with the weapons then being made in town and turned up his nose at a new ship moored on the Rappahannock. "I think her too narrow for her length" he sneered, "and her masts are too taught."[25]

Hazard also got a glimpse of Ferry Farm—probably from Fredericksburg. He declared it to be "pleasantly situated on the north bank of the River," and a little below town.[26] But while he liked what he saw, he also made a curious but understandable error. He called the place "the Hill upon which Genl. Washington was born," as opposed to the place only of his childhood.[27] It was too much to expect visitors to keep the smallest details of his backstory clear. What mattered was that this was a place associated with Washington. In 1777 that was noteworthy enough to warrant a head turn and bit of ink spilled in a diary.

For Ferry Farm, though, it was far more than that. The Washington that rose to such great heights of fame was a man of Fairfax County. His home and estate were there—his wife, adopted children, and his heart were all gathered in a colonnaded home perched on a tall bluff over a bend in the Potomac. Mount Vernon was his base of operations and in the later years of his life he entertained his adoring countrymen in numbers so large as to be rather annoying. Mount Vernon was rightfully Washington Central. Even at Pope's Creek, family members owned the land well past the time when Washington became the most famous man on Earth. At these places, Washingtons could control the story.

Ferry Farm, though, was an orphan. With Mary and Betty living across the river and George long gone, all that was left were a few aging buildings and whatever stories anyone there cared to share. There was no Washington—no one who could speak with the family's authority—to set the record straight and offer mild corrections such as "actually the General was not born here." And despite decades of his association with the town, Fredericksburg actually had very little to show from the man that became its most famous son. He had left town before his star rose; that departure turned few heads at the time. And even on his returns, he still did not always command the greatest respect—certainly the women rummaging through his clothes by the riverbank were not exactly over-awed.

Yet once he achieved his reputation and standing, one would have expected that his old town and its people would try to reclaim their former resident. But instead there was a noticeable silence. There were many who could point out the site to visitors like Hazard, but there did not seem to be much more in the telling than some confused information about Ferry Farm and the role it had played in George's then young life.

In fact, chances to celebrate a uniquely local Washington passed unused. National days like the Fourth of July had the appropriate parades, but no hint of a distinctive Fredericksburg-area Washington lore showed itself. When, in 1800, the nation celebrated the first birthday of the general and president after his 1799 death, the resulting patriotic outpouring looked much the same in Fredericksburg as it did almost anywhere else. If there ever was a moment for locals to step forward with their personal local memories of "our George," the 1800 celebration of Washington's birthday speeches and bunting was it. And yet the local papers reported a public gathering of patriotic men and women recalling the great deeds of a fallen national hero. A Fredericksburg lawyer offered the keynote, but it was all boilerplate—no local color, nothing to suggest that the teary eyes in the crowd were all the moister for the Father of their Country having been, like them, a denizen of this place by the Falls.

Right as Washington became a national treasure and interest in him blossomed, there was no one ready to step up and offer a local version of the Washington story and no one to set a guiding hand on the rudder of Ferry Farm's Washington past. No one, that is, until a colorful preacher and writer from Maryland stepped into the empty space between Washington and the land itself.

That man was an American original. A rather folksy painting of him in what appears to be his middle age shows a balding half-grinning figure in black leaning confidently back into a red-cushioned chair. The fingers of his right hand rest on the pages of a bound volume—the vehicle of his fame—while his elbow seems to be knocking over a small pile of books behind his chair. His left hand is thrust into his coat with a Napoleonic air—or is he reaching into his jacket to pull out some newly penned piece of pamphletry?[28]

But it is the grin that most catches the viewer. It all rests on the right side of his face—the same side of his frame that touches the books. His cheery eye narrows as if caught in midwink. The corner of his mouth rises and wrinkles his creased face. Its shadowed left side looks wistful, perhaps even stunned—his wide eye looks past, or even through, the viewer and his lips level out. He has a single Janus face: one side playful and endearing, the other piercing and pious.

His name was Mason Locke Weems, but generations of Americans would know him by one of the handful of titles he could legitimately claim: "Parson" Weems.

He was a fully trained, and as far as anyone could tell, deeply sincere evangelical Anglican preacher. Trained in England at the time of the Revolution, he returned to a new American world and devoted himself to the art of the sermon. He had pulpits from which to preach, but his real ability was in the writing—his stock and trade the moralizing pamphlet. From the perils of masturbation to the evils of drink and gambling, Weems had an aptitude for the lurid tale deployed in aid of moral lessons.[29]

On the other hand, he was a driven self-promoter, completely at ease with inflating his bona fides or fabricating a tale or a source if it made the writing better and more marketable. It was not enough to pen sermons and occasionally deliver them, he eagerly repackaged others' work under his own byline, sometimes even labeling new works as second or third editions to give the impression of already being bestsellers. Like some sort of early republic cross between Samuel Johnson, John Wesley, Johnny Appleseed, and the Pied Piper of Hamlin, Parson Weems wrote, ranted, and country fiddled his way into the American psyche.

Weems would personally encounter the man who would become his muse sometime in the late 1790s. In 1795 the parson made his home in Dumfries—a small crossroads about a dozen miles from Mount Vernon. This placed him in the orbit of Truro Parish. On the eve of the Revolution the vestry which included Washington, William Fairfax, and George Mason had completed the new brick Pohick Church to serve as the parish's main place of worship. On Sundays, they all heard sermons from Reverend Lee Massey—a friend of the Washingtons and Pohick's full time rector. It was Massey who was the link between Weems and Washington, for he was friends with both the general and the local parson-slash-bookseller. The two almost certainly met at the Pohick Church. There is also some reason to suspect that Weems at least once visited Mount Vernon, perhaps in the company of Dr. James Craik—another mutual friend.

It was sometime during this at best fleeting association that the parson thought to pen a biography of Truro's most famous parishioner. The idea was not entirely unique—others were at work collecting the needed material. An aide of Washington's had started such a project as the Revolution ended, but never finished, and future United States Supreme Court chief justice John Marshall set off buoyed by access to the family papers.

Weems, though, was made of more ambitious literary stuff. He approached Washington about a biography and received a rather generic letter from the man himself offering some bland encouragements and what could be taken as an endorsement. But then on December 14, 1799, George Washington breathed his last and everything was born anew for Weems.

His years of selling books had taught him to understand his customers, and his fleeting connections with a man whom they almost universally revered were more than strong enough to withstand a little profit-motivated embellishment. In January 13, 1800, Weems wrote to Philadelphia publisher Matthew Carey fairly bursting with excitement and martial allusion, "Washington, you know is gone!" but now, "millions are gaping to read something about him, I am very nearly prim'd and cock'd for 'em."[30] Ready, aim, fire!

What Weems proposed was to "give" a version of Washington's life story, "sufficiently minute" so that it would allow the reader to "accompany" Washington "from his start" through his glorious life and on "to the throne in the hearts of 5,000,000 of people."[31] The text would emphasize the subject's patriotism, industry, magnanimity, his temperance, and sobriety, and "thus hold up his great virtues" for "the imitation of Our Youth."[32] It would be not just a bestseller, it would be a building block in a new republic—Weems's own battle in a Revolutionary War that he had actually missed.

Weems also told Carey he was just the man to pull this off. "6 months ago I set myself to collect anecdotes of him. You know I live conveniently for that work."[33] And in less than a month of that letter he was sending Carey a "sample of History of Washington," assuring the printer that "it is in our power to make this thing profitable and beneficial." After all, "everybody will read about Washington."[34]

Even though Carey foolishly initially passed on the offer, Weems nevertheless very quickly printed a fairly short book made thick by padding supplied by appended letters and orations. *A History of the Life and Death Virtues and Exploits of General Washington Faithfully Taken from Authentic Documents* extolled Washington's character and prowess in terms not that much different from those of countless public patriotic orations. It was in most respects like the almost innumerable panegyrics authors all along the coast were churning out to mark the great man's passing.

But Weems was a salesman. And thanks to his drive and frequent reprints, each with a new addition or two, his little book grew and did well enough to convince himself and Carey as well that a more ambitious effort would be rewarded with even greater custom. Weems understood that his readers wanted something intimate, human, and relatable about a man they were quick to call the father of their country—and he meant to give it to them.

Edition by edition he folded in a steady accretion of ever-more anecdotes until by 1809 he had completely transformed his original conventional pamphlet into his embroidered masterwork: *The Life of George Washington with Curious Anecdotes Equally Honorable to Himself and Exemplary to His Countrymen*. He even remade himself as rector of the fictional "Mount Vernon Parish" to bolster his authority.

In his desire to give readers the Washington "behind the curtain," Weems filled in what he needed to add color and feeling to his muse's childhood. He gave George an education in a little "old field school" under the caring tutelage of a quasifictional tenant of Augustine's named Hobby. Weems turned Fielding Lewis into a "play-mate" of little George's who recalled how he would throw stones over the Rappahannock "at the lower ferry of Fredericksburg," a feat few could copy.[35] Weems placed George at Chotank with his cousins when his father—"his best of friends"—took to his deathbed.[36] George came rushing home, making it back just in time to fall "upon his father's neck" and kiss him "a thousand and a thousand times," breaking his tear-filled embrace only to cry out "O my father, my father."[37]

In adding that color, he also memorialized and made famous a vision of Ferry Farm. Weems had certainly seen the old place. He had been in Fredericksburg many times—it was on his regular book sales flyway and he had crossed the ferry many times. He had frequented its taverns, knew many of its citizens, and had even turned to a few of its printers to knock out new copies of his manuscripts. Like Hazard before him, locals no doubt showed him the town's claims to fame.

What he would have seen though was not Washington's home of the 1740s, but rather the tenant home as it looked in the 1790s—run-down, reoriented, marred with an unaesthetic addition, and put to shame by the far grander newer homes of the local gentry. What Weems saw was more modest than even his own home in Dumfries.

So when it came time to recall Ferry Farm in writing, he described the rural rusticity of the home's current "low and modest front of faded red" as he saw it then and imagined that same shambled frame filled with Washingtons.[38] Weems coyly projected the home's "weather-beaten" condition back to the 1740s and used it to help give America a dirty-kneed farm boy George with his "bright plowshare that he loved." Washington, Weems claimed, was not "born with a silver spoon in his mouth."[39] Instead, an American "buckskin" was Weems's Washington, running wild in his humble father's edenic farm "strewed with fruit" and "sweet flowers," chasing butterflies, jumping at birds' nests until, exhausted, he would fall back "on his grassy couch" and sleep to the music of chirping "little crickets."[40]

Weems told his readers that his sources for all of this wonderful detail were credible authorities, some living in Ferry Farm's vicinity. Fielding Lewis got credit for the rock-throwing story. From "a very aged gentleman, formerly a school-mate" of Washington's, Weems learned that little George was an arbiter of disputes amongst the local boys and John Fitzhugh told Weems of what a fleet runner George had been. An "excellent old lady of Fredericksburg" related a complicated tale of a dream in which five-year-old George extinguished a sudden house fire by carting water up and down a ladder "with the nimbleness of a squirrel."[41]

But Weems's best informant by far was an "aged lady" whom he called "a distant relative" of the Washingtons who as a girl had "spent much of her time in the family." It was her anecdotes that most rooted Washington to the land from which he sprang.

She recalled to Weems a childhood walk with George and his father in the arbor of his well-tended trees all "bending under the weight of apples" and shading a ground "strewed with fruit." Amidst that living horn of plenty she saw George overawed by a bounty of more than one "could ever eat" and promised that he would evermore be a generous soul.[42]

From her he also learned a tale in which Augustine scratched his son's name in some newly turned earth and filled the furrowed letters with cabbage seeds. In time, the seeds sprouted and George was astonished into "a lively sense of his maker" upon seeing that very earth itself grow the name "George Washington."[43] Given the chance to explain the seeming miracle, Augustine taught George that all around him was God's possession—even Ferry Farm's "great big house," its garden, "and the horses yonder, and oxen, and sheep, and trees, and everything."[44] The parson credited this revelatory moment and the "profound silence" and "pensive looks" that followed it as "engrafting" on George's soul "that germ of piety" which in time yielded "so many of the precious fruits of morality."[45]

Weems also claimed to have learned a tale he knew then and there was "too valuable to be lost" and which he assured the world was "too true to be doubted." In it, a young George became "the wealthy master of a hatchet." True to his little boy "rogue" form, he took to chopping the little sticks in his mother's pea patch. Soon, he turned the blade on "the body of a beautiful young English cherry tree" which he thus "barked" so badly that Weems mused that "the tree ever got the better of it."[46]

The next morning, when Augustine learned of the damage to the tree "which was a great favorite" he encountered his assembled brood in the house. He asked George—hatchet still in hand—if he knew "who killed that beautiful little cherry tree yonder in the garden?" Possessed of a burning need to tell the truth, the little boy "bravely cried out, 'I can't tell a lie, Pa: you know I can't tell a lie. I did cut it with my hatchet.'" This was the right answer. His arms opened in love, Augustine called his son to him for the promised embrace and not the earlier threatened "beating" for a lie. The honest confession of misdeed, he declared, was "worth more than a thousand trees, though blossomed with silver, and their fruits of purest gold."[47]

These stories all worked to create a little George of the land—a farm boy much like the ones he targeted when he told Carey that he would make Washington's morals "the imitation of Our Youth."[48] And although the body of tales had its skeptics from the very start, they nevertheless took firm root in the fertile imaginations of generations of patriotic Americans.

Weems also made Ferry Farm a place. It had been a meeting point between worlds, it had been homes and fields, and above all else, it had been and continued to be property. More than any other force, it was Weems that gave Ferry Farm an enduring story, a public face, a set of attributes beyond its monetary value and the price of winter wheat. Washington himself had cast the place in prose in letter, advertisement, and survey. He had bought and sold. But Washington's greatest effect on the land was his very fame and the long, lingering shadow his name cast.

It was Weems who grasped the size of that shadow and turned Ferry Farm's otherwise hidden Washington years into a new kind of saleable property. It was Weems who gave America Ferry Farm as a verdant republican idyl, an American Elysium made part of the national story by the fact that its country charms and fertile fields produced "Washington the Great."[49] The parson rooted Washington's "greatness" in a landscape, and thus imbued that landscape with Washington's greatness.

5

❧

Memory Encamps on a Field of Clover

John Gadsby Chapman thought that art was the key to a future of republican virtue and prosperity: Americans were "an independent and intelligent people" and they needed only to "be shown the truth" through good art, and they would "know and maintain it."[1]

So on the eve of Washington's one hundredth birthday, in 1832, Chapman took his oils, brushes, and his Italian training and sought out uplifting American topics. He returned to his native Virginia and set off to paint the sites of Washington's life. Light fell in streaks from pregnant boiling clouds, and vines wound around gnarled trees at the edges of Chapman's Virginia. His eye landed on ruin. He painted the old church tower remains at Jamestown sitting amidst a spill of tombstones and bent trees. He painted Pohick Church, capturing its flopping shutters and knocked-out windowpanes sitting forgotten and forlorn in the bold sunlight.

And he painted Ferry Farm. Chapman set his easel not too far from the gate and "little tombstone" where Mildred Washington lay. He faced westward so that his view caught the drop down to the floodplain, the river, and the town beyond—just the view that Washington had described in his sales ad, except that by then Fredericksburg had sprouted a new crop of church spires, waterfront homes, and a bridge that crossed the Rappahannock along with the ferry. He painted a brooding, almost swirling clouded sky pierced by light reflecting in the water and making a heavenly spotlight landing right where Washington once walked.

A casual viewer could be forgiven for thinking that this was actually a portrait of Fredericksburg as seen from this uniquely fine angle. But the real sitter for the painting was set on the right of the frame, bathed in a warm orangish glow emanating from some unaccounted-for source. It was a gray and white clutter of stones resting right at the edge of the bluff. A few stones stood ranked in such a way so as to show that they had once been a wall. Lying prone at their base were their rocky fellows, toppled over, their binding mortar fractured on impact, their weight pulling them gradually into the ground more and more with each new rainstorm. Surrounding the pile was a cleared empty space; no vegetation dared intrude; emptiness and peaceful solitude contrasted with the busy place of ships and roofs and spires across the river.

The stones were all that was left of the Washington house in this first actual view we have of the place, Washington's childhood home. Other artists had shown the place in their renderings of Weems's stories. One of the earliest, from around 1810, showed Augustine and George, well dressed in top hat and tails, standing in an overflowing, neoclassical garden filled with pots and a rather pointless classical column with a federal-style home in the background. Above the whole scene floated a banner emblazoned with the words "the love of truth mark the boy."

Some drawings showed the building as being a huge, shambling mess of dormers and windows while others echoed Weems's vision of the humble home. One lithograph by German-born, Philadelphia-based artist Augustus Kollner showed Augustine confronting George at the doorway of a dwelling that would have been more at ease in Tuscany or Provence than on the banks of the Rappahannock. None of these were meant to be actual reliable depictions of the house—the kind of thing we today would call "historically accurate." But each little sketch or etching helped keep the lost home alive even after it was no longer there. Each rebuilt the old Washington place in the latest style or remodeled it to a new drafter's fancy.

But these were allegories, while Ferry Farm was quite real. Around the time that Washington passed away in a back room of Mount Vernon's second floor, the people then living in his old home at Ferry Farm gave up on their cobble and clay cellar and let it fill with trash and dirt. It became a sort of in-house landfill that little by little spilled its way into the better-built original cellar. Jumbled up in that stinking, fetid slurry were decades of accreted meat bones, tobacco-pipe remains, broken bottles and plates, and all the other detritus of life.

The smell of the trash, the bending walls, and falling plaster finally became too much for even the most inconsiderate of landlords. By the time Weems's Washington was fully set in the American firmament, the old home with its front of faded red was an empty ruin, and the now-empty lot was soon turned to the plow. The home's rotted or reusable wood was all gone, the foundation stones carried off or pushed into the cellar holes with the rest of the refuse by the time Chapman crossed the ferry and looked back at the view.

Chapman turned that emptiness into his brand of nineteenth-century romantic landscape. There was no smell of decay or trash on the ground in Chapman's Ferry Farm. Warm light bathed the ruin and the cleared, open, flat land near it; the toppled little tombstone was more charm than tragedy. Emptiness spoke of past yielding to a bustling present across the river.

For Judge John Coalter, emptiness meant farmland. The judge lived just over a mile up the river at the large Georgian home that William Fitzhugh commissioned right when Washington was hassling with Anthony Strother and doing his last survey of Ferry Farm. Fitzhugh named the place Chatham and by the 1830s it was home to the Coalters, who acted like every other landowner living opposite Fredericksburg: as riverfront properties came up for sale they gobbled them up.

The land was then a set of outlying fields in the large Chatham plantation. The plow pushed its way through the soil year after year. The steel blade carved up the dirt, making it soft and ready for crops. But each pass also, bit by bit, erased the footprint of the buildings in the yard and what survived of the posts of Clark's old house. The rotted wood and the thin lines of foundation stones and bricks were all knocked loose and folded over, season-by-season. The shards of plates and wine bottles that once littered the work areas were all turned back into the soil as if they could sprout new cups and saucers. With each new planting the old signs of life and activity faded more and more from view. At last, only the biggest and most belligerent of the cellar stones stayed in place. Like a captain going down with his ship, the gray chiseled Aquia blocks stayed on watch until the last of what had once been sank below the surface.

By the time the last of the holes had been filled in, the land had changed hands once again. The new owners were a pair of speculators from Massachusetts and New Jersey. John Teasdale, the sometime minister of the Fredericksburg Baptist Church, and businessman Joseph Mann bought the land together after Judge Coalter's death. The two planned to farm the land, but also invited Northerners to come down and buy up affordable parcels.

Curiously, though, in all of their documents and advertisements to sell land, there was not a single solitary mention of Washington. Instead, the old place seems to have been called only "Mercer's" for its most recent solo owner. The two partners planned to share the land's purchase price and then profit by farming the acres and selling off the old-growth timber still standing behind the fields—the same trees that had stood there since the time of John Smith. The plan failed, though, when Mann could not make good on his side of the deal and Teasdale found his aggressive business plans at odds with his evangelical values.[2]

For local folks, Washington's shadow was passing off the land. Oddly, right at the time a Pennsylvania teacher named William Holmes McGuffey began to produce a series of schoolbooks that would teach generations of Americans to read with stories like Weems's Cherry Tree, Ferry Farm had lost its Washington bloom.

Late in life Washington had called Fredericksburg the place of his childhood. But in response to that honor, the town and environs, oddly, made very little effort to claim Washington as their own. Weems had credited his best-loved tales of Washington's childhood to local sources—those good old ladies so eager to share their stories. But these storytellers somehow managed to open up only to the Parson—no one else ever heard, or even claimed to have heard, any of his novel material before.

In 1826 Washington's step-grandson, George Washington Parke Custis—the only one of the line with a flare for promoting his famous name—published a new version of the Cherry Tree Story. This one had a teenaged George trying to break Mary's new "sorrel colt." He rode the horse so hard that it burst a blood vessel and died. When confronted about the dead animal, Washington of course owned up. Even though it bore something of a Washington family blessing, and was no doubt a Ferry Farm story, no one seemed to take much note.[3]

Not only did these stories find no local tongue, on top of that, visitors to the area commonly misplaced Washington's birth at Ferry Farm and there did not seem to be too many locals eager or able to set them straight, as in Hazard's day. Weems himself had noted the error, recalling that visitors commonly confused Ferry Farm with Washington's birthplace back at Pope's Creek. After the Revolution, Fredericksburg's town fathers renamed the streets from Royal family tributes like Caroline, William, Princess Anne, and Prince Edward to more American titles like Commerce and Water streets. But even then, no Washington Street made it onto the map. When it came to George, there was largely silence. The new nation enshrined Washington as a patron saint—named counties and cities after him, erected statues, and littered their homes with his square-jawed gaze.

But the good people of the Falls—many of them new arrivals—effectively forgot that they could claim this defining American as one of their own.

Instead, in Fredericksburg, it was Mary, George's mother, who emerged as the one most worthy of commemoration during the Washington centennial years. Mary, after all, had been their neighbor for many years. In her day anyone could have walked over and said hello, while Ferry Farm's Washington memory was more and more only a thing of art and writing. The town's eyes and hearts turned toward their former neighbor Mary around the 1832 centennial of the birth of her famous son. As early as 1826, Parke Custis suggested that a memorial to Mary was overdue.[4] The call was echoed in 1831 when some Fredericksburg patriots expressed concern that "the remains of the Mother of Washington" lay all but forgotten "in a common field, marked by not even the simplest stone."[5] One correspondent lamented that "tradition is already our only guide to her grave" because "the field is used for agricultural purposes" and what was worse, "the period cannot be far distant" when the last memory of the location was lost for good. Indeed, it was only a matter of rapidly passing time before "the ploughshare and the harrow will obliterate every remaining trace of her who bore and reared George Washington."[6] A harrowing thought, indeed; the old ties of memory were breaking, as new arrivals knew not the stories of older folks.

The answer was clear. Mary's bones had to be saved and her life commemorated. A local committee called itself into being in order to solicit subscriptions to make sure that the memory of this greatest of "American matrons" would not be forgotten. The group were all fairly new arrivals to town, and all were members of the Presbyterian Church then engaged in building a new church—the pastor of which was then occupying Mary's old home.

The denomination prided itself on its role in the republic and boasted that "no American church" had a better claim on "the shaping of our republican institutions" than did the Presbyterian.[7] Weems himself claimed to have consulted with Presbyterian clergy, and a made-up story circulated that Washington himself had actually received Presbyterian communion during a wartime open-air service.[8] Mary's care could not have been in finer ecclesiastic hands.

Their idea was to erect a "marble monument" to celebrate "a mother to whom Rome would have raised her statues" and then to collect "the remains of this venerable woman" (or, at least something they would certainly have called Mary's remains) and encase them in a special shrine and bury her anew within the walls of the purpose-built Presbyterian Church. They called theirs "so Holy a work" and were confident that the American public were in agreement and would open their purses.[9]

They were not, and they did not.

Instead, people saw the plan for just what it was: a sectarian fundraising scheme to fund a new church and along the way claim Mary Washington as their own. Push-back was immediate. The nationally promoted plan caught the eye of a flamboyant New York shipping magnate, Silas E. Burrows, who had a very different vision. In 1831 he wrote to Fredericksburg's mayor Thomas Goodwin to express his grave concerns. Although he had no personal connections to the Washingtons or the area, Burrows nevertheless professed horror at the prospect that "the ashes of this good American mother" should be removed from that portion of "mother earth" that Mary herself had selected to serve as her eternal "pillow." Instead of the misguided Presbyterian plan, Burrows proposed letting Mary stay right where she was and that he personally be "allowed the honor of individually erecting" a monumental tribute to "Mary the Mother of Washington" in a style "to please the Washington family and the Citizens of the United States."[10]

Of course, Burrows seemed to have no idea that there were no actual white Washingtons left in Fredericksburg to endorse his taste in monuments, nor were any actively involved in any plan to mark Mary's grave. Nor was he too worried about the very real fear that no one was quite sure of the exact location of what he called, "the sacred spot where reposes the great American Mother." By all accounts she had been buried a bit north of Betty and Fielding's home, most likely right at the place where the high and dry acres drop off sharply to the floodplain—a swampy stretch that contained a large African burying yard nearby. But even that was contested. A letter bearing the Weemsian title of "A Near Neighbor to Mary," offered the rather remarkable opinion that Mary had been buried in the black burying yard of St. Peter's Episcopal Church after a service at St. George's. It may be that this was a confusion of the free Mary Washington and the enslaved Mary Washington, whom Augustine had left to his daughter.[11]

On top of that, a new family owned the land north of town. In the early nineteenth century, a family of Scots immigrants took up at the old Lewis place, and it was this clan of Gordons that gave the place its enduring highland-inflected name, Kenmore. By 1826, a small bricked-in family cemetery sat near a large rock outcropping—perhaps right where Mary lay.[12] As the living memory of Mary faded, the little Scots (and probably Presbyterian, at that) family cemetery became another assumed last resting place for Mary as well.

Burrows's eye landed on the Gordon family cemetery as the place to erect his Mary monument. With the help of his own local committee and much of his own money, he bought a pile of stones for a pedestal and commissioned a chiseled marble obelisk that would, when completed, become the first monument to an American woman.

Burrows's cause gathered antebellum steam. Soon a troop of dignitaries rode, rolled, and cruised into Fredericksburg for a full day's celebration of speeches, feasts, and parades, culminating with a grand ceremony in which President Andrew Jackson (no friend of Washington's politics) would help lay the monument's cornerstone. On May 7, 1833, a "dense mass" of people gathered in town to hear Mary praised for having "encouraged and fostered by precept and example, the dawning virtues of her illustrious son." After the speeches, the president set the stone near the graveyard, acknowledging that Mary "asked as her dying request" that her "mortal remains" might rest at this "sacred" place; "hallowed be this wish."[13] Amen.

But while all eyes were on Mary's grave, her longtime home at Ferry Farm was an overlooked ruin. Mann and Teasdale had planned to farm the acres and profit from its harvest. But they also had their eye on the same road network that had so defined this place as a crossroads. Road and river were still making the Falls a busy place—perhaps busier than ever. But the transportation network was pretty flawed, as testified to by no less an observer than Charles Dickens. The author passed over the muddy and rutted roads near Ferry Farm during the Virginia leg of his 1840s American tour. He was simply horrified as his carriage pitched and rolled as it sank "down in the mire nearly to the level of the coach windows" amidst which the mud-caked riders "scream dismally" and drivers flew "back among the luggage on the roof."[14]

In the 1830s, steam trains were the newest form of high-speed transportation, and cities and private companies were fiercely trying to get lines that could connect people and places. Rail promised easier travel than Dickens had experienced. In 1832, the Virginia Assembly authorized a rail project, and by 1837 a public/private partnership called the Richmond, Fredericksburg, and Potomac Railroad had laid tracks through hills carved out by enslaved labor and made a line connecting the cities. The goal had been to tie Richmond to the capital of Washington with a "great iron chain" that would "bind together the North and the South despite the machinations of the abolitionists" and be one more link in a vast, new, transcendent national project.[15] The iron chain would allow for uninterrupted rail travel at speeds pushing a dizzying forty miles per hour, and serve as a large feather in the local cap.

But the Rappahannock stood in the way.

The answer was simple enough. All that was needed was a rail bridge to carry cars, engine, and riders over the water and then link up with a new stretch heading up to Washington. Ferry Farm, with its long-standing crossing, was a perfect location for the proposed bridge. That is what Mann and Teasdale had hoped for—in fact part of their interest in the old farm was the possibility of skyrocketing value thanks to sitting squarely in the railroad's projected path. The addition would have made Ferry Farm the meeting place of rail as well as of road and river.

But local folks were not thrilled with the idea of a bridge to the old Washington farm. That concern had nothing to do with Washington. It was based on a fear that a bridge at the old ferry run would cut off the still quite active wharf from the lower reaches of the river. Meetings were called and partisans on each side talked long into the night about the consequences of change. The plan pitted merchants tied to the older water-borne trade against railroad supporters and the landowners who stood to gain should the new line inflate land values.

The wharf supporters won the day and a new bridge went up in 1842, less than a quarter mile upriver from Ferry Farm's northern boundary. The bridge tied the rails and made the area even more of a trade hot spot. But in the whole discussion, no one mentioned the land's Washington associations at all. The public voice of local memory saw no reason to invoke the Great Washington when discussing the place and its many possible futures. Local boosters saw value in what Ferry Farm could be, not what it had once been.

The next owner of the land—a local farmer named Winter Bray— acted as unceremoniously as one could. He built a new home and outbuildings right over the site of the ruins that Chapman had captured twenty years before. Bray's barns and home rested on many of the same stones Strother and the Washingtons had once used—a good stone was always recyclable. With each year, the Washington memory became less and less significant in the landscape, even as little surviving bits of its foundations were put to new use. A new farm, ordered by the rules of mid-nineteenth-century agriculture, was sitting now at the juncture of road, river, and rail.

Fredericksburg, the rail and river hub, was a prosperous American city and Ferry Farm had a front row seat. An 1856 print of the town from the Baltimore lithography firm of E. Sachse and Company caught Fredericksburg in the full flush of its antebellum prosperity, which was rendered in the firm's trademark bird's-eye map portraits—art which combined accurate street-level detail with majestic, unachievable grand vistas. In this case, the bird in question hung in the sky high above Ferry Farm's northern edge.

The print showed a busy downtown of fine brick buildings surrounded by a cheery and welcoming spray of colorfully painted, well-spaced dwellings, fields, gardens, and wood lots all shown crisp and clear. The etching put the town's commercial and manufacturing vitality on display in the form of factories, tall smokestacks, and the canal north of town. Church spires vied for skyward reach with the smokestacks. The new railroad bridge and the rail lines running out of town were all in clear view.

The old Washington place itself sat on the lower left, oddly, under the only patch of cloud darkening an otherwise bright, sunlit expanse. The draftsman showed the corner of the farm as a plowed field with a team of oxen working their way over its rich brown soil. The land dropped off onto the Ferry Lane upon which our draftsman placed a four-oxen-drawn wagon and a fancy black private coach—twin symbols of bucolic activity and well-earned prosperity. Two framed homesteads straddled the rail line, trees both autumnal and verdant dotted the land, fences separated field and woods.

There is no hint of Washington at all—in fact, nothing seems less relevant to this busy, modern place. The only nod to the Washingtons is that the draftsman obligingly went ahead and finished the Mary Washington monument. His drawing places the obelisk in its pedestal where it can point to the sky along with the church spires and smokestacks.

In reality, Mary's commemoration was still incomplete, Captain Burrows having run out of funds. The blocks of the pedestal were all there and set up, but the cut marble needle they were to support lay supine at their feet. The lithographer showed a bright white triumph where really there was an almost forgotten, half-finished project. With each passing year, souvenir hunters chipped away at the rocks with hammers. Sachse and Company went ahead and finished in print the project that Silas Burrows and friends were unable to complete in stone.

So there it was—Washington's old home had become a small corner of a thriving river and rail city, an American place to be proud of. The river brought the ships in as they had for nearly two centuries, King's Highway still brought traffic to the ferry crossing, or up to a new bridge near the old Fitzhugh place, and now the trains crossed them both and offered new avenues, north and south.

Americans also had two widely available images of Ferry Farm itself that they could frame and hang. One was from a historical writer in the Weems vein named Benson Lossing. He had visited Ferry Farm during his travels but understandably claimed that "nothing of interest" was by then "left upon the soil" where the Washington "mansion-house" once stood.[16] Nevertheless, he published a drawing of a low-roofed, humble home just like the one Weems had described. The New York lithography firm Currier and Ives made their own version of Lossing's take on the old home as well, except that they labeled it as "The Birth-Place of Washington at Bridges Creek, Westmoreland Co. Va." That image hit the stands in 1860—a fortuitous year for Ferry Farm and Fredericksburg alike.

In 1862, Sachse and Company offered another image of Fredericks-burg.[17] By then the name had entered the American lexicon anew. Weems gave Americans Washington's childhood, and artists and travel writers had recommended the town again and again as a "wonderful old town, filled with people of the good old Virginia stock."[18] But in a nation divided and at war with itself, the old city's name became a watchword for war and suffering. Where the first print was all blue and bright skies, the new one of 1862 was dark and dulled. The cloud that originally shadowed only Ferry Farm now blanketed the whole area. At Ferry Farm, still in the lower left, a lone mounted officer stood surveying his army's positions.

Sachse's lone soldier was a solitary stand-in for a far greater number of invading troops that had been at Ferry Farm since the spring of that year. They had come as occupiers. Their goal was to take and hold the town and its road, rail, and river links as part of a larger plan to move on to Richmond and thereby end the rebellion that was centered there. The Northern young men succeeded in taking Fredericksburg fairly easily— although retreating Southern soldiers had burned the Rappahannock's bridges.

The occupying army settled into the land. Chatham became the headquarters of a small dress parade of "West point and white gloves" generals who took turns overseeing the operations through the summer.[19] Ferry Farm, though, became the occupation's muscle: a vast, tented field filled with the men who daily patrolled Fredericksburg's streets and endured the slurs and insults, and even an occasional chamber pot, slung by the town's more resentful citizens—mostly a collection of "a few old hoary headed white men" and "rosy cheeked damsels (all in their sweet sixteenth)," declared one observer.[20] Another soldier called the locals "bitter secessionists" who nevertheless mostly held that view to themselves.[21] Still another stood on Ferry Farm looking at Fredericksburg and labeled it simply "one of Virginia's strong 'nest eggs' of treason."[22]

While in the area, the soldiers saw the sights and remade the place in their own writing. A few called the town an "ancient looking" one "set in a "beautiful valley surrounded on either side by romantic hills and beautiful scenery."[23] But more often the soldiers saw Weems's earthly paradise as a landscape of danger, decay, and death.

The soldiers related stories like that of the four Brooklyn boys someone had come across "tied together" and drowned, or the fate of two other men found "in a barn with their throats cut."[24] One soldier wrote home about seeing the decapitated body of a horse near the Falls, and a pile of earth marking the mass grave of its onetime teammates. The men described little piles of freshly turned earth in the field they passed, church pews stained with blood, and occasional trails of the stuff on the ground. Where once Weems had mused over Washington laying down for a refreshing rest in the clover, soldiers now laid their dead friends once and for all. Where Parke Custis said his step-grandfather had once ridden his mother Mary's new horse to death, mangled mounts lay in open air, buried in shallow graves, or sometimes piled up and burned.

The glistening river where Weems claimed Washington fished and swam became a muddy flow with its own dangers. Wisconsin private Homer Lillie learned this when he "was seized with a cramp" while bathing in the Rappahannock. With a "shriek" he called out "boys, o boys" and before his friends could even get close to him, Private Lillie "was beyond help," his "body had gone lifeless down the stream."[25] They found him two days later and buried him not far from the camp.

How much the view from Washington's old doorstep had changed as well. The river was choked with the remains of "fifteen steamers and other water craft" which retreating Southern troops had "fired and destroyed" as the invaders inched closer to town.[26] Sitting at anchor near this ruination below the wharf were dirty gray gunboats covered with guns, impromptu sun shelters, bored men, and clothing drying on the lines. When Southern saboteurs set these inelegant chockablock vessels alight, they burned to the waterlines, leaving only their rusted boilers and riblike staves settled down and poking out of the mud. Bodies floated by. The stone pillars of the burned rail bridge were encased within a vast, impromptu seventy-foot-high card house of poles that held a new tightrope line of teetering tracks. When the trains ran again they looked as likely to topple over into the river as to make the other side.[27]

A vast bridge made of long boards set upon a dozen canal boats lashed side to side, "bow up stream," replaced the old ferry's run.[28] This floating pathway was the main link over the river, tying Ferry Farm to the wharf on the other side. A team of army engineers stayed on hand to refasten loosened boards and keep the huge canal boats tied tight. At intervals throughout the day and night, squads of soldiers went across. Guard and relief, back and forth for the whole spring and summer as Northern soldiers tramped from Ferry Farm into town and back again.

With less attention paid to drums, bugles, and orders of the day, battalions of enslaved Africans made the same trip in reverse. The region's enslaved people understood quite rightly that making it over the river to Ferry Farm and to the army encamped all over Stafford County was to achieve freedom. With the white population in the hinterlands fleeing the invading army, the gate was open for the enslaved to take it upon themselves to end their generations-long plight. The only surviving image of this large and significant short-lived bridge shows a squad of soldiers formed up and ready to walk from town to Ferry Farm. A sentry stands near the bridge's end and another sits by a hodgepodged guardhouse. But on the Stafford side, in the lower foreground, are three civilians—what appear to be two men and a woman. They are Africans, formerly enslaved, now freed.

They fled the plantations as well—but in the opposite direction of their former masters. These enslaved people (technically they were "runaways") came to the Northern lines by foot and they came in wagons and oxcarts. They came individually or in groups, sometimes "in squads as large as twenty."[29] One Union soldier marveled that newly freed Africans "are flocking" into his regiment's Ferry Farm camp "by scores and hundreds everyday." This mass (and quite literal) exodus, caused him to muse on the irony that the "rebellion that has been excited" by Southerners whom he called "these same slave dealers" was in the process of enacting "the liberation of their slaves."[30]

These newly freed people were eager to share "generally reliable" information about the area and the positions of their former masters. Sometimes the soldiers would hire the refugees "at very cheap rates to cook and do other things for them."[31] Others just watched this most alien parade with a mix of humor, pity, and fascination. The newly freed themselves understood the moment with full clarity. As one Wisconsin soldier wrote home about their new friends, "ask one where he belongs 'I'se a free negger sah' is his reply."[32] A vast demographic shift was afoot as residents poured out of the area and soldiers moved in.

Most of these soldiers—a few thousand in total—were really just farm boys, members of a rural generation raised on Weems and the McGuffey readers. They came from homes in faraway Minnesota, Wisconsin, and New York, homes that had the Sachse or Currier and Ives lithographs on their walls and the historical works of Benson Lossing on their shelves. Like their fellows all over the nation, they had enlisted out of a mix of patriotism and desire for adventure. And like their fellows, they would learn that war was far more awful than colorful prints had led them to believe.

Like an army of young Georges, they chopped at every tree in sight to make fires and dry shelter. When the trees were gone, they turned to fence rails, and when those ran out, they pulled the clapboarding off of abandoned homes—after that, the bare frames themselves went into the cook fire. They dug ditches for their latrines and pits for their cooking fires. When one of the men died they sank grave shafts into the ground. They supplemented their army rations with any plant, pie, or morsel they could find. They effectively collapsed the local economy as they "bought up" all the "eggs, corn meal, and bread" they could find and used a confusing mix of local, national, and counterfeited currencies in the act.[33] When money was not on hand, or no one was looking, soldiers sometimes stole a stray chicken or pig.

They set up long lines of tents in the fields right around the Bray home and gossiped about the war and the area. They told stories about the Bray home's residents—an overseer named J. W. Smithers whom the men called "a mean bitter old secesh" for his pro-Southern secessionist worldview, and the enslaved woman "black as the ace of spades" with whom Smithers lived as man and wife.[34]

But amidst all this grim war, they also knew fully well that they were encamped on the place of Great Washington's childhood. For some it was the newly freed themselves who served as the "living historians of 'Virginity'" and told the soldiers stories of "the balmy days of yore" when "Massa George Washington" used to "roam over the very ground" the army had "converted into the 'tented field.'"[35] For others, like Abraham Lincoln, who visited the farm in May of 1862, it was a wide array of writing and art that told them where they were. After a stop at Chatham, Lincoln and escort rode down to the canal boat bridge on their way to Fredericksburg. The accompanying cavalrymen reined in their mounts; aids and attendants fluttered around the carriage, steadying its team, taking down its retractable stairs, and pulling open the door through which Lincoln stepped onto a landscape he already knew, by reputation at least, if not yet firsthand.

Lincoln was, like most of his countrymen, an admirer of Washington and a self-confessed fan of Parson Weems's "small book," which the president recalled from "the earliest days" of his "being able to read."[36] As he walked onto the acres where Washington came to manhood, for a moment presidential storytelling converged: Honest Abe Lincoln the Rail Splitter stood at the farm where The Boy Who Could Not Tell a Lie used his own axe to chop at his father's cherry tree.

And like their commander in chief, the boys of the army Washington himself had helped create did not lose sight of the land's patriotic significance and its echoes of Weemsian meanings.

They wrote home of bedding down in a "beautiful clover field," deliberately recalling Weems's "clover-covered pastures."[37] They excitedly reported that they were on the "'ol' plantation' where Gen. Washington spent the early days of his life," while a few called it "Ferry Farm where Washington was born," keeping alive the already venerable birthplace confusion.[38] A few went further and saw the very-much-1850s Bray buildings as the original Washington ones and imagined that here was in fact the very home George had once inhabited. One of the Wisconsin soldiers wrote home that this was the place where "The Father of the

American Republic" first took into "his young mind, those principals of love, purity, and fidelity" which so shaped his life's course. In a similar feather, another soldier mused about the sad state of the current conflict and wondered, "when will the Washington of our crisis appear?"[39]

Some of the men recalled how Young George "found his name growing in the cabbage bed," but most simply described the farm as "where little George hacked the cherry tree" or where "little Geo" "went with his little hatchet," an event one claimed through which "we all have been, morally, much benefited, of course."[40]

An "old cherry tree" growing on the farm had been "nearly all cut into pieces" by soldiers who used its wood to "make all sorts of crosses, pipes, rings, etc., that can be sent away by mail." Some soldiers even claimed this was indeed "the original tree of the famous hatchet story."[41] Other soldiers gathered up cherry pits from Ferry Farm and mailed them home so that Northern farms could be graced with trees descended from the most famous cherry of them all. The bravest of the soldiers—or perhaps the most bored or foolish, or maybe just the most Washington devoted—went so far as to pass time at the river's bank "attempting to throw stones across the Rappahannock" even with cannon shot "constantly flying each way" over their heads. Most did not have the arm for the task, except apparently for one "huge fellow from Michigan."[42]

But when not larking under fire, the effects of war were a cause for anger and sadness. Letter writers lamented that this "consecrated" or "hallowed" ground should be so "desecrated" by the "hell deserving bandits" of the South.[43] More than a few took a walk over to Mary's unfinished monument only to be horrified at what they saw. It was poor fundraising and changing priorities that left the marble obelisk lying prone next to the block base. But the monument's marble blocks and carved Greek columns also bore the scars of long neglect and the half-finished obelisk itself lay prone and half sunk into the ground adorned with a garland of weeds.

To these martial tourists, it was the war itself that was to blame for what they saw. Local enslaved Africans circulated a story that Southern troops had used the monument as target practice. It was probably not true, but it was a creative bit of manipulation that certainly hit its target—the patriotic sentiments of these liberating invaders. Whipping up their anger only made it less likely that the formerly enslaved themselves would be returned to their masters when these occasionally came calling to retrieve their human property.

The soldiers took the bait—and many different versions of the story made the grand rounds. One rather precise correspondent claimed that "this piece of architecture" was scarred by the "marks of seventy-five bullets" after having been used as a "target during last winter."[44] In another version, a soldier-correspondent decried "the marks of a thousand bullets or more" fired perhaps by "the ladies" of town. He claimed that "the darkies" told them of Southern officers leading parties to the site for "practice rifle shooting."[45] Another simply said that the "head stone" of "Washington's mother" was "all battered with bullets shot at it in sport by secession soldiers."[46] One soldier even told of a plan to repair Mary's monument that a few of the men had concocted. Like the Presbyterians before him, he was sure that "hundreds would willingly contribute to such a humane project."[47]

The famed Mathew Brady had James Gardner—one of his traveling photographers—even stage a shot of the forlorn monument. In it a small group of men in civilian dress inspect the stark white stone pedestal. In another commercial photograph, a lone sentry walks his beat guarding the "toppled" first monument to an American woman.

In Gardner's photograph one cannot make out the—alleged—anywhere from seventy-five to one thousand bullet marks. At any rate, these were mostly the chips and dings of countless souvenir hunters' hammers plus a few stray shots from earlier fighting. But what a fine metaphor the damaged unfinished monument was for a war that not only tore the still-young nation apart, but also was then turning Ferry Farm and its historical neighborhood into a wasteland.

By the end of the summer, the soldiers had packed up their camps and marched off to fight elsewhere. They untied the canal boats for reuse. One stray floated upstream and came to rest half under water near the pylons of the rail bridge. As soon as the Northern troops had left, returning Southern soldiers burned the new rail bridge, once again ending rail travel north.

Ferry Farm's Old Secesh was able to clean up the rubbish left behind, fill in the holes, and even get out the plow to cut some furrows for planting. There was damage and detritus everywhere, but nothing that small repairs could not put right. As the remaining area residents set about getting back to business, many must have felt that they had more or less dodged a bullet.

That winter though—just a few short months after the army pulled out—a force over ten times the size of the summer occupational force returned. Coming in from the southwest was a similarly sized Southern army. Each dug in on opposite sides of the river and prepared for battle.

In the gray winter, vicious and sustained shooting began right away—first with small arms and then with heavier guns. Over 150 cannons lined the Stafford side, including two batteries of highly mobile 12-pounder fieldpieces which deployed amidst the remains of the Bray farm. When all of these guns opened up on Fredericksburg and its entrenched and hidden defenders, there was not a part of town that was not clobbered. Homes became rubble or Swiss-cheese-pocked shells of broken windows and kiltered doors and shutters. Soldiers hid in their trenches and families clung to each other in cellars and waited for the rain of iron to end.

And when it did, it only got worse. The soldiers who last summer had patrolled the streets with an orderly, even almost-friendly, air, crossed into town in the thousands in a foul martial mood. They vented their collective rage, frustration, fear, and boredom on the battered city, raiding every shop and home they could, breaking windows, eating what food they found, dressing in nabbed clothing, and dragging furniture and other possessions to bonfires in the street. The officers stood by and let the men do as they wished until finally, brigade-by-brigade, they marched west through town to die in horrific numbers on the gentle rise of ground leading out of the shattered city. When it was all over, bodies and ruination were everywhere, all covered by a fresh snow, and Fredericksburg had become a watchword for suffering.

The soldiers who had mused about the Cherry Tree and lamented the fate of Mary's stones could not now be bothered to pay a lick of attention to such trivial topics while their battered army settled back on the Stafford side to recover. No one cared any longer that the old Washington farm was dotted with rifle pits, earthen-walled cannon emplacements, and the tracks and rubbish of thousands of men, wagons, and army animals. In the summer, when the men stole a hen or pilfered a fence rail, it was commonplace for officers to march the culprits out to make it right again. But in a war that could demolish a city and litter its homes and fields with dead and wounded, the fate of a historical landscape was of no real account. This was a cold, cold winter, and Ferry Farm was now enemy territory and nothing more.

With nary a tear, the invaders took apart the Bray home and its outbuildings when they needed the wood for other purposes. Many still thought that they were actually destroying the old Washington home to cook meals and insulate their tents against the damp cold. But in this new climate, such matters no longer were worth the worry. Board by board, they reduced the Bray place to open cellar holes and a few bricks on the ground. They filled the open holes with their ruined canteens, broken guns, and unwanted bits of clothing. They cut down the shading trees that lined the drive up to King's Highway and fully denuded huge swathes of Ferry Farm and surrounding Stafford County.

And even when they left, they only came back again and again with each new campaign. Ferry Farm and its neighbors were picked clean by wave after wave of soldiers and their repeated encampments. The town's dusty streets were lined with empty, fractured buildings, gap-toothed here and there by a burned or toppled structure. In the empty, still shell of a town, life wore a blue uniform. Thousands of men and dozens of women sat, leaned, and lay down in a town that now became a vast combined hospital staging area and graveyard.

Death wore blue, too. Every garden and roadside played some role in covering the dead that mounted from violent campaigns to the west. Burial teams laid over ten thousand men in hasty graves all over town— lining the roads and filling gardens. Everywhere were the dead—laid out in stockinged feet, half-covered perhaps with an army blanket, or bearing to their hastily dug grave a cloth tied to keep a lolling mouth closed— their cold sunken faces looked like gray stone. Their graves carried little more than a wooden board with charcoal initials to recall the people they had once been. After the first rain, the letters washed off and the boards fell over and the names and bones of the men moldering below were forgotten.

One afternoon in the spring of 1864, a photographer drove his black wagon through town and down to the old ferry crossing. He crossed the river to Ferry Farm on a wobbly army bridge made of planks sitting on narrow wooden boats. He would have to have worked his horses a bit to get them up the steep embankment and along one of the many paths that now converged at the old Washington farm landing. His route took him past the tents of the men guarding the bridge. He passed the deep trench the men had cut along the edge of the land and the pitted area where the Bray buildings had stood two summers ago. He rode his way up to the top of Stafford Heights, the rise and plateau at the back of the farm. In 1864, though, it was a place covered with cannons' protective earthen embankments. The guns' crews would lay boards on the ground to keep the cannons' wheels mobile and mud-free. On Stafford Heights, some of those boards had been part of the Bray farmstead—no doubt some of the men who put them under their cannons believed they were putting Young George's old home to a sad new use.

Once the photographer was in the spot he liked, he took out his large box camera, set its tripod stand in the ground, and turned the lens back on Fredericksburg.

There it was—the commanding view Washington had used to sell the land, the sunlit vista of promise and memory that Chapman had brushed onto his prepared board. It was the cityscape Baltimore's Saches and Company offered in two views, one in prosperity's light, one in war's shade.

And now it was the camera's turn at the dawn of the photographic age. And what the camera showed was Ferry Farm and the town beyond— cold, dismal, worn-out, spent.

6

Mary Washington's Grave and the
"Terrible Advertisement"

There was snow on the ground in Fredericksburg on Wednesday, February 27, 1889. About noon on that day, William Kirtley stood on a street corner chatting with Mayor A. P. Rowe about the wonders of a new leafy vine called kudzu. Many local farmers were interested in the new feed crop and Rowe promised to give Kirtley a pamphlet extolling the values of the potentially profitable imported agricultural marvel.

After a bit, their chatting turned to another popular topic: land sales.

In recent weeks, Kirtley and a dry goods seller named J. W. Colbert had teamed up to start a new real estate agency. The town was growing, and buying and selling land was a going concern. The man who changed the topic from kudzu to land sales was George Washington Shepherd, an older, locally prominent businessman with a spotless reputation and a finger in many pies. Locals called him the "Winder Up" of difficult deals and he served for years as Fredericksburg's official property assessor. He was so adept at the ins and outs of real estate that he was known to draft his own sales documents and deeds without the aid of lawyers. His skill had made him rich and respected. He lived in a fine brick home and owned properties all over town. He was widely regarded as one of the town's leading lights in matters commercial and civic.[1]

Someone must have pointed Kirtley out to him, or perhaps the mayor introduced the two. After brief "how-do-you-do's," Shepherd informed the new real estate agent that he had a few local plots for sale and might be interested in including them in the firm's listings. Kirtley was, of course, interested. The pair agreed to walk just out of town to take a look at the two choicest parcels, about a dozen acres on a low ridge where Mary Washington had been buried back in 1789.

Shepherd and Kirtley trudged up the hill leading westward from Fredericksburg's downtown businesses and storefronts. They walked up the same hill General Lee had held twenty-seven years before during the war in which both men had fought—Kirtley as a sergeant with a long combat record, Shepherd as a regimental clerk.[2] Their destination was the rise of land just west of downtown, crowned by Fielding and Betty Lewis's Kenmore and by the brick walls of the city's main cemetery. Block by block, the old battlefield clogged up with homes, and the near-town acres of the old plantations like Kenmore became home lots. Open land was valuable land.

Shepherd already owned Mary Washington's home and lot—he had bought it just after the war when the whole parcel was locally known as the "Tan-Yard Lot" due to an adjacent tannery.[3] In 1888, Shepherd had supplemented his collection of old Washington and Lewis family properties with the ten "Kenmore acres" for about one hundred dollars, and the two grave-filled acres just to their north for 250. Now he sought a profit on his investment. But once Kirtley and Shepherd reached Mary's grave, the problem that would land the would-be collaborators in court began to emerge.

According to Kirtley, the two men stood facing one another, each with a foot resting on part of Mary's still incomplete pitted and chipped monument. What the two said there in the snow soon became a matter of deep dispute. Kirtley claimed he asked Shepherd, "Do you own this

lot?" meaning the two-acre lot containing Mary's grave. Shepherd allegedly replied, "I do." [4] Kirtley went on to ask "Mr. Shepherd, do you own
that monument?" and "Mr. Shepherd, do you own this shaft?" with
both questions receiving the same formal matrimonial "I do."

According to Kirtley, Shepherd felt sure that Mary's grave could be
"disposed of to great advantage." [5] A syndicate of interested parties could
find the right buyer—the right person or people with a patriotic spirit—
and they would offer a good price for the honor of finishing Mary's
monument. Moreover, the 1888 election brought into power a new admin-
istration, and both men held out great hopes that it might mean more
federal money for commemoration projects like Mary's long-neglected
memorial. The rest of the land could be cut into home lots and sold off.

The money side was simple. Shepherd had paid "ninety-nine dollars
and some cents" [6] for the ten Kenmore acres and $250 for the two monu-
ment acres. He hoped to get $5,000 for his ninety-nine and change, and
a full $2,500 for the grave lots. The Realtors would later claim to have
understood that they had an option to buy the land at that price and sell
it for what they could find.

But Shepherd's recollection of the walk was somewhat different. He
did not dispute the street-corner meeting, his expressed interest in selling a few properties, or his offer to take Kirtley to see the lots. The main
difference in the two stories lay in the substance of the conversation.

Shepherd denied any discussion of the sale of the monument. Instead, he claimed that he offered Kirtley a recounting of his own personal memories of the early days of Burrow's plan to build the monument.
Shepherd recalled how the neglected stones were a sad embarrassment
for the city and told Kirtley how sincerely he hoped that someone, local
or otherwise, would now step in and finally finish the project. In Shepherd's version of the conversation, his history lesson was all by way of
saying that he had only the fondest, most patriotic, least self-interested
intentions for Mary's grave when he brought Kirtley up to the site.

As the two men walked back down to town, they took away very different understandings of what had just transpired in the snow. To hear Kirtley tell it, the two laid out a shrewd, if a bit cynical, deal to sell off Mary's grave. To hear Shepherd tell it, he offered a piece of land for listing and a brief history tour to an ambitious but not particularly promising land trader.

Once back in town, pens were set to paper and Kirtley began to get to work on his version of the deal. Kirtley visited Shepherd to tie things up and received more papers dealing with other possible sales. After sharing these with his partner Colbert at the latter's dry goods store, Kirtley walked by Shepherd's office once more and then returned home to draw up what he understood the deal to be: to wit, that G. W. Shepherd gave to him and Colbert a "sixty day option on the lot containing the Mary Washington monument and large marble shaft thereon for the sum of twenty five hundred dollars" and that "Colbert and Kirtley have full authority to sell said property at the price named above."[7] The note he drew up also outlined the same option for the Kenmore acres, for a price of five thousand dollars.

The next morning—the twenty-eighth—Kirtley once more returned to Shepherd's offices. This time the man was there but was "occupied" with affairs. Shepherd must not have seen the note Kirtley had left the previous evening as he absently asked the eager sales agent to "write up such a paper" as he wanted Shepherd to sign, and said that he would come to Kirtley's office later and sign it.

Kirtley returned to his office and once more wrote the terms of the agreement, this time dated February 28, 1889. Then he and Colbert began to write the text of the newspaper notice and handbill they planned to issue to find a buyer.

Later that day, Shepherd came to the Realtors' office. He read over the note and commented, "I will add here that Colbert and Kirtley have full authority to sell, and that I will make title when sold."[8] After adding more or less these words to the document, Shepherd signed it in a practiced hand that looked elegant alongside Kirtley's rougher penmanship.

Colbert and Kirtley sensed gold and were eager to close this deal as fast as they possibly could. Kirtley recalled that Shepherd handed the paper back to him saying, "I hope you will be able to find a purchaser." Kirtley replied, "We will do our best."[9]

With that exchange, Shepherd took his leave. It would be the last friendly words the two men would share.

On Saturday, March 1, Colbert and Kirtley took out their ad. It ran in the local papers, *The Fredericksburg Daily Star* and the *Free Lance,* but they also had it placed in papers in Washington, D.C., where they planned to hold the auction. Washington was the biggest nearby city and a place with lots of potential moneyed buyers.[10]

The ad was brief and clear, reflecting Kirtley's understanding of his charge from Shepherd. On Tuesday, March 5—the day after Benjamin Harrison's inauguration as the Twenty-third President of the United States—Colbert and Kirtley "will offer at public outcry" the full "12 acres of land, embracing the grave and the material of the unfinished monument of Mary, the Mother of Washington." The first ad, in fact, even included Mary Washington's home in the sale. Subsequent ads dropped mention of Mary's home, perhaps one of the other properties Kirtley and Shepherd had discussed.

Even before the auction was to take place, preliminary offers began to come in. On March 2, Colbert already had a staggering offer of ten thousand dollars for the two acres and the grave. Before the Realtors could tell Shepherd the good news, a mutual acquaintance and local farmer named James D'Atley ran into the Winder Up in the street. D'Atley related that a prospective buyer had already telegrammed Colbert with a fine offer. Shepherd was unimpressed. He responded only that "$10,000 was not enough for it" and that he planned to "go to see Colbert about it." As he headed back down the street, Shepherd turned and asked D'Atley if he "remembered the name signed to the telegram?" The answer was no, only that "the last name was Graham, or something like that."[11]

The ad certainly created enthusiasm. But not all of the responses were quite like Mr. Graham's offer. Another sort of reaction was quickly taking form in town.

The morning of March 1—the very day the ad ran—Kirtley recalled that there was a "fine gray stallion" on William Street right in front of the *Free Lance*'s new metal-fronted building. Virginians have always appreciated a good horse, and a small crowd had gathered to size up the beast.

Absorbed in his own appraisal of the animal, Kirtley missed the approach of his client. The street was noisy, so Shepherd leaned close to his agent's ear and "not in a whisper, but in low tone of voice" told Kirtley "if you will allow the expression, you have kicked up the devil." Kirtley must have known just what the issue was because he replied, "I do not propose to kick up the devil—but I want to sell the property."[12] It would seem that both parties already knew that they were treading on dangerous ground—or perhaps "sacred ground" is a better way to phrase it. Word was out, people were not happy, and someone had clearly gotten to Shepherd, who was beginning, even then, to find a way out of the deal.

The next morning, Kirtley headed over to *The Fredericksburg Star* offices to have the details of the sale printed up in two thousand handbills. At the office, he was accosted by Hampton Merchant, a *Richmond Dispatch* reporter and the son of the *Star*'s owner. The elder Merchant had already editorialized in his paper that the proposed sale would "never never take place."[13] The younger Merchant was then in town visiting and writing a piece on the sale for his own paper. Now it was his turn to weigh in on what was becoming the talk of the town.

He stopped Kirtley at the door saying, "You are the man I want to see." Merchant had been doing his homework. "I notice that you have an advertisement to sell the Mary Washington grave." With visible astonishment the reporter told Kirtley, "You can't do it!" He then told Kirtley that after careful review of the deeds and applicable paperwork it was clear that the land had been reserved permanently as a grave and that any sale was illegal. Indeed, it did not matter one bit what Shepherd may or may not have said—no one could authorize the sale of a reserved grave plot. The sale had to be shut down—the sooner the better.

Kirtley, though, was unfazed and replied only, "I propose to sell it." Stunned at this brazenness, Merchant stammered out "The hell you do! You can't do it!"[14]

Merchant was not the only one stunned. Conversations like the one at *The Fredericksburg Star* offices were taking place all over town. Word was spreading faster than kudzu on a warm moist day, and by March 3 people were up in arms against the sale of so important a site, and citizens were in the street handing out flyers announcing a "mass meeting" to be held the following evening at the courthouse to decry the proposed sale and, if possible, shut it down.

That Monday, Fredericksburg saw what the *Free Lance* called "an intensity seldom displayed in this quiet old town."[15] The courthouse main room filled with angry people, and the crowd spilled out onto the street. The smell of cigar smoke mixed with the fumes of gas lamps, and the sound of rustling handbills and newspapers mingled with murmurs and side chat. There was more in the air, though, than smoke and the patriotic chivalric defense of the Damsel Mary, Mother of Washington.

For one thing, most of the gathered were Democrats, who that day had witnessed the inauguration of former Yankee-general-cum-president Benjamin Harrison—a candidate who could not even garner the bulk of the popular votes. Only an Electoral College victory made the Republican the Twenty-third President of the United States. In the deep South, citizens voted for sitting Democratic president Grover Cleveland by eight-to-one majorities. In more moderate Virginia, Harrison fared a bit better. But even so, about six out of ten citizens that night were on the losing side. For some Southerners, Harrison might mean a return to the hated Reconstruction years. For the people at the meeting, the sale of Mary's monument seemed like another assault on the South and its heritage.[16]

Virginians were already angered by the plan of a group of Northern investors to buy and relocate Richmond's Libby Prison. In the North, the half-whitewashed walls became a familiar, much-invoked symbol of Southern cruelty. Songs and art lamented its overheated, airless detention rooms and celebrated a daring escape by a group of tunneling Union officers. Just a year before Shepherd and Kirtley's walk, papers were full of articles and editorials decrying the sale of the old warehouse to what they always pointedly called "capitalists" or "speculators" who planned to remove the building lock, stock, and barrel and bring it up to Chicago where it would be a pay-by-the-visit attraction.[17]

Citizens complained that "the historic landmarks of the South should be kept where they are" and not "sold to the Barnums of the North." Many feared that "glib strangers" would buy up places like Libby and even the old battlefields themselves, only "to coin money out of them."[18]

Was Mary's grave the next Southern monument to be sacrificed to crass commercialism? It was true that the people of Fredericksburg had done little to maintain the old stones. Even though anger at commercialism, capitalists, and greedy syndicates was the current mood, it was nevertheless hard to avoid the reality that a measure of local indifference had played a role in the lead-up to the sale that the courthouse crowd now gathered to condemn.

But there was no sign of that local indifference as Fredericksburgers of "all classes, professions, and politics" gathered to defend Mary's grave and their Southern heritage.[19] As the hubbub of the noisy crowd settled down, Mayor A. P. Rowe called the meeting to order and offered a few preliminary words of outrage. The next one to address the crowd was none other than G. W. Shepherd himself, who asked to "make a personal explanation." And what he said was nothing less than astonishing.

To begin with, he told the gathering that "he had never given authority to Colbert and Kirtley to sell the land containing the grave of mother of Washington" and claimed never "having in any manner authorized any person or persons to sell the monument," despite that fact that not five days before he had attached his signature to a document that did just that.

He went on. Shepherd claimed to have only given the two Realtors an option on the Kenmore acres, nothing more—and despite the fact that he would later testify that he and Kirtley discussed the monument's sad story at the site, he told the assembled citizens that "nothing was said about the monument" during their February 27 walk in the snow. Before a crowd of his angered friends, neighbors, and business associates, Shepherd protested his innocence in an affair that "had been gotten up without his knowledge or consent." He "disclaimed," "disavowed," and "vigorously denounced" the sale and the sellers.[20] It would seem that Shepherd's whole performance on March 4 was designed to staunch the growing "unenviable and unpleasant notoriety" the Winder Up had just helped bring on himself. And if that maneuver came at the expense of the two realtors' public reputations, it was a fair price to pay.

Most people accepted Shepherd's protestations—and indeed the realtors became the overnight villains in this infamous land deal. The meeting authorized a committee to draft up a statement of sentiment reflecting their commitment to stopping the sale, on the grounds that "the authorities of Fredericksburg have an indisputable right and power to protect this sacred soil."[21] Their manifesto went on to absolve Fredericksburg of any responsibility for the monument's failure. By the time the meeting was over and people headed home in the night air, a narrative had coalesced, and quiet consensus had been reached, and the roles of victim and villains had been cast. They also had achieved at least an initial goal: the March 5 auction never took place.

Afterward, Shepherd talked in the street with two friends—friends who perhaps knew better than to accept all the denials on their face. They simply asked, "how could you do it?" In a revealing introspective moment, Shepherd answered, "a man sometimes loses his head."[22] Shepherd later denied that chat took place.

Sometimes men lose more than their heads, though.

Colbert and Kirtley were not at the March 4 meeting. How could they have been? No doubt they knew about it, and no doubt the sinking feeling they must have felt was the decline of their public standing. The *Free Lance* ran a long column covering the meeting the morning of the fifth. To its left were a series of spots advertising the fine dry goods "for sale cheap, at J. W. Colbert's." To look at the page in light of what happened next, the ads look like little obituaries.

The two men felt set up by the older, more established Shepherd. In their view, the well-known figure had clearly planned to hide behind the relatively untested sales agents and let them be the public face for a sale anyone could have seen would be controversial. Standing before the assembled citizens of Fredericksburg, Shepherd laid all blame at the realtors' feet and hung them out to dry, suggesting they were devious and unscrupulous—perhaps others would add "unpatriotic" and "grasping" to that list. The community and its leaders were happy to accept this narrative. Men who were the week before upstanding citizens suddenly became symbols of crass commercial rapine—perhaps not Northerners, but Barnums just the same.

As early as March 1, the firm had been called upon to defend the sale. They did so in language reflecting an interest in the common good. They pointed out that Congress had made no effort to finish the monument and that with "the general depression of all kinds of business," sale to a buyer seemed a good way to "enliven up things" and maybe "bring money here from other sections."[23]

But lacking the public forum that the city gave Shepherd, the two Realtors turned to the only vehicle they could use to defend themselves: the local papers. In the battle of the newspapers, Shepherd again fired the first salvo. On March 9, *The Star* ran a long column in which he claimed it never dawned on him that such a fracas could emerge from what he called "the loose language of a hastily written paper."[24]

On March 12, Kirtley and Colbert took out their own column in the *Free Lance,* offering a robust defense of their plans and their declining reputations. They wisely shied away from attacking the well-respected Shepherd and instead professed their regret that "any act of ours" has brought "unpleasant prominence" to "the good name and fame of one of Fredericksburg's most highly esteemed citizens."[25]

They then made Shepherd's reputation the backbone of their argument. "The citizens of Fredericksburg and vicinity need not be told who Mr. George Washington Shepherd is," they wrote. "[He] is conceded to be one of the shrewdest, keenest, and sharpest business men in this section." Therefore, how could anyone imagine that such a figure "was as childlike and bland as the historic Heathen Chinee," who would have "fallen an easy dupe" to the "evil machinations" of a "pair of scheming tricksters." In short, "no bunko or confidence man would ever pick Mr. Shepherd if he knew him." To the Realtors, the idea that a man of such skill and acumen could have been tricked, or that a man so steeped in real estate deals and charged with overseeing the city's land valuations would have been casual in a legally binding bond of sale, was unlikely in the extreme. Instead, they were the ones being ill used—so much so that they claimed that "only a court of justice can relieve us."[26]

They coyly concluded their case through the logic of land pricing. Shepherd had last year paid $250 for the two-acre plot, they recalled for their readers, but was now asking $2,500 for the option the Realtors believed they had bought. To Colbert and Kirtley, it seemed obvious that Shepherd saw the stones and grave as "the valuable part of the option" and for their part, they "never questioned" his "right and title to it." Indeed, they asked, if it were not for the intention of selling the monument, what else made the price jump so high in one short year? "We had never heard that such a 'boom' had struck the vicinity of that lot," they sarcastically declared, "as to increase its value so much in so short a time.[27]

The path ahead was clear. With fighting words, they stated that the Winder Up had "attempted to discredit us and injure our business standing" and had "grossly misrepresented us and done us serious injury and damage." The only answer was to "seek redress before the proper tribunal."[28]

It was almost a year before the work of recording depositions and collecting evidence was done and the docket was clear. On January 15, 1890, *Colbert and Kirtley v. G. W. Shepherd* was ready to be heard in open court. The seasons passed in their course, from warm to cold, but the tempers and passions that underlay the case were as warm as ever. On the eve of the opening arguments, Merchant's *Fredericksburg Star* ran a poem by the Bostonian poet Edna Dean Proctor entitled "Mary, the Mother of Washington." "Let us crown her grave, the river by, with column to stand eternally," Proctor urged from afar. "And say to earth, and to star and sun: Mary, Mother of Washington!"[29]

The action that day centered on the main courthouse—the same one that had housed the grand meeting the previous spring. Judge William S. Barton usually wielded the gavel in local cases, but he had been a key organizer of the anti–monument sale meeting on Inauguration Day, and had been outspoken in his opposition to the sale. For good reason, he recused himself from the case. In his place was Judge William McLaughlin, usually of Lexington, Virginia, presiding now in Fredericksburg Circuit Court with a festive crowd in attendance. McLaughlin's gavel came down, and the opening arguments began.

Each party came armed with a brace of attorneys and everyone knew that fireworks were in the offing. After Shepherd's legal team's failed attempt to stop the case, the barristers made their opening comments—first W. S. White spoke for the realtors, followed by St. George Rose Fitzhugh for the defendant, Shepherd.

White made the case that Shepherd had changed the terms of his deal with the Realtors in midstride. The papers, he argued, would show that the arrangement was just as Colbert and Kirtley had always stated, and that Shepherd's reneging had done real and substantive damage to White's clients—damages that could be fairly covered by $20,000. He further argued that his clients had been so slandered in the press by Shepherd that only an additional $10,000 could put the pieces of their reputations back together. It was a rather staggering sum to ask for over a deal that began with a figure of $2,500.

For his part, Fitzhugh called the whole thing balderdash. His client was being fleeced by an unscrupulous pair of flimflam men, and all of the town could see what was happening. He asked that the two cases be tossed out as transparent frauds. Failing that, he aimed to put an end to this robbery forthwith.

It took more than three hours to set the stage and then it was time to move onto the main event. Kirtley took the stand first and endured four hours of questions. It was rough going from the start. Fitzhugh demanded to know if Kirtley had ever claimed that Mr. Shepherd had "told him that he owned the monument and shaft, and that he wanted to sell it."[30] It was an odd question—of course he had—that claim was the whole basis of his case! But when Kirtley answered with a simple "yes sir, he did" Fitzhugh lost his temper. "Mr. Shepherd will stamp that as a lie," he boasted to the court, "and I believe you know it to be a lie when you so state it."

The crowd gasped at the open provocation, and something in the old Confederate sergeant's temperament began to snap. With thinly veiled menace the combat veteran replied that he held Fitzhugh "personally accountable" for that slur. Fitzhugh replied, "I don't care for your threats." The courtroom erupted as Judge McLaughlin banged his gavel and demanded order. But it was too late. He adjourned the court until the next morning. The new battle of Fredericksburg was well and truly engaged.[31]

The next morning the crowds and legal teams streamed back into the courthouse, if anything even more eager for a good show, having had their appetites whetted the day before. Kirtley returned to the stand and glowered at Fitzhugh, who set in to pick up where he had left off. Before the questioning could continue, Kirtley made clear that he had been "grossly insulted the evening previous" and that he wanted "the protection, if there was any, from the court" and that, failing that, "he would protect himself."[32]

But an unimpressed McLaughlin looked down from the bench and said, "I will place you under bond, if you make threats." Kirtley had marched under Stonewall Jackson, he had faced Yankee riflemen on the hill just outside of town, and in Gettysburg as well, and now he had to sit tight and guard his tongue while far wealthier and more influential men called him a liar in open court. For over a year he and Colbert had suffered many little jibes and whispered slurs, they had seen countless disingenuous smiles, and had business opportunities silently closed.

But they were all there in that courtroom. They were there in the smiles of the townsfolk who had come to watch simply for the entertainment of the drama. They were there in Fitzhugh's imperious manner and insults, as well. The indignation that Kirtley saw the previous year when the reporter, Merchant, warned him against his intention to sell the monument was back again in Fitzhugh's tone and accusations. "The hell you do! You can't do it!" the reporter had said as the deal unfolded, and since then similar threats and warnings must have been repeated over and over by friend and foe alike. And there in the courthouse Sergeant Kirtley was once again being told what he could and could not do.

Sensing the level of emotion rising in his court, Judge McLaughlin stepped in. He told the assembled that he had never had a hard time maintaining order in his court, and he was not going to give up that prized reputation just yet. He called upon Fitzhugh to "withdraw the offensive language used to the witness the evening before."[33] Fitzhugh was in a corner and knew it. He swallowed the pill the judge ordered, but did so with the most resistance he could muster. He said he would "comply with the request of the court," but he wanted to reiterate that Kirtley's "statement had warranted" Fitzhugh's "very sharp expressions."[34]

With that parting jibe, it became Colbert's turn to step up and come under fire. The questioning continued more or less as it had before, until the realtors' attorney, Abner Dickenson, asked a question that bothered Fitzhugh. He rose to object to the question, and Judge McLaughlin sustained the objection. In good lawyerly fashion, Dickenson found a way to rephrase the question so as to elide the objection. Fitzhugh aggressively objected once again, at which point Dickenson told him where he could put his objection.

"Anger was now beaming from Mr. Fitzhugh's eyes" as he shouted at his opposite number, "I will not stand your insulting remarks any longer." Squaring off, he declared, "unless you stop them, I will thrash you!" Dickenson turned and met the attack—"if you come outside I will mash you into a jelly!"[35]

The two lawyers then rose and fell on each other. Fitzhugh was there first and struck Dickenson across his head with his rattan walking stick "breaking the cane in a number of pieces." Dickenson, lacking a weapon at hand, grabbed a nearby wood and glass inkstand, which he hurled at his assailant. His missile overshot its target, smashing instead into an iron railing behind the jurors' box. Juror Douglas Knox, a local businessman and Confederate veteran, was covered in black ink and "presented a dark spectacle."[36]

The whole of the crowd leapt to its feet, while a few jumped into the fray to try to pry the lawyers off of one another. Sergeant Kirtley saw his moment and, with cane uplifted like ol' General Armistead himself leading his men at Gettysburg, he charged into the engagement. His drive was stopped by one of the assembled, who threw himself on the plaintiff and brought him down. Amidst the yelling, the insults, and the mix of people fleeing the chaos and others rushing in to see it, the court's Sergeant Edrington pushed his way in and formally arrested the two battling attorneys.

Through a combination of gavel banging, physical restraint, and plenty of shouting, the court's order gradually settled back in. Judge McLaughlin, his proud record of keeping an orderly judicial house now shattered, began handing out retribution to the litigants who had reduced his court to riot. A fine of fifty dollars each went to Dickenson and Fitzhugh, and a thousand dollars bond each to ensure that they would "keep the peace for twelve months." The same bond was ordered against Kirtley and Shepherd to make them hold their punches as well.[37]

Once the dust had settled, witnesses continued to take the stand. Attorney Marye and Reverend T. S. Dunaway reminded the court about the level of indignation the sale's announcement brought about. Their testimony caused little trouble, though. Not so that of James D'Atley. The respected farmer claimed to be "partial to neither party in this suit," but he did have some pretty damning information about Shepherd's case. His recollection was that the Winder Up had declared the initial ten thousand dollars to be too small for the grave. Fitzhugh's hot temper flared once again at the prospect of such dangerous testimony. He was reported to have fumed, in his familiar manner, that if D'Atley dared to say as much, Fitzhugh would "call him a liar then and there, and prove it." For his part, D'Atley threatened to purchase newspaper space in which to brand "the jackanapes lawyer" as a "shirking coward" who used his office to "insult better men than himself."[38] Rumors spread that the two men were headed toward a duel to settle the matter.

On Friday, January 17, Shepherd himself took the stand and, in an hours-long session, reiterated his version of the notorious business deal. On Saturday, the court reconvened and each of the parties had the chance to restate their cases. Fitzhugh fumed, not just about the case itself, but about the dishonor of the bond McLaughlin had slapped on him. This ignominy he claimed loosed "a lot of yelping curs barking at my heels" who, but for his need to keep the peace, "would not dare do so for one minute." This was made all the worse by the "spirit of blackmail" that had hung like a pall over the town for "the past twelve months" thanks to the plaintiffs. He called upon the judge and the court to free him and all of the town lest, "no citizen's character would be safe from assault."[39]

Dickenson, still recovering from having Fitzhugh's cane broken over his head, was not in court to make the closing arguments. In his stead, Colonel R. J. Washington rode down King's Highway from Westmoreland County to step up and make the case, once more, that the Realtors had been done wrong. Washington had no previous involvement in the case, but his sudden arrival and name was nothing less than a counter appeal to the sensibility and patriotism of the court. As a last gambit, the Realtors and their lawyers used connections to bring in a genuine Washington ready to lend his name and prestige to the Realtors' claim. The partners, he argued, had been made promises, duly signed, and those promises, now breached, entitled them to fair damages.

It must have been a singularly odd scene. Here was a lawyer named Washington—the only man with any claim to some distant relation to the venerated Mary Washington—making the case that the Realtors were fully within their rights to sell at auction, in Washington, D.C., Mary's grave, then owned by another man, himself named in tribute to Washington. Mary's veneration was really a project to which the Washingtons themselves had no real connection. Indeed, they had not erected a durable marker on her original grave, they had sold off all of their local holdings, and now a distant kinsman was in town to defend the men the new Cult of Mary most vilified. It was an odd and fittingly confusing end to over a week of entertaining courtroom drama. And with that, the whole case was finally in the hands of the jury—a group that included Isaac Hirsh and John Griffin, both of whom had been members of the antisale committee. By the end, though, there were only ten jurors left "on account of sickness"—genteel code, perhaps, for wounds incurred during the court riot.[40]

The reduced panel deliberated for a scant two hours and four minutes before H. R. Gouldman, a local tailor and jury foreman, handed their verdict to Judge McLaughlin.

It was as short and sweet as it was predictable. "We, the jury, on the issues joined, find for the defendant."[41] Colbert and Kirtley could hardly have been surprised. The papers had been running stories reminding folks of the national opprobrium the two had incurred "for their attempt to so desecrate the grave of that illustrious woman."[42] The *Star* also kept the public aware that funds were coming in, dollar by dollar, to save Mary's grave. The court had even been able to hear witnesses attest to the scale and emotion of the public meeting against the sale—a not-so-subtle tactic to remind jurors just where their neighbors, customers, and business associates sat on this issue. Even the spectacle of having a genuine Washington sum up for the plaintiffs could not really turn a tide that first rose in the March 4 meeting, nearly a year earlier.

The moment Gouldman read the verdict aloud, Mr. White petitioned the judge to stay the verdict so that his clients could build an appeal. McLaughlin replied that "there was no ground for any such motion and that he would over-rule the motion at once." [43] They were free to take another stab at their case, but in the meantime, McLaughlin was heading out of this disputatious town as soon as he could get his robes off.

Colbert and Kirtley had lost, but they never really had a chance. It may well be that Shepherd had set them up to be the front for a potentially unpopular deal. But once opinion hardened against them and the sale—once they became just so many "Barnums" selling off parts of prized Southern heritage—there was no way that they could ever come clean of the taint.

They appealed in February. They failed again. The papers barely noted the case. Colbert and Kirtley's loss was a foregone conclusion, and by that time fundraising to complete Silas Burrow's old project was in full swing. In most people's eyes, the matter was settled. On top of that, Shepherd had one more trick up his sleeve that doomed the appeal once again, before the gavel fell.

On January 24, he deeded Mary's grave and the two acres in question to Fredericksburg's Ladies Mary Washington Monument Association—the same group whose fundraising tallies had been diligently recorded in *The Star* right next to the trial coverage. Shepherd wrote into the deed exactly the kind of language he claimed he had always held by. The grant was for the land "but excluded therefrom" the actual monument itself.[44] How different that language was from the slippery document he signed back in '89 offering "a sixty day option" for "the lot containing about two acres of land with the Mary Washington Monument and large marble shaft thereon for the sum of twenty five hundred dollars."[45]

The new deed appeared in full in *The Star* and went a long way to making Shepherd's version of the original deed the official one. The gift lost him his $250 investment, but that was a small price to pay to end the case once and for all. The Ladies were happy to take over and set in to completing the project that began back in the 1830s.

After their February loss, Colbert and Kirtley took their file to the Supreme Court of Appeals of Virginia. They failed there as well. The court reviewed the case and ruled that "the jury is plainly right" and that in upholding that original verdict against the partners, the February court "did not err."[46] But their finding still had room for a bit of commentary. The whole of "this horrid transaction" they opined was "stamped all over with the fraud, false pretense, and deceit of the plaintiffs in error."[47]

Like the two Fredericksburg courts before it, the appellate judges overlooked or attached no importance to Shepherd's quiet admission that "sometimes a man loses his head." They also paid no mind to that scrap of paper buried in the case file in which Shepherd carefully added a line in his own hand to the draft agreement—an agreement of which he later denied knowledge. They cared not that James D'Atley had sworn that Shepherd had rejected the price of ten thousand dollars for Mary's grave, nor did they object to the fact that two of the jurors had been activists against the sale. Instead, they saw only what they objected to in the sale, and not the circumstances that led to what would soon be called "The Terrible Advertisement."[48]

In town, winter slowly turned to spring. Much of the work of removing the countless bones of dead Civil War soldiers had been completed. The far end of the old battlefield's ridge was filling with these bones and small stones, each saying "unknown." Living survivors of the army were back in town as well—this time, though, in the form of engineers with ambitious plans to dredge out the Rappahannock. Where Weems's Washington once swam, where charred and rusting ship ruins settled, there was now so much silt that navigation was becoming difficult.[49]

All over town a small building boom began to set in. New homes filed into the valley where Northern soldiers had fought and died. They crept in to block the line of fire the Southerners had once used to such great effect. One by one, the old views of the battlefield were lost—the sites of the worst fighting were the first to be filled in. Even as large swathes of outlying properties remained as they had been, developers took the actual sites of combat and carved them into ever smaller slices to be filled with modest homes. It was almost as if it was an intentional plan—as if crowding the battlefield with individual homes would somehow erase the memory of the town's collective suffering.

G. W. Shepherd and other developers like him did well in this game, selling the open land and profiting along the way. The same people who were outraged at Colbert and Kirtley's proposed sale and the loss of their Southern heritage took no notice at all as the old Fredericksburg battlefield filled with houses. Mary Washington was history—she was a past they wanted to hold up and venerate. Her presence in their heart and community was a vital tie to America and her values. And the "late unpleasantness" of the war? That was something else. That was pain. That was suffering. That was not history—it was something to put behind.

Of course, locals honored veterans' service and even proudly trotted out the old Stars and Bars on occasion. They had commissioned a big iron gate to mark the large burying yard behind Kenmore, and renamed it the Confederate Cemetery. And even though the families of many of the old veterans chose not to recall their service on their stones or in obituaries, the dead were nevertheless remembered.

But the actual places of the war? These were a different story. The physical scars the landscape still bore—the hundreds of names and initials carved in brick all over town by bored and recovering Northern soldiers, the trenches and earthworks still open and even serviceable, the innumerable bullet and cannonball holes that had to be patched and covered—all of these were bitter memories and damages better silenced and hidden. Filling in the old battlefield with homes made good commercial sense and it went a long way toward healing the town's still sore wounds. The war-era vistas and remains were meticulously erased, and most were glad to see them go.

The money kept flowing in to local and national Mary Washington Monument funds. Soon, a group of proud American matrons were able to announce that they had what was required to build for Mary a brand new and fully fitting monument. The mothers of America would complete Burrows's vision: a tribute to the mother of all mothers. In October 1893 they set the cornerstone and quickly raised the pedestal and column. On May 10, 1894, President Grover Cleveland, himself a Presbyterian, and the man who most of the people in town had voted for back in '88, retraced Old Hickory's 1833 commemorative bunting-lined footsteps again in the company of local grandees, Washington descendants, and cabinet members, and once again a president came to honor Mary the Mother of Washington.[50] This time, though, it was to dedicate a completed monument and not to start one from scratch—much better to crow after the egg is laid. In this case, the egg was a tall, uniformly gray obelisk pointing skyward right near the spot all now called Meditation Rock. It looked much like the monuments going up all over other Civil War battlefields—indeed, the stone was provided by two former Union soldiers active in the veterans groups.[51] The stone itself came from Buffalo, New York.

Fully paid for, skillfully carved, and lovingly tended by adoring Americans, Mary finally had her grave marker. It might even sit right atop Mary's actual grave—no one even really remembered anymore to worry about that detail. Before the big dedication day, the stones of the old monument were quietly sold and hauled off. No ceremony, no complaint. They just were bought as so much scrap.

The matrons had achieved their goal, but they had also given birth to something new in Fredericksburg—historical preservation. It was an odd beginning and an odd subject to preserve, right when so much of the area's recent history was rapidly going away. But Mary had long mattered in Fredericksburg. She might not have birthed her famous son here, but her memory spawned a sense that there was a past here worth saving.

It came at a cost, though. Colbert and Kirtley paid it.

Two months after the appeal, Colbert lost his seat on the city council. He had been an active and engaged member for some time. But his standing had fallen so much that he came in eighth in the next election for his Upper Ward seat—a staggering loss for an incumbent. He lost to J. S. Knox—a member of the anti–monument sale committee.[52]

Soon after that, the paper carried a notice that, due to hard times, J. W. Colbert, Grocer, was closing up shop and leaving town. He took up residence in Portsmouth, on the Chesapeake, and started anew.

In June of 1906, he was struck by a streetcar. The ghastly accident took off his arm, and after a week, he was dead. In an act of forgiveness, his body came back to Fredericksburg and was carried to his grave in the Confederate Cemetery by the sons of the jurors who had helped drive him from town. J. W. had served his time in exile, and in death, his former neighbors were ready to take him back.

But not so for Sergeant Kirtley. He had always been the more outspoken of the two, and so more of the local scorn attached to him. Moreover, he was a shadowy figure. He first burst on the local scene with the "Terrible Advertisement," and he all but disappeared once the deal was shut down. Perhaps that is why it was easier to make him the villain—he had so few kin and allies in town. Or perhaps it was his way of looking at the town's better-connected grandees, and simply and defiantly telling them what they did not want to hear. They had embraced the logic of the marketplace, but they were not yet fully comfortable with the people it had created. When those people were Northern Barnums, well, it was easy to resent them. But when they were simple, ordinary Southerners, men like Kirtley who had marched with Stonewall, well, it was a bitter pill to swallow.

So Sergeant Kirtley marched off to fight his next battle—wherever that was, we do not know.

7

❧

The Farmer and the
Bicentennial

On September 7, 1909, the *Free Lance* announced that Ferry Farm had a new owner. His name was James Beverly Colbert.[1] He was distant kin to J. W. Colbert and had been a businessman in town since the days of the "Terrible Advertisement." He lived in a fine, lightly ginger-breaded house with a wooden-lace-trimmed porch that looked up the gentle rise to Kenmore's tall brick walls. He did not have to strain too much to see Mary's new obelisk, and the daily walk to his downtown businesses could lead him past her old house and other reminders of the Washington family.

He was a country boy—born in Massaponax the year after the conclusion of the war that left his native county an impoverished wasteland. Like many of his generation, he came to town to make his fortune in commerce, even though he never lost his country airs. He had amassed a small empire in the dozen or so years he had lived in town. He gained some notoriety for his 1903 attempt to monopolize the local ice trade—a venture that landed him in a public brawl with his main competitor.[2] He owned properties all over town and ran a saloon and a small hotel. He and a partner named John Jones sold furs and fabrics, and he was always on the lookout for nearby farm properties. Colbert was not one to keep all his commercial eggs in one venture basket.

He was front and center for the lessons of Mary Washington's grave and these would not have been lost on such an enterprising mind as Colbert's; there was money in a historical property if one handled it correctly.

Ferry Farm was just such a place, even though its value was mostly potential. After the Civil War, a new family from Pennsylvania came down and cleaned up the damage on the acres including the old Washington home lot. The Corsons filled in the holes that were all that was left of the 1850s farmstead. They dumped in building refuse and corroded materiel the soldiers had left behind. They picked a site about midway between where the Washington and the Clark homes had stood— right where the old kitchen was—and erected a new two-story home sitting near a pair of barns. They cleaned up the old farm lane and added a one-room farm office at the end of it. This was built more in the local vocabulary with a small brick chimney and simple wooden shingles on the roof.

This was the farm that Colbert purchased in 1909—a plain, useful farmstead without flash, elegance, or ostentation. All it took was the right mind to reimagine it as Washington land once again. Under Colbert's management, the old place became "The George Washington Farm—J. B. Colbert, Proprietor"—a name he made sure the newspapers used. His specially printed farm stationery showed the new name in large bold Gothic letters. The letterhead filled a full quarter of each page and boasted, "Old home where Mary Washington Lived and the Famous Cherry Tree grew," and "Old home where Geo. Washington lived and threw the Silver Dollar across the Rappahannock."[3]

These wonderful Weemsian remembrances flanked a portrait of George himself. It was, rather fittingly, a simple line rendering of the Gilbert Stuart portrait (of dollar-bill fame). But this Washington showed the distinctive drooping eye and knowing grin of Jim Colbert, Proprietor.

J. B. knew just what he was up to. His name and Washington's were now both of the same place, the same rural corner. For Colbert, this was all a manner of arrival—a way of positioning himself in the best light, associating himself with the most famous name around, and claiming for himself the mantle of a legacy of greatness. It was a stroke of brilliance that Washington, Parson Weems, and P. T. Barnum himself all could have appreciated. Colbert perfectly blended his own commercial goals with the grand language of all things patriotic.

His initial purchase only included about two hundred acres—the main home area and the waterfront and a nice stretch back from the river. But like Strother and Washington and Fitzhugh and Mann and Teasdale before him, he gradually snapped up each new adjoining parcel as it came up for sale. A few dozen acres in 1910, a few more in 1911; bit by bit, Colbert reconsolidated the lands Washington had surveyed back in 1771 and made them his own.

But this was no preservation effort—no attempt to somehow keep these lands off limits in a special reserve. This was business. J. B. planned on using every single acre he bought for productive farming. He built himself and his family a new and enormous farmhouse right where a Bray building once sat—itself above the old Washington kitchen. A set of low-roofed milking barns would house his growing herd of dairy cows and he filled the fields with fine alfalfa hay. Colbert had his men build a fifteen-foot-deep icehouse right next to the old Corson farm office. They used Washington and Bray foundation stones to line the large pit.

The old office reused stones as well, and as Colbert modified the farm that small, one-room framed box with its brick chimney and curling cedar shingles began to look older and older. That look of age, coupled with Colbert's heavy use of the Washington name, led to something remarkable.

It is hard to say when or how exactly it happened. Photographs are our best guide. For some reason, the old Corson farm office made its way into an oddly large number of visitors' snapshots. A few feature members of the Colbert family, standing by the office as if it were a prized possession. One shows J. B. himself in his Sunday best chatting with a bespectacled man in bowler hat and long Edwardian jacket at the office corner. The office's ramshackle condition is clear to see—the unpainted clapboards pull away from one another and there are large gaps in the foundation stones. All of this makes it look far older than it in fact was, and photo-worthy.

A few of these pictures have handwritten captions on them noting "The Geo. Washington Farm" or "the office." One shows a tree with the words "Cherry Tree of Geo. Washington Farm" written in the margin while another names it "George Washington's Cherry Tree." Visitors could also see some old stones in the cellar of the new Colbert house— stones the owner claimed were part of the Washington home.[4]

Colbert grew fine alfalfa hay and raised show-quality dairy cows. But he was also busy growing Weemsian stories from the clovered fields where Washington had once bounded as a boy. Was it Colbert's idea to serve up these stories in aid of his own ends, or were visitors bringing their beloved Washington tales with them? There is no way to know for sure, but J. B. was orchestrating these stories—adding to them, accommodating them, making the most he could of them, and seeking ways to profit from them. He may not have set this Ferry Farm Weemsian renaissance in motion, but he certainly kept it rolling along and was its principal beneficiary.

By the 1920s, under Colbert's ownership, Ferry Farm, or the Cherry Tree Farm as some called it, was more awash in Weemsian stories than ever before in its history. Colbert was the first owner to build the old stories into the promotion of the place itself. On top of that, he presided over the invention of brand new Weems-inflected stories and objects— some of which may have been his very own creations. As Americans all over the land took a renewed interest in their nation's colonial past, Colbert saw to it that his George Washington Farm lived up to the reputation the Parson had given it so long ago.

The centerpiece of this reawakening was the Corson farm office which soon had its own newly minted Weemsesque backstory.

Augustine had a set of surveying tools listed in the probate record taken after his 1743 death. Given that Washington made so much of his early fortune and his start in adult life as a surveyor, it was just too tempting for Washingtonphiles to connect those very selfsame tools to the start of George's career. But Colbert went them all one better.

It seems that these surveying tools had been stored in a special building. And that building, unsung as it was and yet so deserving of recognition and renown, was still standing on the farm where Washington had come of age. That building was the Corson farm office—of course though, true believers all called it the Washington Surveying Office.

If Colbert made that up himself, then he was a Washington storyteller almost on par with Weems. If the story coalesced from fragments of popular imagination, misheard memories, and patriotic priorities without a guiding single agent, then it is a wonderful illustration of the folk process settling on a landscape. What it was not, though, was a viable historical claim. There are too many actual photographs of an empty buildingless Ferry Farm during the war to allow any argument that any structure survived intact from Washington's days, and its construction is all late 1800s. The Surveying Office could have been many things, but it cannot be an eighteenth-century building.

But that sort of dismissal is for those who lack the romantic imagination to appreciate a good story. And there was no shortage of appreciative visitors posing before the building for a snapshot, or just communing with the relic as a way to connect with the Great Washington. Colbert could push the story pretty hard when he wanted to. When colonial historian Joseph Dillaway Sawyer visited Ferry Farm around 1923 during his research for his two-volume opus, entitled *Washington*, Colbert offered the scholar the deluxe tour which of course included a walk-through of what Sawyer later called "George Washington's workshop." Sawyer praised the office as an "indissoluble" link to the farm's past.[5] The Surveying Office had arrived.

Others got on board as well. Local historian and project supporter Chester Goolrick penned a few newspaper stories about Ferry Farm that featured the "old office of George Washington." He even recounted a made-up family tale about how his own grandfather used to take his father (then a youth) out to Ferry Farm to admire the office and remember Washington.[6] The local stationer named R. A. Kishpaugh even produced a special hand-tinted Surveying Office postcard. The image featured the aged building itself and also showed the large tin roof Colbert had built over his prize to keep the rain from leaking through its loose wooden shingles. The back of the card retold the Surveying Office story, although it hedged its bets a bit, saying it "is said to have been used by Washington."

It certainly was said—and more and more people were saying it.

One of them was a science fiction and travel writer named George Allan England. On one of his annual migrations from New England to Key West, Florida, he stopped in Fredericksburg and threw himself into local history. The preservation bug that the citizenry first caught over Mary Washington's grave had spread. George Washington Shepherd had sold Mary's home to the Association for the Preservation of Virginia Antiquities, who began to remake it as they wanted it to be—regardless of what it actually may have looked like in Mary's day. Similar attention fell on Hugh Mercer's home and apothecary shop, and on the Rising Sun Tavern at the old edge of town—both places with some Washington associations. Kenmore, with its solid brick, watertight walls, also became an object of preservation. To help the preservation cause, "George Allan England, novelist," with his characteristic dark-eyed stare, dressed in a loose-fitting, colonial-style coat and misplaced mop of a powdered wig. He may have been a visitor, but England knew how to work his way into locals' hearts and favorite causes.[7]

On one of these trips to town, someone suggested he might find good material across the river as well. It would not have taken much to make England curious to see the place famous for the old Cherry Tree and so many other fine yarns about Washington's childhood. So pretty soon England was in his best colonial garb at "the place of young Washington's exploits."[8] From the moment Colbert and England first clasped hands in greeting, a truly unique and creative partnership was born.

The two men could not have been cut from more different forms. Colbert was short, round, and drooping in his eyes and mustache. His surviving photographs all show him with the puckish, knowing grin and dark suit of a character to be reckoned with.

England, on the other hand was a lanky, angular, stick insect of a man. A straight-hafted pipe often gripped in his teeth, his dark ringed eyes had a searching intensity and even in cold black and white, his images give off an air of nervous energy.

As different as they looked, their backgrounds were even more at odds. Colbert was a creature of the farm—an eighteenth-century man using twentieth-century tools to pursue age-old goals. England was Harvard educated, well-connected—there was a story that he had tutored a young Franklin Delano Roosevelt—and very much a self-styled, well-traveled, multilingual man of the world. There is no reason to believe Colbert ever traveled as far as even Baltimore where his second wife was born.

Both were men of the outdoors—Colbert having been raised a farmer and eagerly keeping his hand in the game while also digging icehouses around the area. There is a photograph of him out back of Ferry Farm's barns, amidst piles of lumber, in a Homburg-style hat and a long woolen coat sitting on a fine, shining horse. The rider exudes vigor and confidence in his attempt to look like a Washington or even a Robert E. Lee.

But the casual, sloppy, industrial-farming background of the shot reveal a man who has not quite mastered pretension. It is easy to see this Jim Colbert as the newspaper once described him—standing and whipping the reins of a team of horses pulling a wagonload of men up a Fredericksburg street at breakneck speed as they tore out to douse a raging fire that was consuming a wood lot he had just bought.

England's outdoors was a different place. Although born on a Nebraska army post, he sought out an Eastern city office life of starched collars until lung problems drove him to the woods of Maine for a new start. His outdoor life was one of choice. It was a world of sportfishing in the Florida Keys, book-research adventure travel on an icebound Newfoundland seal hunters' ship, hair-whipping biplane trips to Mexico, and membership in various adventurer's clubs. One photograph of the novelist shows him in full sealer's rig—his deeply lined face ringed with a fur hood. Another shows him in an absurd array of argyles, plaids, and jodhpurs at a Florida golf resort with Lou Gehrig and a few bankers. Clothes made the man for this army minister's son turned self-made literary personality.[9]

Colbert was conventionally New Southern: dedicated to local groups and local commerce, active in his Baptist Church, and with a few lodges, but never really in the upper reaches of Fredericksburg society. Never an officeholder or a Winder Up, never a name in the list of the great and good. England was an outspoken and prolific Socialist who joked about being the most unpopular man in Maine due to his terrible showing in the 1912 governors race on the Socialist ticket. He boasted over a dozen languages at his command, including Esperanto, whose utopian utility he repeatedly advocated. England wrote hundreds of words a day, and published article after article, story after story. Colbert had a hard time spelling.

Tall and skinny, short and round, they were like some sort of Washington-inspired Laurel and Hardy (a reference they would both have gotten and both resented). Yet, in their ways, both men were deeply sophisticated and both understood—also in different ways—the value of a good story. The two were in all ways useful to each other as far as Ferry Farm was concerned.

The stories of cellar stones and Washington offices began under Colbert, but were built on a bedrock of Weems's storytelling. It took a bard to champion the cause, to pick up the standard of Cherry Tree and Surveyor Office and bring them to a larger audience than the one who happened by the farm.

In Colbert, England found a man with a story to tell, and in England, Colbert found a man who could tell it. And in Colbert and England, Ferry Farm found a pair of champions with vim and vision.

Between face-to-face meetings and letters, this odd couple hatched a plan. The idea was to raise the farm's profile, remind the world that this was the site of the Cherry Tree, the Sorrel Colt, the coin toss, as well as countless other memories of Washington. There also was the Surveying Office and the cellar stones as living monuments to Washington. The plan was to find the right backer or group thereof to step in and buy the site. Here was a chance to take Ferry Farm from working farm to national shrine. Here was a chance to save the last links to Washington's childhood so that their value and lessons could be passed on to posterity. Here was a chance for Colbert and England to do well by doing good.

The time was right. Americans in the 1920s were fascinated by the images, tales, styles, and feel of the Revolutionary era. They restyled their own homes to look more like how they imagined those of their colonial forbearers. On top of that, there was something else on the horizon. The year 1932 was going to be the two hundredth anniversary of George Washington's birth. For a nation already fascinated by colonial styles, the prospect of celebrating perhaps the most famous colonial American was delightful. Scores of independent foundations and citizens' committees and fraternal organizations took it upon themselves to get things in line so that George's two hundredth would be a date to remember. Their work was egged on by President Calvin Coolidge's call that Washington's two hundredth birthday be "appropriately observed."[10]

The result was a National Washington Bicentennial Commission coordinating a vast national fete. The whole thing would be ringmastered by a New York congressman named Sol Bloom. No man was better qualified. Not only was he a member of Congress's Committee on Industrial Arts and Expositions, he also had a long career behind him as a vaudeville show promoter and theatre owner. There even was a story that he was the impresario for "Little Egypt," the famed "shimmy dancer" who scandalized the Gilded Age with her bare midriff.[11]

Local and national bicentennial planners all knew the growing importance of the automobile and the sort of mass visiting they were making possible. By the time England visited Ferry Farm there was already talk of turning King's Highway into a "60 foot [wide] concrete tourist route."[12] The new road, rechristened "The George Washington Memorial Road," would link the great man's birthplace in Westmoreland County with Fredericksburg, and then up to Mount Vernon. History-minded motorists would be able to smoothly cruise right through the heartland of Washington's youth.

Fredericksburgers wanted in on the anticipated boom. They began to promote their host of colonial sites and talk a bit more about the Washington they had so long overlooked. They even re-renamed the main streets in town, undoing the Revolutionary-era changes to American-sounding names—like Water, Commerce—and returning to the pre-1776 royal tributes of Sophia, William, and Caroline, in an effort to better invoke ye grande olde dayes.

The stars were converging to make a singular profitable opportunity for The George Washington Farm. And for a professional spinner of yarns and a hard-nosed, fearless, and proven aggressive farmer/businessman, the bent limbs of Weems's fruit trees must have never seemed to have been hanging any lower.

England got to work as early as December 1925 when he introduced

Ferry Farm to prospective buyers in pages of the *Daughters of the American Revolution Magazine*. England's written call to arms forthrightly labeled Ferry Farm, "the most historic farm in America" and in many respects, "by far the most valuable." England made no attempt to hide that this was a pitch. He urged the "patriotic women of America" to "rescue from oblivion a landmark that should be a priceless national heritage."[13] Well, perhaps not completely beyond price.

Other pleas appeared in the nation's major newspapers and other venues. Each pitch was targeted to a specific audience, but each asked the same leading rhetorical question—"why some patriotic individual or society" has not yet stepped up and made Ferry Farm "a national shrine is a profound mystery."[14] And in each piece, England and his typewriter dressed the farm up in full Weemsian finery, while adding his own distinctive touch of romance and overstatement.

Here was what "local tradition" called the "scion of the original cherry tree that young George hacked with his immortal hatchet." It is true that the whole story had "some critics," but England rebuffed the deniers—"time and popular belief have crystallized" the story itself "into solid reality" and "the lover of history," he assured his readers, will experience "a genuine thrill to behold the place of that tradition."[15] Here one can "find the spot on the riverbank where the youthful George threw the Spanish dollar across the Rappahannock," and walk the fields where Washington had "his memorable though disastrous encounter" with his mother's "ungovernable sorrel colt."[16]

In one pitch England included a picture of "the Old Survey Office" and heaped praise on J. B. by name for his selfless and deeply patriotic attempts to protect this "humble but priceless" (there was that word again) "little house." Its "ancient and handmade shingles and clapboards" were even then showing "marked signs of deterioration" which "if not soon arrested "would certainly lead to the loss of this "irreplaceable landmark of pre-Revolutionary days and Washington memories." Indeed, while "Lincoln's birthplace is protected by imposing marble," this "soul-stirring Washington antiquity" sits vulnerable to "destruction by the weather or fire."[17]

He tried invocations of beloved stories, a carefully introduced sense of urgency, and even some shame. He could even shoot right at the heart. He told the Daughters of the American Revolution that Ferry Farm had been the home of Mary Washington, who had been the object of such well-deserved love, admiration, and preservation energies—her grave was well marked, her home in Fredericksburg bought and restored to the colonial revival gem it never had been. Yet, Ferry Farm, the home she inhabited "for by far the greatest portion" of her life, "finds no monument—not even a simple wooden tablet" to mark the spot.[18]

He told readers of the *Washington Post* that someone should buy the land and donate it the Boy Scouts so that it may serve as their national headquarters. After all, was there any place more associated with the Scouts' goals than the site of the most famous American boyhood story of them all? Patriotic values all but grew on the farm's celebrated cherry trees, and certainly there was no better place for teaching the "lessons of Americanism" as well as "history and patriotism to the youth of America."[19]

On top of that, the land was already "ideal for tennis, football, baseball, hockey" and, curiously included on that list, "aviation," and a river "admirably suited to all water sports," making the farm perfect for building the "moral integrity" of American youth as well as "developing" their "physical health."[20]

England certainly believed the stories he shared. Even though he had a small financial stake in the outcome—a finders fee for a buyer—there is no mistaking his genuine sincerity for the project. After Weems, England was the land's most effective storyteller, largely because, like his predecessor, he really believed in the moral value of the wares he had to sell. Weems certainly knew he was fibbing, but England was a true believer.

And there were others. And they heard England's call to action.

Very soon, a group called the George Washington Foundation (one of many with that name in the 1920s) filed incorporation papers and set about raising the money to buy the farm. Led by a government statistician named E. Irving Fulton and a New York lawyer named A. Stedman Hills, this group of concerned citizens managed to pull together enough funding to make a first payment of the staggering $125,000 Colbert asked for the farm.

The deal was vintage J. B. Colbert. Rather than get a mortgage from a bank, Fulton, Hills, and their associates agreed to have Colbert be the receiver of separate payments—some in the form of postdated checks. These payments came from the foundation's fundraising efforts and would arrive at Ferry Farm at regular intervals. The real kicker was that Colbert and his family would continue to live on and operate the farm as they always had, with no legal lien or impediment to their activities "until such a time as all of the purchase price thereof shall have been paid to him in full."[21] Not only that, but the buyers also agreed to pick up the outstanding mortgages on the other adjoining parcels Colbert had grabbed along the way.

In other words, Colbert continued working his farm while the checks came in. And what happened if the George Washington Foundation defaulted on its payments? That would leave the Colberts right where they began, with of course some extra cash gained along the way—ownership came on full, not partial, payment. If England told stories that Weems would have embraced, Colbert set up a deal to sell Ferry Farm that Washington himself would have envied.

In the bright, shining days of the prosperous twenties, enjoying a mild case of Washington and colonial fever, it seemed to the partners that the sky was the limit and they had found the ideal way to make good and serve the nation as well. But perfect as the plan seemed, it quickly ran into speed bumps—all having to do with fundraising the cash to meet Colbert's $125,000 asking price.

The main problem was that Ferry Farm was not the only game going. It was as if every town on the Atlantic seaboard between Maine and

Georgia had some sort of eighteenth-century ramshackle house that now needed to be restored, rescued from private ownership, or moved to a safer location. And while there were preservation projects galore, Virginia was singularly larded with them—Fredericksburg alone accounted for at least a half dozen.

Some were private ventures, like that of Daniel and Helen Devore who in the 1920s tried to restore Fitzhugh's Chatham to its former greatness, or James Monroe's law office, opened to the public by his descendants in 1927. Others, like Mary Washington's house and Charles Washington's home, the "Rising Sun Tavern," were already in their second decades as projects of the statewide Association for the Preservation of Virginia Antiquities. Groups like the Kenmore Association and the Fredericksburg Citizens' Guild, who owned Hugh Mercer's "apothecary," were task-specific local entities with large reaches beyond the area.[22]

Ferry Farm was an odd duck in this preservation pond—a stand alone. No well-connected grand dame or prominent Revolutionary Daughter stood at the project's helm. Instead, it was J. B. who was the project's principal local face—and even as late as the 1920s, the Colbert name was not always associated with the best side of local preservation. Ferry Farm's sale had to compete for funds with these and dozens of other worthy efforts in letters and appeals that all went to the same kinds of patriotic people. True, Ferry Farm could boast the best name in colonial revival sensibilities—the veritable gold standard, the biggest man there was. But what did the farm really have of him to preserve? The cellar stones and the Surveying Office were the main surviving attractions and dubious as they were made pale shadows compared to still-standing Kenmore or Mary's house.

What made the place memorable, though, was its stories. Weems's tales had always had an audience—even if it was just to turn up one's nose at them. That was the beauty of his work—the stories were useful to believer and denier alike. For "serious" people and a rapidly profession-alizing generation of academic historians, knocking Weems was a way to show that one was "one of us," real, credible, truthful, and not yet an-other storyteller or fabulist of past generations. True believers and ro-mantics like George Allan England might see the tales as valuable, but the new century of progress and wars to end all wars had no time for such silliness. Just clear-eyed objective historical truth, please.[23]

Ferry Farm's value depended on what one thought of Weems. For his fans, the place of the Cherry Tree was a gem; for his deriders, the land was as rejectable now as when the real flesh-and-blood Washington turned his back on it and lived his great life elsewhere.

These were all mere challenges, though. Ferry Farm's real obstacle came in the form of an aging patrician professional genealogist from New York. He made his living flattering his rich clients that their pedi-grees were as good as they had hoped they would be. He exuded all the sense of privilege and condescension of the prickliest of the most turf-conscious academics tied to a contractor's insecurity. His name was Charles Arthur Hoppin and he was the chief historian for another one of the Old Dominion's many preservation projects. It was called the Wake-field Association and its goal was to reconstruct the "birth home" at the Westmoreland County site where it once stood.[24]

Of all the regional preservation projects, Ferry Farm and Wakefield had the most thematic overlap. The two were most directly in competi-tion for resources and status in a contest that pitted birth, ancestry, and well-heeled backers against Weems's boyhood stories and the begin-nings of Washington's glory-bedecked career. Both sites made claim to being the place where The Great Washington began, albeit in very different ways. Both were also preserving open landscapes that lacked much in the way of Washington survivals. Like Ferry Farm, Wake-field's eighteenth-century buildings were long gone. Despite some early nineteenth-century monumentalizing, their very locations were something of a contentious conundrum. Some heavy-handed excavations had found a variety of brick foundations, but claiming them as being the Washington home was tricky.

Hoppin understood very early that the reconstructed home and enshrined landscape he wanted to see at Pope's Creek could only be harmed by a rather similar project up the peninsula. He made it part of his job to discredit and undermine Ferry Farm's historical claim to Washington itself, and its homespun enshrinement, at every turn.

Acerbic, snide, and dismissive, Hoppin was a man who loved a fight— especially if battles could be won with snarky jabs at an opponent's credibility, ancestry, or even wardrobe, packed into dense, single-spaced, multipage letters. He had made the controversy-ridden and vicious world of the distant pre-Virginia Washington genealogy his personal forte. Sol Bloom wrote that rivals in that contentious field were "each ready willing, and anxious to poison the other."[25]

And "poison" was a fine word for Hoppin, who himself had no love for "Bloom, The Jew" and the dog-and-pony-show celebration he orchestrated.[26] He and a small circle of like-minded critics fumed and fussed in print and to one another about all of the "Bloom Commission's" sins. Bloom was "a business man first." He was "second hand clothes, what?"[27] He tried to pass off a "fake bust of Washington" while "knowing it was a fake" and that it was "executed by a foreigner."[28] His commission's published Washington historical pamphletry was "packed with ignorance and mendacity," not to mention "blunders, mistakes, and misstatements," and of course "slander, and perhaps even treason."[29] Bloom's own ancestry and his crass showmanship meant that Washington's commemoration was in the hands of, well, shall we say, the wrong sort. This was a constant irritation to Hoppin and friends. But there was nothing much Hoppin could have done about that other than write long letters. And in this one new Battle of Fredericksburg, writing mattered.

Hoppin took on Ferry Farm exactly the same way that England had been promoting it—by attacking in print its very historical validity and its core claims to the American heart and purse. Wakefield was the real Washington bicentennial project—the only one rooted in sound historical work (his own, as it happens) and not in "popular belief" or in "so-called tradition" and "cherry tree stories." Indeed, there was no room in the larger discussion for such "Weemsian flotsam and jetsam which no court would admit" and which "real investigators of history have rejected." That kind of evidence would not gain one "ancestral eligibility," and it should not be the basis for creating a historical site.[30] The Cherry Tree may have "crystallized into reality," as England argued, but the self-appointed guardians of things Washington did not see it that way.

But Hoppin went much further than attacking the rather easy target the always questionable Weems presented. He argued that in fact Ferry Farm had virtually no Washington associations whatsoever. His arguments were a scattershot collection of "if this then that" style false equations and some willful misreads of the land record evidence.

Hoppin stated that Augustine Washington had never "owned this cottage, never lived in it" and rather astonishingly "never owned the land around it."[31] Washington, he argued, never even owned this land at all, or at least if he did it was "not until late in the life or after the death of his mother."[32] That remarkable claim sought to distance the words "Washington" and "boyhood" in the Ferry Farm promotional writing and worked to muddy the waters by suggesting that the place may have been one of Mary's other properties as opposed to the one left to George in Augustine's will. He even moved Mary away from Ferry Farm entirely, placing her at her Little Fall's land despite much evidence that she stayed right where she had been. On top of that, Hoppin placed the site of the old Strother home as one or perhaps two miles eastward or downriver of Fredericksburg itself—thus denying the entire town any good Washington claim at all.

Hoppin's anti–Ferry Farm claims, though, were so widely fired and so off the mark that they set off unintended alarm bells. His goal was to stir up enough dust, to create enough confusion, and deploy enough dismissiveness that backers would simply reserve their money for his own project at Wakefield. But Hoppin actually caused a rallying to the cause by people in town when he tried to take their Washington away from them.

Fredericksburg local historian and George Washington Foundation member, Chester Goolrick, took up the defense, writing well-researched pieces defending Ferry Farm's and Fredericksburg's Washington claims—essays, interestingly, that concentrated on land ownership and not Weems's stories. When one of Hoppin's incendiary pamphlets made it into Goolrick's hands in March 1928, he wrote to Josephine Wheelwright Rust, Wakefield's dame in chief and Hoppin's nominal boss. Rust in turn called Hoppin to the carpet for publicly promulgating easily disproven falsehoods in the name of her project. Caught out, Hoppin distanced himself from his own claims in language so obsequious, so oily, that only an extended quotation can give it justice.

Referring to Goolrick's complaint, Hoppin replied, "if the objection is predicated upon the idea that the use of the said words in the said folder was to annoy any person or persons, to misrepresent or to serve, consciously or unconsciously, some purpose that may or may not exist in the mind of still another person or persons, then the objectors' ontological predicates have been metaphysically mixed." There was a story that Hoppin used to feign deafness in public. Not muteness, though.[33]

Despite his errors in the famously murky land records of early Virginia, Hoppin's poisoned arrows did hit their mark. Historians were distancing themselves from Weems as never before. So even though he still had his fans and advocates, people were not willing to put money behind projects that seemed silly or frivolous when so many seemingly "real" causes presented themselves—real projects like rebuilding the Washington birthplace at Wakefield. But Ferry Farm's promoters put Weems front and center on their own. Those unwilling to back a Weemsian project didn't need Hoppin to dissuade them.

The fusty genealogist's real achievement was to kick up just enough dust to leave remaining at least some taint of scandal and uncertainty around Ferry Farm—just enough friction to ensure that it would remain a marginal local endeavor and not make the national scene. That may have been all he had hoped to do. He later recalled that "people in Fredericksburg" had tried to "kill the scheme" to rebuild at Pope's Creek. "I stopped them," he boasted. He warned his friends, though, that they may still yet receive a funding request from the George Washington Foundation—"doubtless" they "will know where to find a waste basket for it."[34]

But in the end it was not Hoppin's campaign that truly doomed Colbert's vision. Fundraising was proving harder than the farmer and the writer might have imagined. In May 1929, Colbert wrote to England in his unschooled way to urge him on and remind him of what was at stake. If the author failed now, Colbert lamented that "I would probaly loose the sale, and you and Jones would loose all your time, energy, money, and commission." England had "a good friend" who might want to offer money, so Colbert urged England to "induce him to furnish the money to pay for the farm, the sooner it is pay for the sooner you and John Jones will received $5,000 dollars each." Colbert went on. "What I need now is some money" so "line up and get your friend to put the money up." He concluded with a postscript, saying "turn over a new leaf go and see the man and tell him everything is all right and satisfactory and see what you can get him do."[35]

This may be all that survives of J. B. Colbert's daily voice—a letter that leaves little doubt about who was calling the shots and orchestrating the preservation of The George Washington Farm. It had indeed been "J. B. Colbert, Proprietor."

And amidst this panicked scrambling for funds and staving off false claims from opponents, the sky fell in. On October 24, 1929, a high-flying stock market took a nosedive and set off a wave of collapses that devastated the world's economies. Farm failures, mass unemployment, and all of their attendant suffering left preservation projects like Ferry Farm's seeming like quaint luxuries from a bygone era.

The effort to find backers ground to a halt, and the George Washington Foundation was no longer able to meet its obligations to Colbert. On top of that, the grace and gaze of the federal government and its Washington Bicentennial all but passed by Fredericksburg and Ferry Farm. In January of 1931, Sol Bloom and company came to Fredericksburg. Local boosters pulled out all of the stops and feted the great showman and his entourage of "heads of departments" and members of his commission's "executive force."[36]

The dignitaries saw all the sites—Kenmore, Mary Washington's home and grave, the Masonic Hall where Washington first entered the craft, Charles Washington's Rising Sun Tavern, Mercer's Apothecary Shop, and James Monroe's Law Office. And of course, they crossed the river to Ferry Farm—sitting directly opposite the lower end of town as it always had, and not two miles downriver. They probably received a personal tour from Colbert, Proprietor, and Preserver in Chief.

Bloom walked a virtually rose-strewn path through the fruit of decades of preservation in a town eager to forget its horrid Civil War past by becoming America's most historical city. The party took "many notes" at Bloom's direction as they "made a very thorough inspection" of all that Fredericksburg had to offer. He had high praise for their work and expressed his hope that the area "should have a big part in the great celebration."[37] For many, it must have seemed that the greatest and most welcome of Northern Barnums had arrived at last.

The congressman liked what he saw during his visit, but there was much to do and he offered cautions. He singled out Ferry Farm, expressing hope that "some means would be devised of quickening the progress of plans" and seeing the project to completion. And then the bad news. Bloom reminded the preservation leaders that his commission was not "sponsoring local programs," he would only lend them the government's influential endorsement.[38] As Bloom himself later noted, the strings on the nation's purse were tied tight, and there was no room for the "mad squandering of the public funds."[39] Bloom's smiles and encouragements might have been large, but the government checkbook he wielded was deceptively small. The people of Fredericksburg had done fine work on their own, and now Bloom and Uncle Sam urged them to continue on— alone, as they had been doing—with a hearty thank-you and a pat on the back, but not much else.

If all it took were good words and hearty endorsements, Ferry Farm would have been a Washington "shrine" in time for George's two hundredth birthday. But words, as they say, are cheap. Money is somewhat more costly.

As the national depression deepened into the 1932 bicentennial year, there was little evidence that the foundation and its friends were going to be able to make good on the deal they had cut with Colbert. While bigwigs all across the country were able to martial patriotic paper endorsements, none stepped up to pay the bills, and their fine words could not separate others from their dwindling cash. In Fredericksburg, the big two hundredth year came and went with a whimper, at best. No great fanfare, no national spotlight, no great highway linking Washington sites. Like the previous Washington centennial, Fredericksburg's was not all that different from any other in the nation. And instead of becoming the national shrine—the fate that befell Hoppin's Wakefield—Ferry Farm remained property—better known, more famously storied, and more bedecked with Washington relics than it had been a few short decades earlier, but property nevertheless. And thanks to Colbert's creative deal making, it was now property with a very confusing and ambiguous set of deeds.

J. B. never got to see the bicentennial he had been preparing for. He had always been "a man of an exceedingly active nature," whether whipping the reins in a wagon flying up Marye's Heights, brawling in the street, or keeping a firm hand on the tiller of a dozen ongoing ventures.

But J. B.'s age and activity were catching up to him as he waded into his sixty-sixth year. On the afternoon of April 23, 1931, Colbert was off being active as was his wont—this time supervising the excavations needed for a new ice factory venture north of town. As always, he was hands-on.

At 5:30 P.M., J. B. Colbert, Proprietor of The George Washington Farm, Manager of the Cold Spring Ice, Factory Dry Goods Seller, Hosteler, Saloon Owner, Land Sales Agent, Church Member, Two-time Husband, Father, probable inventor of the Surveying Office, Dairy Farmer, and producer of the finest alfalfa hay from the fields where George Washington played as a child, stopped in his tracks and collapsed in a heap.

His friends and crew rushed him back onto Marye's Heights—this time in a car or truck and not a wagon—to a new hospital named for Mary, the Mother of Washington. As he lay half conscious, bouncing along the dirt roads, the places of his greatest triumphs were laid out on the left. If he opened his eyes through his labored breath and pain, he might have seen the spires of town, and even beyond them perhaps, if the day was clear enough, the farm he championed. To the right, the first red of the sun was setting into the western mountains—the place the Algonquians once saw as being the top of the world. That day, it set for J. B.

He was dead before the nurses could even rush him to an examination room. Five days later John Jones and five others carried J. B. to a grave in the far end of the old Confederate Cemetery. His plot was barely in sight of Kenmore—new homes had filled in the land between his new grave and Mary's older one.

Colbert was the lynchpin that held the whole Ferry Farm project together—its driving force, its visionary, and its main advocate. It was his from the start. Without him, the wheels came off for good.

8

⁂

From Weems to Walmart

The February 3, 1940, auction of Ferry Farm was big enough to make national newspapers. Stories recalled that "it was on Ferry Farm" that a young Washington "performed the legendary feats of chopping down the cherry tree and hurling a silver dollar" over the river.[1] One story even noted that the old showman Sol Bloom wanted to pull together backers to preserve the place, despite having passed it over once already. Local papers saw it differently, with "Public Ignores Auction," being the headline.[2] By 1940, the Washington moment had passed and the bloom was off the cherry blossom.

On that chilly morning, a small group of locals tugged at their collars and blew on their hands as Stafford's Elliot B. Brooks, "red faced in a biting wind," rang his big bell and sang his auctioneer's song. After a full fifteen minutes of prompting, the crowd of "townsfolk and rough clad farmers" heard only two bids called out.[3] And when this nondrama was all over, Jim Colbert's daughter Maybelle was $25,000 in debt for the 470-acre farm where she and George Washington had grown up. Newspapermen pointed their cameras at Miss Colbert of Ferry Farm looking smart in a long woolen coat and feathered Alpine hat, and snapped away as she looked over the bronze plaque the Fredericksburg Chamber of Commerce had erected five years earlier marking the site where "young Washington is reputed to have chopped cherry tree (sic)."[4]

The sale itself was the culmination of nearly a decade-long tangle of lawsuits stemming from the confused state of affairs surrounding the farm at the time of J. B. Colbert's sudden 1931 death. By that time, Colbert and his family had received somewhere in the range of $85,000 from the George Washington Foundation. But that left much of the agreed price of $125,000 still unpaid. The Depression made raising the rest a near impossibility and the buyers had to default, even though they continued to try to pay their bills.

The contract they had with Colbert stated that the family would continue to live on the farm until six months after the last payment check cleared. As that check never came, there was no pressing reason nor legal obligation for the Colberts to leave what was still very much their farm, even though the foundation held the actual title. On top of that Maybelle, her stepmother Virginia Colbert, and her older brother Clinton fell into conflict over who exactly had the best legal claim to J. B's estate. Meanwhile George Allan England and the George Washington Foundation also had claims they took to court. So family, friends, and interested parties all lawyered up, formed a circular firing squad around J. B.'s will and property, and opened fire. For much of the 1930s, stepdaughter sued stepmother, estate of husband sued estate of wife, brother sued sister, and friend sued estate of friend. Case by case, the property division became more and more impenetrable, and all the while bits and pieces were sold off to pay bills or settle disputes. Suit by suit, the pile of papers in the Stafford County Courthouse got bigger and bigger while the actual holdings under contention got smaller and smaller.[5] Finally, the matter was so contentious and so convoluted that the Stafford court ordered the 1940 on-site auction in the February snow through which Maybelle bought formal title.

That certainty may have ended the confusion over ownership. But it did little to forward the old vision of the farm as a Washington shrine. A 1946 *Washington Post* article claimed that "only one small building used by the youthful Washington as a Surveying Office, remains at Ferry Farm."[6] She was an aging damsel in distress still awaiting a savior.

Maybelle was more interested in running the place for profit. Within a few years, real estate developers were eyeing the farm's acres, hoping to subdivide them and turn them into new homes for returning World War II veterans. Maybelle was happy to go along. Newspapers carried notices that surveyors were again out at Ferry Farm to mark out house lots and new road paths on the land so recently passed over by official preservers.

Echoes of Colbert's fading vision, though, still sounded. At regular intervals concerned citizens banded into similarly named "George Washington's Boyhood Home Foundations" and did what they could to buy and commemorate the core area surrounding the Surveying Office. Nineteen forties plans foundered on the financial rocks. In 1958 another iteration was on its last legs and had to default on its payments. For the want of fifty-five thousand dollars Ferry Farm and its "run down one story building" faced the "dim prospect" that its "few decaying timbers among the weeds" would soon be lost forever to development.[7]

During these years, Ferry Farm was a historical orphan occupied by an ever-changing array of renting or sharecropping farm families. These families learned to supplement their incomes by profiting from the small stream of visitors that still stopped by to touch the young Washington. They offered impromptu tours of the Surveying Office and the bronze plaque that then still sat near the Cherry Tree—the same one photographed in the 1920s. By the 1940s all that was left was a large hollowed-out trunk. By the '50s it was so frail that it took a wire frame to keep it in place. There is no counting how many pocketknives sliced off a small sliver of the true tree. The demand was strong enough, though, that industrious renters kept a spare log stashed away in the shed so that there were new splinters-a-plenty to sell when the old trunk ran out.

Somewhere in the rather dizzying and poorly documented parade of small-scale and unsuccessful preservation efforts, someone attached Washington significance to the icehouse Colbert dug next to the Surveying Office. By the 1950s, well-intentioned preservers placed a shingled colonial-style cover atop the fifteen-foot hole to give it an authentic air. Now two post-Washington Washington-era buildings sat side by side, twin sentinels recalling a bygone era that had produced neither one.

Even if the land and its relics could not attract a savior, its stories still had value to some. The idea that Ferry Farm was of innate value as a place for bettering "the boys of America" went at least as far back as the days when George Allan England called for the Boy Scouts of America to step in and make Ferry Farm their own. That notion became the heart of an ambitious plan concocted by a group of Midwestern Seventh-day Adventist pastors and teachers.

Under the banner of Youth for Christ International, the pastors hoped to protect American children from juvenile delinquency and international communism, and to prepare the next generation for American citizenship and leadership. In 1963 Youth for Christ International became the latest party to take on the farm's monthly payments. Their idea was to establish the farm as the George Washington Boys' Home—a residence and school where wayward youth could benefit from living and learning amongst the places of the Great Washington's childhood. This was Cherry Tree true belief at its height, brought together with religious faith and a Cold War inflected concern for America's future.

The pastors and their families moved to the area and took up residence in Colbert's old farmhouse—then showing its age with sagging floors that made walking around a fun-house experience and sheet plastic covering the windows to keep out winter drafts. The pastors took over the running of the land—then reduced to about 101 acres—and assumed the payment of the site's fifty thousand dollars.[8]

Once on the land, the new owners learned and uncritically repeated all of the old stories of the Surveying Office, the cellar stones, and the Ice

House. They quickly connected with local Ferry Farm backers—the people who had long wanted to see the place turned into a Washington shrine. One early project ally was the local painter Sidney King. At a time when the art world was celebrating minimalism and post-abstract expressionism, King's strong-handed, rustic, realistic work was not destined to make a splash at Manhattan art galleries.

But King was prolific and powerfully drawn to historical scenes. Living in the Fredericksburg area made Washington and his childhood's lore a natural subject. King produced many versions of the Cherry Tree Story, the Sorrel Colt tale, and other scenes documented and undocumented from Washington's upbringing. King was also a true believer, and was dedicated to the idea that Ferry Farm's lore was historical reality.

By 1966, anyone driving down King's Highway saw an enormous Sidney King painting of Washington and the Cherry Tree marking the entrance to the Boys' Home. King also painted a large bird's-eye view of the Washington Farm the pastors hoped to build. King showed it all—a school and youth home, a "Temple of Truth," a "Washington Chapel," a riverfront Boy Scout encampment, horse trails, a restored ferry, and the centerpiece: a rebuilt Washington farmstead. This was to feature a somewhat small rustic home very much in debt to Weems's "front of faded red," as well as a restored Surveying Office and the colonial-style Ice House. It was a beautiful tableau of the Weemsian fantasy, Cold War nationalism, piety, and misinformed historical speculation Ferry Farm had become.

Not much of what the painting showed would become a reality. The "colonial and rural" chapel never got started.[9] Reconstructions like the planned carriage house and a colonial-style workshop also fell out of the discussion fairly quickly. Instead, old Corson farm buildings served as storage for farm equipment and as the shops where the boys learned industrial skills and made souvenir statuettes. The "Temple of Truth" appears to have been nothing more than a Sidney King Freemason-inspired fantasy that never got any further than the canvas.

The pastors did stage a few rebuilt ferry crossings, and team member

Paul Millikin ran a small museum on the first floor of the old Colbert home, while his family lived amidst the plastic sheeting and warped floorboards upstairs. The museum boasted no real Washington relics but it did have an old carriage, a Civil War drum, some colonial-era coins and trinkets, and a nice collection of Sidney King paintings.

Their most impressive object was a twice-life-size bronze bust of Washington made by noted American sculptor Paul Wayland Bartlett for the Washington Bicentennial. The bronze was an indirect donation by the artist's daughter and came to rest on a simple wooden stand erected near the entrance to the Surveying Office.

But the main achievement was the actual Boys' Home—a two-story faux-colonial mansion built a few hundred yards to the south of the old Washington home lot. The home was capable of housing as many as fifteen boys and a host family and boasted a full kitchen, a dining hall, public rooms, and a grand central stairway. The walls carried religious and patriotic art and the residents' beds' coverlets bore portraits of Washington and scenes from his celebrated life. The effect was a powerful use of Washington-inflected patriotism and historical architecture in the shadow of King's towering painting of young George and the Cherry Tree.

By 1966 the new home was built, but within two years the pastors were announcing that they were out of money and were on the verge of closing their doors. By the time the home was done, the organization was heavily in debt, having gone from $50,000 in the hole to a full $120,000 down. Fundraising was hard. Their project operated at a national professional level—local boys received no special consideration. Officials even noted this problem, admitting that "critics are honest in wanting to know" how the home can "expect local aid when it refuses to take local boys into its care."[10] On top of that, there were even some locals who assumed that the "Boy" in Boys' Home meant African Americans and were not thrilled at the mistaken prospect that the home would be a haven for black youth.

With the price of the land to cover as well as the mortgage on the new building and operational costs, the pastors faced a tough financial challenge. A possible answer came from the new Interstate Highway System. By the late 1960s a new highway was wending its way through Stafford County, and builders were in need of crushed stone to go in its bed. Getting that stone entailed grading six feet or more from Stafford farmland, which pretty much killed it for farming. In exchange, federal road builders were willing to hand over a handsome one-time payment. Having divided Ferry Farm into three "zones"—a "historical area," a "residence and school area," and "a farm area,"—the cash-strapped pastors went ahead and sacrificed the "farm area" for the larger project.[11] The graders came in and scooped out the whole southern stretch of the Washington Farm's remaining 101 acres. Promotional photos of the Boys' Home show a pair of smiling eleven-year-olds climbing an enormous heap of churned-up Washington earth.

But even that was not enough. In the summer of 1968 the Boys' Home closed its large colonial doors and sought out new private homes for the ten children then in residence. The pastors looked around for a buyer to save them from their debts. That salvation came in the form of an offer from an Arlington, Virginia-based developer. In 1969, Samuel and Irma Warren became Ferry Farm's new owners.

The Warrens made it clear that they understood the historical value of the farm and expressed an interest in doing what they could to preserve the site. But that goal was secondary to finding a way to profit from their purchase. No sooner had they claimed the parcel, than they began to seek a "B-1 Commercial" rezoning for the whole of the property.[12] Developers had bought off chunks of the site ever since Maybelle Colbert's ownership, but there always had been the sense that there was a core area of greater value than the rest. Over the post–World War II decades that "core" area shrank more and more from the over 400 acres Colbert owned, down to the 101 acres from which the George Washington Boys' Home carved off the graded southern part of the land. Once the Warrens owned it, the area shrank once again, down to the few acres centered on the still-standing Colbert house and the Surveying Office. It was little more than an old "rundown property" which the *Washington Post* was now claiming "no longer has original dwellings from Washington's youth."[13]

Never had the old place looked more down for the count. Overgrown and overlooked, the forlorn farm watched silently as shopping malls and fast-food restaurants sprouted on the land that Washington once knew so well. One editorial wag summed it up this way: "it is hardly surprising that Ferry Farm long ago ceased to be what it once was; like much else, Ferry Farm has changed beyond recognition, and its past will never be brought back to life."[14]

Through the 1970s and 1980s the Warrens waited and the county looked for a way to create a good deal. More than once in the past, Stafford's officials had passed on the chance to take over some part of the farm and run it as a public historical site. Each of Stafford's six districts brought in some commercial revenue; only Ferry Farm's "George Washington District" did not. Rezoning in exchange for the core area increasingly became the most appealing way to change things. Negotiations with the Warrens continued and offers came and went.

Some versions had the Warrens giving the county two acres, others envisioned as many as thirty-four. But the basic outlines were in place— the Warrens would give the county the last sliver of Ferry Farm, and the rest would be rezoned and sold off for development. By 1990 the deal was done—the Warrens would donate to the county the twenty-four acres around the old Colbert house and the Surveying Office in exchange for the rezoning of the rest of the land. These acres could now be sold off to the highest bidder at a price almost ten times the value that the land could have claimed when it was zoned agricultural.

The county assessed the whole ninety acres the Warrens then owned at $452,800, based on their then current agricultural zoning.[15] But the Warrens claimed the twenty-four acres they planned to give to the county were *alone* worth four million dollars—a creative sleight of hand pulled off by retrofitting the increased land value of rezoned land onto acres never intended to be commercial. This donation would then qualify the owners for a massive tax deduction—something they would need, as they hoped to sell the rest of the land (using their figures) for just over ten million when it was rezoned. Not a bad profit for land they purchased for close to $200,000 twenty years earlier.[16]

Many hailed the deal and rezoning as the perfect solution to the fact that Ferry Farm had been "bypassed by the historic preservation movement" and that it had been "slowly eaten away at for years."[17] The Warrens' lawyer Grayson Haynes said, "I think this is a good compromise." Stafford County would gain title to the historic core, "without paying a nickel" and his clients would be able to "realize the highest value for the property they could."[18] A planned fifty-foot barrier, some pine trees, and six-foot-high fence would separate the old place from its new proposed commercial neighbor.[19]

But others raised strong objections, right after the rezoning, to the possibility of a shopping plaza or a motel sitting right next to the Washington Farm and screened by a few trees and a backyard fence. One concerned opponent was so incensed that he claimed that in other states "the National Guard would be brought out to protect" a relic of Ferry Farm's caliber.[20] As it happened, the hotel or plaza was slow to develop— market forces still called the shots even for rezoned land. The first plaza was a nonstarter, but the county still owned the historical core, the crumbling Colbert home, the Boys' Home, the Surveying Office, and the Ice House, and wanted to make the most of it.

Into this situation sprang a high-energy little cricket of a man named Robert Siegrist. Ever since the early 1970s, this former congressional aide, radio commentator, Republican activist, and Washington aficionado had been hoping to buy Ferry Farm and turn it into the shrine others had tilted at. His offer (or maybe it is better labeled "offer of an offer" since Siegrist had no money himself and spoke for no deep-pocketed backers) had been rebuffed by the very patient and focused Warrens. Siegrist took it upon himself to serve as the self-appointed guardian of and spokesperson for the property's historical value. But having had no luck with the Warrens, and rather miffed at their unwillingness to play ball on his pitch, he went before the Stafford Board of Supervisors to try to make a deal right as the Ferry Farm donation was coming together.

Like many before him, Siegrist was an outsider coming into the Fredericksburg area late in his life and with a mission in mind: to be nationally celebrated as the man who saved Washington's Ferry Farm. Dictatorial, self-impressed, and full of determination, Siegrist regaled the supervisors with his vision—essentially a rehash of the long-standing one of the farm as Washington shrine. All other plans had failed—but this would be different, Siegrist believed, confident that he himself had been the missing element. The plan he shared would preserve the farm and turn it into a significant tourist attraction for the county, and leave Robert Siegrist the acknowledged hero of the day and reigning overlord of the project.

After sitting for Siegrist's song and dance, the county elders rather indifferently gave him their blessing to manage what came to be called the Ferry Farm Project. In 1989 they even promised money—as much as $500,000 over five years, although that demonstration of commitment and goodwill only partially materialized. But it was clear that their vision was that the historical core would shift from county hands to private ones, and Siegrist, with his bluster, his affection for self-aggrandizement and name-dropping, and his eagerness for the project, made him, if not the ideal man for the job, at least the man most willing to take on the job.

With the county's imprimatur and some of its money behind him, Siegrist set about building his empire and becoming famous as the man who saved Ferry Farm.[21] He thought in grand terms: Of the deal that established his tenure he said, "I don't look a gift horse in the mouth." Indeed, who knows, maybe it was "divine intervention" or "the grace of God, or even the celestial "intercession" of his "late daughter Mary" that guided the project. For Siegrist, Ferry Farm was once again in Mary's hands.[22]

Siegrist's Ferry Farm vision was largely right out of the 1920s. Although he was openly skeptical of the Cherry Tree, he nevertheless worked to celebrate it however he could and also uncritically passed along newer lore, like the Surveying Office and the Ice House, which he had cleaned of its accumulated trash and covered with a new specially built protective shelter. He even added his own little short-lived contribution to the farm's expanding body of Washington lore.

Bartlett's bust of Washington had stood on a column near the Surveyor Office from the days of the Boys' Home. In 1972, a few bored youths stole it and sold it in town for twenty bucks. After some wrangling, the two hundred-pound bronze ended up displayed in a Fredericksburg alley near a public men's room until it was rescued from this ignominy and put on display (inside this time) at Ferry Farm once again.[23] But in 1990, the column which once supported it near the Surveying Office still stood surrounded with a small cluster of boxwoods. In Siegrist's imaginative hands, this column came to mark Mildred's long-lost gravesite. Mildred was indeed buried not too far from the home, but the statue's placement right on the grave would have been an epic coincidence.

To prove his theory, Siegrist even went so far as to have the grave excavated to "prove" somehow that it was Mildred—a conviction in which he never wavered—even when the data did not line up. Nevertheless, the fantastic story became one of many with which Siegrist regaled his visitors.

The trick for Siegrist was to tell his stories to the right audience—to find the perfect influential person or group thereof who could step in, pony up the cash, and make Siegrist the savior of Ferry Farm. During the Washington Bicentennial project years, project backers collected letters of approval from as many United States governors as they could—even President Hoover wrote to endorse turning the boyhood home into a national shrine. But these stuffy letters, full of patriotism and pomposity, were worth slightly less to the project than the official letterhead on which they were printed.

Fifty years after these bicentennial efforts, and in a very different national climate, Siegrist still adhered to the same "White Knight" strategy—in this case inflected with a Reagan-era Republican politics bent. He did reach out to all the preservation and historical entities one would expect, bringing his high-energy style before local groups and Daughters of the American Revolution chapters all over the state. But he went one (or a few) better. He filled his office files with copies of *Forbes Magazine,* using them as a road map to locate the rich and powerful. His letters to these movers and shakers were full of flattery, patriotic boilerplate, and professions of the value of Ferry Farm and its body of stories to the preservation of American values, the fight against international communism, and maintenance of domestic tranquility.

He had his favorites—Richard Nixon, for example, then at the nadir of his political influence, was singled out by Siegrist for special adoring attention. In letters to the likes of anti-Feminist icon Phyllis Schlafly or Heritage Foundation founder Paul Weyrich, he revealed just how much he connected his personal politics and his work at Ferry Farm, and did it in his signature halting prose: "as with you, the concepts I held dear, and for which, like you, I fought, are those which, over the years, brought me to Ferry Farm."[24]

Siegrist was most distinctive, though, in his deep interest in the Colbert house—by the early 1990s an aging shambles. He was a firm believer in Colbert's story that his home had Washington foundation stones incorporated into it. The pastors used to bring people to the basement to show where some chipped-back Colbert-poured concrete revealed older stones set into the wall. For Siegrist, this section of cellar became a sort of sacred trust—so much so, that Siegrist came to see the home as a crucial core of the museum he wanted to manage.

Convinced that Colbert's claim about the house foundations was true, Siegrist commissioned a small-scale archaeological study of the area.

While the team was there, he aggressively directed them, carefully making sure that their work only served to confirm Siegrist's own preconceptions. The diggers knocked out a small part of the concrete floor of Colbert's basement and found beneath it a nice collection of eighteenth-century relics and some foundation stones from the old Washington kitchen. For Siegrist, these promising but preliminary findings were enough to prove definitively what had been said since the 1880s and what Siegrist himself deeply believed—that this was indeed Washington's very boyhood home. And so Siegrist ecstatically crowed over what he called "our archaeological phenomenon."[25]

He centered his tours on the house, placed his office trailer near it, cut down the trees so that it could be viewed from King's Highway—now Route 3—and even had floodlights erected to light it up at night. The issue was not the Colbert house itself—that was immaterial—but rather the secrets it held. He tightly controlled access to the house, padlocking its doors and rearranging entries. And most tellingly, he always referred to it as the "Washington House." This is not to say that he actually *believed* Colbert's WWI–era farmhouse was in fact Washington's home. But rather, that the house, with its stones, was effectively *metaphysically* the Washington home by the transitive power of architecture.

But in the early-morning hours of September 26, 1994, Siegrist's vision crashed, and literally burned.

The Stafford County Fire Department trucks made it out to Ferry Farm fairly soon after a passing motorist reported seeing flames in the old Colbert house some time around 1 A.M. But despite their efforts, the house was quickly a charred ruin. The flames ate out its core, leaving only the home's outer sides. There was no recovery possible. After standing for eighty years, the old Colbert house was finished.[26]

Siegrist made it to the site by about 8:30 A.M. while the remains were still smoldering. He ran around in a sort of panic, taking testimony from the firefighters and darting in and out of his trailer making calls and offering reports and updates to friends and backers. For Siegrist, the

"Washington House" had burned to the ground yet again—and this time right before his eyes. One person who saw him that morning said that he was beside himself; it was as if his world was coming to an end.

And in a way it was. Siegrist's relationship with the county had already soured, partly due to his style and partly due to his lack of success in lining up backers. But now with a fire destroying his Washington House and threatening his "archaeological phenomenon," his vision for himself was going up in smoke as well. He clearly relished issuing pronouncements, making statements, being the expert, and using that position to contact the powerful and influential. His project was as much about Robert Siegrist as it was about George Washington. And the Colbert house—Siegrist's beloved Washington House—was the visible manifestation of that desire and the project that it drove. With that gone up in smoke and flames Siegrist's Ferry Farm Project was dealt a deathblow. The county ended its relationship with Siegrist and began to formulate a new way to carry on without the little cricket who had been so eager to sell Ferry Farm.

Fire investigators ruled the blaze arson, and all kinds of rumors made the rounds. Some thought county supervisors had wanted the fire as a way to get rid of the building—although it is hard to see just how its presence hurt the county. Others thought that officials wanted the fire to get rid of Siegrist. Certainly he was officious and irritating, but he also drew no salary and it would have been easy to send him on his way without resorting to arson. Instead, the official explanation that teens or vagrants had set the fire out of malice or indifference is probably the closest to what in fact happened.

But Siegrist was crushed. Soon after the fire he simply disappeared from the scene, leaving the project for others to carry on. Even though Siegrist and the old Colbert house were gone, the story of its antique foundation stones lived on, and official statements after the fire, for example, always noted that despite the fire there was no real damage to the cellar stones. A team of volunteers even stepped up to build a cover for the "Ferry Farm foundation stones," now called by one and all without a hint of doubt "the 1727 Washington home foundation."[27] When county-hired archaeologists turned up a nice collection of eighteenth-century remains—logical given the presence of the cellar—and many of the remnants were burned, that was enough to serve as confirmation that the story had always been right.

With Siegrist gone, the county christened a new board, the George Washington Boyhood Home Foundation, to continue the task of overseeing the property, working on getting potentially lucrative National Historic Landmark Status for the farm, and raising money for its restoration—a sum some reckoned at close to six million dollars. The county even hired a professional fundraising firm to bring in money, which they did—a total of $25,845. A promising start some might say, except that it cost $150,000 to bring in that fraction.[28] Soon the foundation itself was facing its own bankruptcy. By 1995 it was down to its last dollar and unable to raise funds. The George Washington Boyhood Home Foundation was now headed down the same sad road trodden by every one of its predecessors.

Meanwhile, the Warrens continued to look for a developer to buy their new commercially zoned acres.

But Ferry Farm's darkest day was soon to dawn.

One day in the summer of 1995, a Stafford County minister walked across the land on his way to the now rather derelict boys' home where his congregation was gathered. Along his way he unexpectedly met a group of surveyors who told him an astounding and implication-rich piece of news.[29]

The workmen told the minister that, like him, they were there on a mission, one contained in the blueprints they carried. They foretold acres of paved parking lots, enormous chain stores, and more fast-food franchises. Walmart was coming to Ferry Farm, even though the retailer quickly denied the fact.[30]

As more and more suburbanites had flowed into the area, merchandisers rushed to fill residents' homes with the consumer paraphernalia of American life. And in the midst of that, Walmart's eye came to rest on the few hundred acres of old Washington land, which had been passed over for federal recognition, quarried for the highway, and now sat largely unused. After war and neglect, the bulldozers and earth graders that were planned to follow the surveyors represented the single greatest threat Ferry Farm had faced since Smith's arrival heralded a total reordering of the land. The blueprints showed the Washington acres transformed into a vast shopping plaza with the "anchor" being a Walmart Supercenter measuring in at 105,000 square feet and surrounded by another 30,000, with long-term plans to double that yet again. The county would still run the "core" of the old Washington Farm as a park until a private entity could take it over, but no matter how you sliced it, this was a massive and irreversible change for the old place. If that plan went through, the Cherry Tree Farm would be all but paved over and what remained would be cheek-by-jowl with parking lots, floodlights, and garbage hoppers.

Many saw dark clouds rapidly scudding over Stafford Heights. They saw how the plan would harm the historical tourist trade in Fredericksburg—a town by then surviving on its trees, charm, and antique shops. They saw how it would (further) disrupt the area's still surviving Civil War vistas. But most of all, they saw that the plan would be the final act in the long, slow death of a site long known as the setting for America's most celebrated presidential childhood. Efforts during the 1990s to locate a new business on the tract yielded little fruit. But while strip mall builders or motels go in and out of bankruptcy almost daily, Walmart was a horse of a different color—or at least a commercial force with which to be reckoned. So for those who wanted the land developed and for those who did not, the news that Walmart's advance surveyors were walking Ferry Farm's acres was a sign that something big was afoot.

As the news spread, battle lines that had formed in 1990 hardened anew. On the one side were Walmart, the Warrens, and their supporters on the county board of supervisors. Each had every reason to believe that they had arrived at a Solomonic solution to a long-standing issue.

After all, decades of trying to save the farm had failed over and over. Not only that, but the county had just witnessed its own set of failures at the task. Surely if Ferry Farm ever had a moment, that moment must have come and gone. The "for sale" sign had been up for years, and at any point concerned citizens could have rallied to the cause. Not many did. Furthermore, the rezoning deal was years old, allowing plenty of time to object. That a developer was coming in now could hardly be called a surprise. No one can blame Walmart and its backers for feeling that they had green lights all up and down the line and were clear to move ahead.

On top of that, Walmart backers could point to the fact that a small "core" of the site would continue to be left alone and most of the building would take place on the chewed-over land that they always took care to call "the quarry" or the old "gravel pit." Also, in recognition of the site's historical associations, Walmart promised a columned plaza with a redbrick colonial feel and even special tributes to George and the Cherry Tree. A berm or tree barrier would screen the bulk of the shopping center so that it would not be too visible to visitors to the Surveying Office and the Washington Farm. In fact, these visitors would even be able to park their RVs in Walmart's well-lit parking lot. Not only that, but the expected revenue from the plaza could even aid in restoring and maintaining the site. For Walmart's local friends, the retailer's arrival was not a death knell—it was the best hope at doing something good and profitable with the long-neglected site.

But many were ready, willing, and able to oppose a plan that they saw very differently. Walmart's opposition was made up of both likely and unlikely allies. There were Fredericksburg small business owners—the people who lived by the tourist trade that had become the town's economic backbone over the last decade. Antique shops, art galleries, and Civil War memorabilia and kitsch stores all catered to visitors strolling the town or communing with battle sites. An enormous Walmart with trucks coming and going, and its all-night-long orange light glow from the parking lot immediately across the river, would become a town-trashing backdrop for prized and profitable nineteenth-century architecture and Civil War–era feel.

There were local historical preservation advocates in their many varieties. Historic Fredericksburg Foundation was the guardian of the city's claim to be "The Most Historic Town in America," and through a mix of influence and ordinances was able to steward a large portion of the town's older architecture. The College of Mary Washington had a nationally renowned program in historical preservation, and its faculty and many students were known voices in town affairs. The National Park Service oversaw the local battlefields and also had considerable sway in what happened to local sites and vistas, and had the weight of the federal government behind its charge to protect and preserve.

There also were groups like the Association for the Preservation of Virginia Antiquities, which still owned and operated Mary Washington's Home in town, and the Kenmore Association which owned Kenmore, as well as Civil War Round Tables, Daughters of the American Revolution, Civil War reenactors, and others, all of whom had constituencies (sometimes overlapping) and wielded area influence. None were too thrilled at the prospect of a parking lot on top of the old Washington Farm.

There also was a growing anti-Walmart, antisuburban sprawl movement taking shape both nationally and locally. In 1994, the Virginia Piedmont town of Culpeper had denied Walmart the permits to build locally, and just before that the Tidewater county of Mathews had blocked access to any large chain store. This all meant that there were some Virginians watching Walmart's actions with keen and experienced oppositional eyes.

Topping all of that, the mid-1990s was a high watermark for Virginia historical preservation. The signature example of this was what some called the Third Battle of Manassas in 1994. When Walt Disney Corporation announced plans to build an American history theme park on land near the site of two major Civil War battles, the kettle boiled over. Legions of newly minted Ken Burns–inspired Civil War buffs joined the ranks of more established preservation groups and antisprawl activists and banded together saying "No Passaran!"—or perhaps they would have preferred to see themselves as standing something like a stone wall. In either case, the prospect of a history theme park reviled by those citizens most dedicated to American history (exactly the families Disney most wanted as visitors) became too embarrassing to sustain. Mickey Mouse and Company pulled the plug on the park before the project got far beyond the planning stage, handing historical preservation advocates their biggest high profile victory.[31]

With these lines drawn and arrayed, all eyes turned once again to Ferry Farm. The "Save Ferry Farm Coalition" put preserving the old place in the news once again. The site now appeared in *The New York Times,* for example, as "the most important historic site in Stafford County."[32] In on-site rallies, crowds heard from victors of other fights that indeed Walmart could be stopped. In local and national papers advocates sounded the alarm and more and more people rallied to the cause. On television as well, site preservation backers told the nation that the Cherry Tree Farm was about to be forever lost.[33]

Despite having offered $100,000 toward the preservation of the "core," Walmart seemed oddly tone deaf to advocates' pleas. At first, Walmart attorneys simply said the matter had been settled in 1990 rezoning and that there was nothing that could change that.[34] Its lawyers then publicly suggested that opponents should stop whining and instead work on raising money to save the core. Soon, shoppers at other area stores received flyers claiming that the Ferry Farm backers were "a small group of people" doggedly "pursuing a pipe dream."[35] Spokespeople ignored the historical concerns of critics, preferring instead to claim that opposition came from downtown merchants afraid of a little competition—a claim easily deflected by Historic Fredericksburg's then president and Ferry Farm activist Bill Beck, who noted that "our downtown died twenty years ago" and that the store would not have "any significant impact" on a remade "antiquey and artsy" downtown.[36]

Walmart's senior vice president for corporate affairs Jay Allen reminded people that the store would sit on the "old gravel pit" the pastors
had long ago sold for grading, and said of the public outcry "all this stuff
is really unjustified."[37] But this dismissal was parried by Cessie Howell,
then director of the George Washington Boyhood Home Restoration
Committee and wife of influential Virginia legislator William James
Howell, who simply pointed out that regardless of how the acres had
been used or misused, they were all part of the one and only place where
George Washington spent his childhood and as such were a national
treasure.

In response to Beck's public suggestion that the retailer simply
move its building site and donate the site of Washington's childhood as
a gift to the nation, Walmart's Allen all but snarled that the idea was
"ridiculous," saying that "we can't operate a business and give millions of dollars away," after all, "we're talking reality."[38] When a Walmart
spokesperson made clear to Howell during a joint appearance on CNN
that the retailer was unbowed and planned to move on full steam ahead,
Howell simply replied, "you are going to have to roll over my body before you ever get that property."[39]

While Walmart and its backers continued to read their opposition as
a small group of ideologically driven antisprawl activists, more and more
people came to see saving Ferry Farm as a patriotic duty. Letters began
to flood into Stafford County and Walmart's Bentonville, Arkansas, home
offices. Rallying citizens condemned the plan as an affront to Washington's memory and an embarrassment for the retailer. Other writers
claimed that Walmart's founder and patron saint ol' Sam Walton himself
would never have let a plan like this go through. Letters and newspaper
stories and television reports all invoked the Cherry Tree and the rheto-
ric of the Minutemen and the Revolution itself. Long neglected Ferry
Farm was remade as Stafford County's greatest historical site and a long-
lost national treasure at last returned to prominence.

Everything came down to a simple decision made by the Stafford

County Architectural Review Board. The issue was this: By allowing the rezoning back in '90, the county board of supervisors had officially agreed to the plan. What is more, a few of the members were quite clear about their unshakable support for Walmart's vision. But county law required that designs go through a veto-equipped architectural review board before approval. Any plans not approved could be slowed down or even stopped as they were sent back to the supervisors for reassessment. So suddenly this usually placid five-member committee of county government became all that stood between Ferry Farm and Walmart.

When the board met on March 11, the crowd of sign-bearing citizens spilled out into the hall. Locals and visitors alike gathered to make it clear that they felt the Walmart plan was an assault on the American past. Some carried signs that said "No Walmart By George," others had American flags, and a few dressed in pseudocolonial garb. The crowd harrumphed skeptically when Walmart's lawyers assured the board that the retailer would do all it had to to maintain the historical feel of the gravel pit. But they cheered when Bill Beck and others made the case to save what remained of the site's county feel.

Concerned citizen Rae Ely appeared before the Stafford County Architectural Review Board March 11 meeting and summed up the protestors' mood, saying "one of the wealthiest corporations is in front of you, and all the people of the United States are behind you!" After her rousing words, the crowd of people leapt to its feet to sing "America the Beautiful." Even if Walmart and its allies did not yet realize it, they had just lost the Battle of Ferry Farm.[40]

On April 1, the review board announced that it was rejecting Walmart's design as being just too massive. The retailer's spokespeople announced that this was a mere setback and that they were not giving up on their plan—but of course it was clear to everyone that the game was over. Soon Walmart's lawyers were looking for a way to back out of the deal in a fashion that would save face and recoup their money. The pieces came together very rapidly. One was a new possible building site just under a mile downriver—well off of Washington land, well out of sight of Fredericksburg.

The second one was Vernon Edenfield—the director of the Kenmore Association—working behind the scenes to pull together the money needed to buy up the land. His terms were that he wanted to purchase *both* the county historical core *and* the land that the Warrens wanted to sell. Walmart's terms were that they would entertain an offer, but were committed to not losing a penny should the Washington Farm become a preserved place.[41]

In August, Edenfield offered 2.2 million dollars for the whole package. The retailer declined, fearing that they would lose $400,000 in the deal. Phones rang. People called in favors. In the end, Stafford County footed part of the gap between Edenfield's offer and Walmart's asking price. By the end of the month, at a cost of close to $3 million collected, begged, and borrowed—from private sources, the federal government, the Nature Conservancy, and the county—the clouds of development parted. Ferry Farm was at long last a preserved historical site.

9

⁘

The Land Tells Its Story

In the summer of 2002, I brought up from Florida my first group of field school students. They were to join the fledgling team of pros and interns that my longtime digging partner, David Muraca, had been assembling since he took over managing the site, lab, and collection. The team had already begun the usual work of laying out a grid and beginning to learn the land that special way that excavators do.

In the wake of the Walmart fight, the land had become the possession of the newly christened George Washington Foundation. The new owners still faced the same old fundraising challenges that dogged every other effort. The main difference was that they understood that archaeology would have to play a central role in understanding the site. There had been some clunky early efforts, but as the museum professionalized and began to settle into its own, a good and thorough excavation became a real priority. That is where we fit in.

As we knew at the outset, our mission was to locate and comprehend the Washington home and better understand Washington himself and his family's time there. Over our years working together, David and I had honed something of a model for how we liked to take apart big sites. In public talks I often say that this method is very time consuming, but on the bright side, it is also very costly. Its hallmarks are obsessive thoroughness, a preference for large-scale digging, a love of the tiny finds over the seemingly glorious ones, and a skepticism toward most of what we have been told about a place. Ferry Farm was going to test every part of the method.[1]

Earlier excavations—just tiny peeks into the ground, really—had shown that there were some very interesting remains of old buildings and trash pits, and we built our first few seasons' digging plan around these promising areas. Right away though, we ran into the first assumption about Ferry Farm that would cause us trouble. It was the idea that the Washingtons had suffered a terrible house fire on Christmas Eve, 1740. The story comes from a few documentary tidbits, and in the 1990s it had become a central piece of Ferry Farm's narrative.[2] It was also the first puzzle we had to unravel.

If the home, which Augustine purchased from William Strother in 1738, had burned down two years later, then there would have to be *two* Washington homes at Ferry Farm—one prefire, and the other the postfire rebuild. We would have to find both. With that in mind, we set out to focus on the areas with the oldest artifacts in hopes of finding the older one first.

The best concentration of earliest material was in an open patch of grass near a large tree and very close to the bluff. The main feature was a large cellar—a type of hole dug into the ground beneath a home and covered with floorboards or by a wooden pallet. These commonly served as cool and dry storage areas when first dug, but since they were often short-lived and artifact rich they have long been favorites of regional archaeologists. An abundance of ceramics and pipe stems all dating to the early eighteenth century added to our confidence that we had landed on just the right spot. The team set about removing the grass and the upper layers of soil and we slowly revealed the faint remains of our first building—in an act of overconfident optimism, we even began to refer to it as the Strother House.

But as work progressed, that identification fell more and more in doubt. For one thing, we saw that the building was built around eight posts set in the ground—a building style a bit out of place and out of date for Strother. Plus—there was no evidence of fire, just some burned clay markings where a hearth once sat. Then, as we looked into the large cellar and postholes, it quickly became clear that there was no fire. Instead of seeing layers of burned house, we saw the quiet order of a home used, repaired, and then left to rot in place. We found that the large cellar had been used for a few years, but its sheer size and unbraced walls quickly took their toll. The walls slumped, the bottom filled with silt—and even though the owner had tried to scoop the mud out, storm by storm, this was a losing battle. Finally, someone had filled in the pit and, in a redesign of the house, had built a new hearth on the hard-packed cellar fill.

Repair, renovation, and abandonment were what we saw. But no fire.

There was another problem, too. As we saw more and more artifacts from the cellar, it became clear that this building was far too early to have been the one Strother built and sold to Augustine Washington. The ceramics told us that. In our cellar, all the artifacts we saw were dating to well before the 1720s—a time when a new type of British ceramic was beginning to become popular. This new White Salt-Glazed Stoneware should have been somewhere on the site—in some feature or hidden in some layer. It did not have to be everywhere, but it at least needed to be *somewhere* in the mix. That is how ceramics work. Plates broke pretty soon after they were unpacked from their sawdust-filled shipping crates. It was a rare plate or cup that lasted ten years. But once broken and discarded in a well or trash pit, thrown down a bluff, or crunched to bits in a walkway, it had to then be replaced by new purchases in whatever type of ceramic the potters were making at the time.

So, given that we initially thought that this was a house that stood until 1740, the lack of post-1720s ceramics and the early rusticity of the post–in-ground home were undeniable deal breakers.

Instead of hitting Washington on our first foray out, we landed on what was the earliest building yet seen in the area. Everything about it suggested the kinds of buildings archaeologists have long seen in the Tidewater. Here was one of those small, efficient, easy-to-build homes which were "sufficient and safest for ordinary beginners," in the words of that 1684 pamphlet.[3] Here was an altogether typical post–in-ground "dwelling house" of the type that had dotted Virginia's waterways for over a century after the colony's founding. I can't say that we were thrilled to have put so much effort into a part of the site not related to our main Washington mission. Given our background in digging seventeenth-century sites, it seemed a sort of cruel irony that instead of finding George, as planned, we found something far earlier.

A little work in the land records made the dates of the home converge with an otherwise long-forgotten name—Maurice Clark. All that the records contained of his life were a land deed, a will, and a possible reference to his arrival in the colony. By excavating his home, by undoing the postholes he and his servant Dennis Linsy had dug so long ago, and by sifting through the trash that collected in the bottom of his cellars, some small shadow of a new text about him came into view.

Everything about his material life at Ferry Farm in those earliest years of English settlement was so typical. Today we inhabit a world awash in a bewildering array of consumer choices, but options were much more constricted then. The sparseness and simplicity we saw was not the result of some imagined frontier rusticity—far from it. Clark lived well; by the standards of his day and for a man of his station, we might even consider him fortunate. When I think of Clark, I can almost see him and Linsy at work in their field. They are there in the peripheries of my historical imagination. I can see the two leaning over in the hazy air, lifting and dropping their iron hoes in time, master and servant indistinguishable at a distance, both doing the same labor, living in the same small home, wearing the same type of clothing, and eating off of the same plate. At night I can see them, in the earthen-floored main room they shared. Clark never married, so he and Linsy had only each other for company as the two men passed the nights mending tools, tending their possessions, swapping stories, or planning the next day before a fire they both fed when it grew low. Such was life in Virginia for so many small planters.

But a set of small glass and copper cuff links we found also told us volumes about where Clark saw himself in the world. The purchase of those delicate adornments told us that here was a man of ambitions, a man who hoped to be more than a small planter like all the others. He would have seen how his former master and his neighbors positioned themselves in their local version of Virginia society. He would have learned that the trappings of gentility were ways to set himself apart and express ambitions, to show that he was invested (quite literally) in the same game as his friends and neighbors were. He might not have been able to afford jewels and silver, but he planned to, and until then, paste and copper would serve as stand-ins.

The Clark house sits separated from every other part of Ferry Farm's sequence of homes—its cellars and postholes touch no other home or part of the site. Everywhere else, epochs collide and chew into each other in the ground, but not here. Clark's home has rested in peace, as does Clark himself, somewhere nearby. Despite being a farmstead, decades of repeated building on the same spot have made the place essentially as complicated as any urban site. But Clark's home is a small rural island in all of this activity. Somehow, something about the spot Clark chose held little appeal for all subsequent inhabitants. Perhaps it was that subsequent owners had enslaved Africans they could send down the ravine to get water, and therefore did not need to live quite so close. In any case, even though Clark was the first British resident to haul water up from the creek, the first denizen to throw his trash down the bluff, and the first farmer to clear the fields and work them in the English fashion, he faded from the story he helped begin.

But as rewarding as it is to piece together the lives and ambitions of long-forgotten people, we were being paid to find the Washington home, and on that score, Clark was a washout.

As we began our third season, we refocused on a new part of the site. This time, we concentrated on an area right behind the venerable Surveying Office, which by then had become the nocturnal home for our impressive collection of wheelbarrows. Just next to the office was the outline of Colbert's old icehouse's foundation. The Ice House itself had been dug down to its sandy bottom in the 1990s, on the mistaken assumption that the 1970s stories were true, and that this was a colonial feature. That was a hard and dangerous job with a better-than-average risk of wall cave-in, as the excavators went five, ten, even fifteen feet into an unsupported stone-lined hole.

Fortunately for us, the whole shaft had been refilled and planted with grass, and we were spared having to worry too much about it. But even if the Icehouse and the Surveying Office were built long after Washington's day, the ground nearby was far more encouraging. It was full of some very telling ceramics that told us we were onto something.

Going back to Colbert's day, there had been an assumption that the Washington home had stood right where the Corsons, and later Colbert, had built—a few dozen yards north of the Surveying Office. It was that association that led Robert Siegrist to treat the old Colbert home as his own personal Washington shrine.

The fact that there were colonial-era remains there only seemed to confirm the story. And once the Washington Christmas Eve fire entered the narrative picture, evidence of burning in the Colbert house made the whole interpretive package seem unassailable.

But, here again, there was a problem. The artifacts from the cellar, certainly, all dated to the right period—that was beyond question. But they were also all of the wrong type. The Washington cellar in the Colbert home had a collection of very coarse and utilitarian plates, pans, and storage vessels. True, cellars were for storing things, but if a cellar was within a home, then the collection of objects should be more associated with the eating of food than with its preparation and storage.

As we looked over the kinds of ceramics near the Surveyor Office and the Ice House, we saw a totally different picture. Tableware of all kinds, as well as wineglasses and even bits of forks and knives, were there in abundance. Some of it was quite impressive, including a distinctively ornamented piece of 1740s white salt-glazed stoneware. There was a distinct pattern here. Looking at the kind of garbage that collected around it, the Washington-period building under Colbert's house was not a home at all; it was an outbuilding, such as a kitchen or a dairy— both very common elements of an eighteenth-century homesite.

Of course, that left the actual home itself still MIA. But seeing all of these distinctly residential artifacts clustering close to the bluff's edge hinted pretty loudly that a dwelling had to be close by. So we dug more where we were finding the right stuff. We closed in on the edges of Colbert's old Ice House and began to see something new—lines of stones all mortared together, unmistakable signs of an old house foundation. Of course, we were quite excited.

The feature itself was a great digging project. Some features challenge a team's skill more than others. Some can be simply works of art when viewed through appreciating eyes. This was one of those instances. The challenge was that Colbert's fifteen-foot-deep Ice House had dug down right into the center of what remained of this stone cellar. Of course, when Colbert had his men dig out the hole, they clawed through and discarded whatever layers still hid in the old cellar. That data was lost forever. Only a small sliver of the original cellar fill was left to tell us about the building that once stood there. Getting it right was a real test of the craft.

Meanwhile, the artifacts that we found in those cellar layers were not that great—from a Washington standpoint at least. We saw lots of early nineteenth-century ceramics—mostly a pervasive plate type called Whiteware. We found plenty of Civil War refuse as well. Buttons, knapsack hooks, dropped bullets, and even two crushed canteens. These kinds of things have many fans—some of whom will go to great lengths (legal and illegal) to wrench them from the ground for fun and profit.

For that reason we never liked to talk too much about seeing these sorts of things. Everyone in archaeology has their stories of dealing with "pot hunters," as the profession derisively calls these private collectors. In fact, in some cases we have had to take great care to keep a find a secret lest the site get raided at night.

So Civil War artifacts were not the best news. The last thing we wanted was to show up one morning to see our site poked full of holes as if dozens of short-attention-spanned gophers had had a party there. But the real reason the Civil War stuff was less than welcomed was that it was way off, on the date front, if this was the Washington home.

Cellars usually contain remains dating from after their homes were gone and the cellars became exposed, open pits. Finding later objects is not necessarily a problem. John Gadsby Chapman had painted the old home as an open ruin in 1831. That meant that the dirt filling should have contained all manner of post–Washington era rubbish. But the Civil War? That seemed a bit late.

For these and other reasons, I had reservations about this really being an eighteenth-century building. Dave always has impeccable judgment in these matters, but in this case he and I were at odds. As the team opened up more and more of the foundation, the remains went up in his esteem, but dropped in mine. Pretty soon it became a fun part of the day to squabble like an old married couple about who was right on this one, recalling every ancient precedent from our long partnership. Our field director, Paul Nasca, also arrived at the nineteenth-century date and bet various meals with Dave, who was clearly enjoying being the holdout. I began to call the feature "daddy's little disappointment," and cast my aspersions as often as possible.

Meanwhile, the beautiful excavation continued and the evidence mounted. One part of the foundation revealed itself to be a fine set of stone stairs as nicely set today as when the builders first made them. Made them, that is, in the 1850s. For underneath one of these stone slabs, sitting right where it had been the day the masons set the steps in place, was a nice piece of 1830s Whiteware—a sure sign that daddy's little disappointment could not possibly have been an eighteenth-century building at all. Paul got his free meal, I got bragging rights for a day or so but, all told, we were no closer to the Washington home than we were when we began.

What we saw instead was the Bray home—one of the complex of buildings that went up in the years before the soldiers came to Ferry Farm to pull them down. In fact, the remains we saw told us just how connected were the war and the end of the Bray farm.

Civil War field artist, Alfred Waud, had drawn a remarkably detailed and accurate panorama of Fredericksburg during the 1862 winter battle. He stood on the slopes of Stafford Heights near the big guns, and sketched out the view before him. That included a glimpse—the only glimpse—of the Bray farm that Lincoln had visited and some of his soldiers mistook for the original Washington home. Waud showed a typical hodgepodge of framed buildings and a large barn with a distinctive cupola dead center on its roof ridge.

But photographs of the same view the following spring when the Yankees were back, this time fighting west in Chancellorsville, showed nothing left of what Waud had sketched. A year after that another image showed that the trees once shading the farm's lane had been cut down to stumps. The faintest shadows of brick or stone foundations showed at the blurred edge of the collodion photographic plate, but it was clear that what had been there in December 1862 was gone by May of 1864.

Cutting into what remained of the Bray foundations took us even deeper into that sad occurrence. When the soldiers were there in the summer of 1862, their officers tried to keep them from stealing even so much as a fence rail. But as the war got tougher, farms like the Bray's took it on the chin as they were looted and gradually dismantled. Whereas the big cellar in the Clark house had enough time to slump in and fill with rain-washed silt before it was finally filled in during the Strother years, the Bray cellar opened fast and filled with the war's rubbish. The canteens, buttons, and clothing hooks show that soldiers were treating the open hole as a trash pit for old or damaged clothing and gear.

In time, we found other parts of the Bray farm, such as ephemeral slave dwellings that left behind only the sparsest of marks in the ground, as well as plenty of Bray-period artifacts in the surrounding areas. But as interesting as the Bray farm and its martial demise was, the fact remained that our main mission was the Washingtons and, if Clark was strike one, then Bray was strike two.

With the Clark house and the Bray building ruled out as the Washington home, it made sense to do a real study of an odd rectangular cellar outline near the bluff. Once our team had cleared off the backfill from the old excavation, we could set about systematically examining this feature. Its stone outline was visible in the subsoil, but its odd size and shape were troubling. Houses built with full basements leave a pretty logical outline—find the cellar and you know the size of the house. But this stone outline was roughly twenty feet by ten feet—it could not be a building's outline; it had to sit fully inside of some larger structure. Patience is a hard virtue to master, but it is essential in these endeavors. Before we could dig into what was clearly an enticing cellar, we first had to see what other building components surrounded it.

It took some time to clear away the vast area around the cellar. But once we were done we had only begun to figure out the puzzle we were seeing. We saw sporadic lines of stone, and trenches where other walls once rested. We saw small surviving sections of foundations and chimney bases. We saw earthen cellar holes. We saw a large Civil War trench cutting right through the whole thing and another sewer line running down from Colbert's house site also cutting a line across the area. But what we did not see was a clear outline that we could point to and say "here is a house footprint."

This was particularly infuriating. After our near miss at the Bray house, this area emerged as the next best hope. The stone cellar was so large that it had to have been part of a building, and the artifacts in and around it were mostly from the mid-eighteenth century. At Ferry Farm, that meant the Washingtons. But there needed to be a foundation! That we could not see it right away was alarming.

Our team mapped each five-by-five-foot excavation pit as they opened them, and Paul kept a large master map, carefully recording the full compliment of rocks and shadows on one large sheet of gridded paper. We even took overhead photographs. At previous digs I had stood precariously on ladders or climbed out on tree limbs to get a good shot. Sometimes we would rent a boom truck and I would ride out in that swinging little fiberglass bucket to get nice overheads. The crew would clean the site for a day or so before the big shoot to get it ready and then we would gather just before dawn in the big day so that we could get the pictures before the sun got too high and cast shadows that might look like stains in the soil.

The boom truck we used in the past usually went up about twenty feet—just the distance needed to fix a blasted transformer, clip a sparky wire—or fit between the trees to photograph an archaeology site. But the size of the opened area clearly called for something far higher than the usual boom. We would need to bring out something more in keeping with the scale of the work—maybe as high as thirty-five feet? Fifty feet? With all our macho bravado mustered, we called the rental place and asked for their largest boom. The guy on the other end absently asked exactly what kind of job we needed it for. Full of confidence, though, we just reiterated that we needed the really big one, thank you very much. He calmly said that he had ones that were as high as two hundred feet— and asked again what kind of job we needed it for. Reeling a bit from that number, we stumbled "er, what about a fifty-foot boom, do you have a fifty-foot one?" After a long pause, he asked again in a measured tone, "what kind of job do you need it for . . . ?"

When the phone call was over and our industrial-equipment bravado had deflated, we had booked a fifty-foot scissor platform truck for the following week. The team set about getting the site ready for photographs, and pretty soon we had some of the most important Ferry Farm images since the Civil War.

When viewed from fifty feet in the air, the site looked like an earthen game of pickup sticks—a huge tangle of lines crossing lines. Here is how it is supposed to work: A team of diggers finds a corner or section of a historical building's foundation remains in the ground. It can be a deep cellar or just the very bottom course of bricks on which once rested a whole structure. No matter how great or small, the team will gradually open up more and more of the area to reveal the nice, easy-to-identify foundation wall, and begin to understand the house that once sat there. The remains can be shown off, mapped and photographed, and in some cases, even rebuilt upon.

But our site was not going to play by those rules. Instead, we had fragments, isolated bits of wall and ruin, and hints about what might have once been there. The rectangular stone cellar, had—rather unusually, as it happens—an addition added to it, which only further confused the line of the home's walls. A home like Clark's left very identifiable postholes in the ground. No matter how much had been repaired or replaced, that record was intact and all we had to do was expose it and connect the right dots. Brick foundations often leave a nice outline as well. This is because the bricks themselves are only fired clay. In the seventeenth and eighteenth centuries the heat of brick kilns was low enough to leave the product a tad undercooked. In time, the lowest bricks in a foundation would soak up water and become soggy. While the higher-up, better bricks were fine for reuse in other buildings, those on the bottom were not worth a salvage crew's time to dig out. So, colonial-era recyclers often left full, if short, outlines of the building they otherwise disassembled.

Not true of foundations made of rocks, though. Stones (famously) don't gain or yield moisture. The time it took to find them and shape them to purpose was far greater than the effort expended in digging up and reusing the old ones. So, the main reason we saw so little of the expected building outline was that its stones had gone into each subsequent building project on the site. They were there in the Colbert cellar and they were in his Ice House. The Surveying Office sat on stones first found and fitted generations before. We even found a 1920s sump hole filled with eighteenth-century foundation stones. That sewer ran right into the stone cellars where it ended in a deep sump. A large Civil War–era trench cut across the house site, but its enlisted diggers redirected their efforts when they banged into foundation stones too large to move easily.

This all made for a charming architectural metaphysics. Each new structure incorporated parts of its predecessors, and thus, in a way, kept them alive. Each new activity connected the latest changes by reusing old materials or remaking old spaces to meet new needs—even if it was just to change a colonial-era cellar into a 1920s septic pool. Even if the old Surveying Office or the Ice House were not there in Washington's day, it became increasingly likely that at least *parts* of them had been. Viewed that way, the old stories suddenly seemed less a case of simple error and more one of creative definitions—still wrong, but perhaps more interestingly so.

But as we looked at the pickup sticks, our main question was, "was this the Washington home, and how can we prove that with so little of it surviving?" The plan was to begin to excavate the stone cellar complex while also taking a close look at the foundation remains to see what they had to share. We set a few of our team's most able hands to work in the cellar full-time, while the rest of the crew fanned out to slowly pull apart the pickup sticks.

The cellar began to talk to us right away. Its upper layers had a nice mix of colonial and early nineteenth-century remains—none of the Civil War stuff we were seeing in the Bray cellar. That was great news—everything was pointing to this being the same cellar Chapman had painted in 1831. In fact, even the color and cut of the stones looked a bit like what the painter had left for us. As the team got deeper in, the news just got better and better. All manner of small domestic artifacts began to turn up. Fork and spoon handles, glassware and tableware, shoe buckles and other bits of adornment and clothing fasteners, horse furniture, and rusted bits of hinges and locks all fairly shouted that here was a home— and a gentry one at that. Clark had had a few nice things, but all told, there was not that much left at his site. But here was the homestead of a family with some buying power and the desire to choose the better stuff.

The best example of this was the cellar itself. As the team took down the fill layers, we saw more and more of the walls themselves. They were remarkable. Large, well-cut slabs of uniform, carefully chosen stone all set together with such skill that our professional mason consultant was just about beside himself marveling at the craftsmanship. Each stone had been carefully faced with chisel marks still as crisp as the day they were first cut, and they were as straight and solid as one could want. A cellar with this quality of stonework had to be part of a home of some quality, as well.

When Strother built his home, he was a member of the House of Burgesses, and when Augustine Washington moved his family to that same home, they were amongst the wealthiest Virginians. The house we were looking at, therefore, needed to be one that these folks would have called home. The stone cellar was the first thing we saw on the site that fit that bill. It had once had an entrance on the riverside—a doorway at ground level large enough to allow storage items to make it in. At some point late in the house's life, though, a second cellar, built to a far lower standard, had replaced this bulkhead doorway. The second cellar was made of river cobbles and picked—not cut—stones, sealed with mud, and awkwardly fitted around the old entrance. On top of that, the newer cellar sat outside the building's line, meaning that it had to have its own upper floor or roof. Layers at its bottom showed that it had quickly filled with trash and with silty mud that dribbled in from openings and through the poorly built walls.

The two conjoined cellars made a very odd pair. One was the finest stonework a colonial Virginian could buy, while the other was a hodge-podge of rocks and mud. This difference was telling us a significant detail from the home's biography. The evidence showed that it had been built as a costly gentry home. But at some point later in its life, it had fallen far from its initial finery. Whereas the first builders spared no expense, later owners did not care all that much if their utilitarian additions leaked or looked good. Here was a home that had gone from the A List to being a money pit rented out to tenants or used to house enslaved labor. Remembering that Weems recalled the Washington home by its "low and modest front of faded red," it may well be that the "modesty" he saw was really only a reflection of the home's later years. If, in fact, this was the Washington home, the cellars may well be telling us that decades of portraying Washington's "rustic" childhood with its rude home came simply from the fact that later owners had let the once fine home go to seed.

And everything in the cellars was lining up to suggest that we were in fact looking at the place where Washington had lived. The artifacts fit right into the perfect time period, and with each new layer it became harder and harder to account for this building if it were in fact *not* the Washington home. The preponderance of the evidence was piling up on one side of the scale.

There is a popular notion that single finds make an archaeologist's case—that some magical object, some perfect inscription, or some lock-tight-cinch thing or other wins the day. In reality, archaeological sites are collections of tiny conundrums, which all gradually solve themselves in the same direction. There is often a straw that tips it one way or another, but even that can only work its wonders once many others have already pointed in the right way. The cellars worked just that way. The stonework was certainly up to gentry standards. Check. The artifacts were all fitting into the right date window. Check. The cryptic written, drawn, and painted histories of the home were all harmonizing with what we saw in the ground. Check. It would have been nice to find something with the

Washington name or a bottle seal with an unmistakable A. W. on it. But absent these special finds, everything we saw was saying that at last we were digging the Washington home.

But even so, there were unanswered questions. For one thing, what had survived of the home beyond the cellars was a confused mess. For another, there still was the question of the Washington family house fire. We saw no evidence—no burned objects or burned layers anywhere—to support the idea that the home had gone up in flames and then been rebuilt. But we still needed to put that notion to bed once and for all if we were going to be certain that this was Washington's home. After all, the two cellars could have been a result of the conflagration—one pre- and the other postfire. But the clearly earlier of the two had no fire damage in it. That was a big problem for the fire story.

To see a collection of objects all dating to the Washington years and to see also no evidence at all of a fire was too much to let the story stand. Or maybe we were just looking at only one of the two pre- and postfire homes? Here again, the evidence worked against that conclusion. The artifacts in and around the area were just too good. We saw earthen cellars that straddled the periods of the Strother and Washington occupancies, and nowhere else on the entire site did we see collections of the right period objects. No, this one area, this one collection of holes and stones, had to be the place where the house had been. If we had a story about a big fire, and at the same time no actual physical sign that there had been a big fire, then one of the two would have to go. And frankly, it is far easier to dismiss a possibly misremembered and thinly documented story than it is to redirect a pile of physical evidence.

But a small cellar just before the scant remains of one of the home's fireplaces reconciled the pro- and antifire arguments. As one of the crew cut into this feature, he ran into layers of thick black dirt and charcoal. Now, that is what one sees archaeologically if there has been a fire. We slowly and carefully looked over the layers in this pit. They told an interesting story. At the very bottom was a mass of burned rubbish, dirt, and tellingly, burned plaster. This last bit was remarkable. Ceramics and wine bottles can burn anywhere and be deposited in a hole when it gets filled. In fact, it was pretty common for workers to clean out a fireplace right into a cellar before its filling. So finding burned trash in a disused cellar hole is not really earthshaking. But plaster is another thing altogether. There can be no better evidence that a wall suffered a really bad fate than to find burned wall plaster.

But there was more. In layers above the burned plaster were globs of new plaster. What we were seeing was a sequence. There had indeed been a fire during the Washington years—although it had been small—contained perhaps to only this single room. But, rather than consuming the home, it was quickly followed by repairs as the family set it all right.

So, the question of the possible two homes found its answer. If it was on Christmas or not remains unknown, but the home had indeed seen a small but damaging fire sometime before the 1750s, and following that, a set of repairs. We did not have to worry about there being two Washington homes, one pre- and the other postfire. Instead, there would only need to be *one* home—and this was looking more and more like it.

The final challenge was to make sense of the small foundation fragments that appeared in pieces around the cellar. The home had been picked down to its bottom layers. Chapman's painting showed a few courses of stones above ground. People living on the site over the years had taken what they could use and left it so that only a few of the bottommost foundation footer stones were still in place. It was a faint shadow of what had once been there.

But there was one day when it all came together. I had flown up to cover a few small research questions. Dave and I walked over the site while the crew worked on a variety of pits. We had been discussing a particular problem, and being on-site gave us a chance to knock around ideas. What it came down to was that one line of stones did not line up with the others. Houses need to be square, and if one wall wants to make a building footprint a parallelogram, then there is a problem.

All that was left of this troublesome wall was an eight-foot line of stones set in a trench—single ones, not even mortared together. They pointed toward a large flat stone that we had been thinking was a building corner. We talked through every possible explanation for this inconvenient wall. Was it a later add-on, perhaps not even part of the older home? Was it some makeshift repair to a long-gone wall? What would the footprint look like if we just excluded it? All the while, the stones sat there, holding their council and silently thwarting every explanation.

But then, standing on the flat corner stone, I thought out loud—what if this slab was outside the building, like a footer for a stairway—as opposed to the wall's corner? We looked it over and over and ran a few long tape measures to see how things would work.

What happened was remarkable. Just by viewing that single (albeit large) stone as having a different role in the structure suddenly made the problematic wall fall, quite literally, right in line. The parallelogram was gone and in its place we could now envision the full outline of a home, an eighteenth-century gentry home, the home where George Washington came to manhood, the home we had been after this whole time.

I sat down on the remains of Colbert's Ice House in the shade of the Surveying Office and let the moment settle in. The crew continued on digging, and Dave stood over near the corner, his arms crossed, looking at the ground, lost in his own thoughts.

The last door had closed; the last of the problems had been dismissed. The preponderance of the evidence all now aligned, and the scale stopped teetering and the matter decisively slammed down on one side.

Up until that point, we had been pretty sure that we were dealing with the Washington home, but that surety was in the 75 percent range, then the 80s, even reaching into the 90s on good days. But once that wall made sense, there was nothing left to block a public positive identification. And that following summer, that is what we did—first at the National Geographic Society offices in Washington, and then later at Ferry Farm itself with dignitaries, staff, and project supporters.

Once we were sure that we were looking at Washington's home, we could begin to make sense of the things we found in and around it. One ceramic pipe from the stone cellar molded with a Freemasons' compass and square was too late to have been George's, but it did help recall that he had first joined the order across the river in Fredericksburg. Besides, subsequent owners, like members of the Mercer family, were also Masons. The very rare tambour hook we unearthed was the one that Mary and Betty had used to fashion high-style embroidery. Likewise, a spoon handle marked with Betty's initial had to have been part of the set she used as she learned the gentle arts that prepared her so well for a good marriage. A matched pair of oyster shells carefully set in a crevasse in the cellar wall revealed that someone in the household was trying to create balance and order in their world through magical practices. These might have been African or British folkways—we could not say, since whatever the shells once contained was lost.

But either by magic, or careful purchasing, we saw that the Washingtons—both enslaved and free—surrounded themselves with things that made their world work for them.

❧

Once the cellars had been cleaned out and the outline made sense, it was time to go back up in the boom truck and take more photographs. The first time the cameras had gone skyward, most of the holes and trenches had still been intact, new finds. This time, the scissor lift cast its shadow on what we now knew was the Washington home, recovered.

We had had an impact on this land just as surely as had Washington, the soldiers, Colbert—any of them. We had disassembled layers and features that had taken centuries to build up. Honestly, there is a sadness to that. There is no escaping the fact that archaeology is inherently destructive and for that reason we need to always do it with care and professionalism. On the other hand, the great paradox is that preserving the site for future generations was dependent on digging it. Past attempts had always failed, in part because they could not really show anything substantive for their cause. Even though the cellars and other features have to be backfilled with dirt to keep them in good condition, we know that they are there. And from that real and solid knowledge, new generations of commemoration can begin. The artifacts go into exhibits, and visitors have more and more to see about Washington and Ferry Farm's larger history. All of this ensures the site's preservation as long as Americans agree that these kinds of places are worthy of keeping. The excavations do not end history here—they just change what can go into its ongoing making.

Looking at the resulting photographs, I can see that I was somewhat wrong back in 2002 when I first thought that there was not much to see here. It was all a question of angles. The ground never forgets, and when handled the right way it can be made to tell its otherwise hidden stories. A fine colonial home became a faded, threadbare beauty as fashions changed and its owners left it behind. New additions only made it less and less useable until it was finally abandoned—lost to sight, but remembered all too well in art and literature. Its stone foundations were picked over and reused, again and again. Soldiers sought physical shelter amidst its remains while invoking the name and mission of the home's most famous resident. Later, work crews piled up cellar stones in a pit designed to turn foul water sweeter. A pipe brought water from a nearby house down to rest on the cellar's new sump. In that home, tourists and preservationists discussed and fussed over the one-time resident they all uniformly revered. And yet, every time they flushed a toilet or washed their hands, the wastewater filtered down into the home they all thought carried a unique special connection to American history and moral virtue.

In some ways, that is the lesson of this landscape. So often we love and cherish our past while at the same time treating it and its physical remains, as, well, crap.

10

❧

The Truth About the
Cherry Tree

In 1894, the world was introduced to a remarkable German stoneware tankard. It was the find of an American collector named Stewart Paton, who brought it to these shores from its native home of Stralsund. Paton shared his purchase with friends and collectors and all were impressed with his "discovery" in the German resort town. The historian, expert collector of antiquities, and curator of New York's Metropolitan Museum of Art's American Collection, R. T. Haines Halsey was the first, though, to make a serious appraisal of the tankard and to publish his findings. The authenticity of the mug was rock solid; as Haines Halsey declared, "its genuineness is unquestioned."[1] It bore the date of 1776 and was in all ways consistent with ceramics of the period and manufacturing. The mug's pewter cap and foot stand of same were all right in line with run-of-the-mill, late eighteenth-century German ceramics. Haines Halsey had seen dozens, as had every other collector.

But what made this particular tankard noteworthy was its decoration. It showed a rural scene and a man in blue jacket and tan breeches. The figure shoulders an axe and stands before what appears to be a well-pruned fruit tree or even the trunk of a dead one. In the background sits a house, a hill, and some oversized, highly stylized plants. Floating above the scene are the letters and numbers that for an odd moment vaulted this humble stein into the national eye.

Above the tableau sits "G W 1776." No doubt it was those icons of American history that caught Dr. Paton's eye in Germany and later elicited excited gasps from those to whom he showed his treasure. In case the meaning was not clear, Haines Halsey connected the dots for all to marvel at.

The letters mean that the figure is George Washington, the 1776 makes clear that this is an allusion to Washington's Revolutionary War global fame—a parallel made even clearer by the figure's blue jacket and tan trousers, an obvious reference to the colors of the Continental Army uniform which Washington wore. Having established that the figure is none other than Washington, the axe and tree next come into focus. By now the explanation should be clear: Here was a graphic reference to the Cherry Tree Story. But, the 1776 date, incised a second time near the maker's initials of A.S.K., makes this retelling a full thirty years earlier than Weems's first iteration. On top of that, this ceramic telling was made in Germany—a sure sign that the story had indeed been in wide circulation well before Weems brought it to his readers.

For Haines Halsey there was no sliver of doubt possible. Indeed, "it does not seem improbable," he wrote, that the Cherry Tree Story "was wafted across the sea and reached the ear of some potter, who then clumsily pictured it upon a mug of stoneware."[2] Add to that "the interest the German people took in our struggle for liberty" and the conclusion was inescapable. This simple Prussian tankard was material proof positive that Weems did not make up "the Cherry Tree Story dear to all Americans"—indeed "every test of science" and the fact that the mug had been "expertized as to date and genuineness" proved the story true.[3]

Weems had always been a problematic figure with as many detractors as fans at any given moment. In 1899—the same year that Haines Halsey

crowed in public—Henry Cabot Lodge spoke for the historical establishment when he called Weems "simply a man destitute of historical
sense, training, or morals." The parson had one goal in mind and that
was to "take the slenderest fact and work it up for the purposes of the
market." Indeed, Cabot Lodge claimed that "until Weems is weighed
and disposed of, we cannot even begin an attempt to get at the real Washington."[4] Thus, stories like the Cherry Tree were worse than charming
tales—they were dangerous historical obstacles, subversive silliness that
only distanced the real Washington from his adoring public.

These were the stakes of the battle into which drifted the mug from
Stralsund. If it could prove that the centerpiece of Weems's Washington
canon was, in fact, a fact, well then, the tide would turn. "Expertisers"
like Haines Halsey had no doubt that the tankard was a devastating
blow to those crusty historians who so harshly dismissed the story. The
tankard spoke loudly and it did not lie.

Or, perhaps there was another, less dramatic explanation for the mug's
designs. In a later review of the tankard's claims a German ceramic expert
and director of Hamburg's Museum of Arts and Crafts, Dr. Erich Meyer,
arrived at a rather different conclusion.

For Meyer, there was nothing Washington at all about the tankard.
The colors of the clothes? Unremarkable common ceramic dyes. The
telltale initials of G.W.? Germans had those initials as well, and since
it was a common practice for people to commission mugs in honor of
one another, some long-forgotten Gottfried Weissengruber or Gerhardt
Wagenknecht seems much more likely a G.W. honoree than the Great
Washington. The 1776 date? Germans, as it happens, used the same calendar as Americans—that year came and went in Germany without regard
for its importance in the United States. During it, children were born,
fortunes were won and lost, crops failed and thrived, and potters fashioned tankards, and all without reference to the American Revolution.

On top of that, much of the design itself becomes about Washington
only after a healthy dose of wishful thinking. The tree is more pruned

than whacked at by a child. The figure with the axe is also pretty fully grown—far too adult to sustain Haines Halsey's claim that it was a "youth." The tankard's Washington elements only lined up when one already knew they were supposed to.

Meyer saw nothing but meaningless coincidence in the mug's decoration. Another collector and tankard supporter named Arthur Merritt found that a bitter pill. "It requires a remarkably tolerant digestive apparatus," Merritt wrote, "to permit the swallowing at one gulp of so many coincidences." How could such a convergence of details be "combined through pure accident," he asked.[5] But in reality, it was the Weemsians who were asking an impossible alignment of details and seeing what they wanted to see. The Stralsund tankard, like the Civil War soldiers' cherry pits, the Washington cellar stones, or the venerable Surveyor's Office, were well-meaning tributary fabrications that took a thin bit of evidence and stretched it for all it was worth. Weems made Ferry Farm a place with trees so heavy with fruit their limbs fairly touched the ground. In practice, it was Washington lore itself that was the farm's most bountiful produce.

No, the tankard's proof was all merely a set of commonplace elements creatively held together by a net of wishful thinking and Washington piety. The tankard was just an ordinary German mug of no great merit except that, for a moment, it seemed to challenge an establishment view of Washington's life story. It enjoyed a fleeting moment or two of celebrity. It appeared in Halsey's ceramic book, and it made occasional annual appearances in February—the month in which the nation recalls the Cherry Tree and all things Washington. In 1904 for example, the arts and literature magazine *The Critic* ran a little essay hinting at the validity of the mug and by extension, the truth of a story then mostly invoked as the "subject of idle jest and irreverent jest."[6]

Its grand showing in Annapolis, Maryland, in Washington's 1932 bicentennial celebration, was meant to be this ceramic debutant's coming-out party. It was also an attempt by Marylanders to rescue the reputation of Weems the native Marylander in this most Washington-themed of years. Newspaper coverage there was, though the exhibit itself made less of a splash.

The mug made appearances in the pages of a three-volume collection of Weems's writings, which were accompanied by a "reader you be the judge" kind of insinuation of validity. It surfaced again in 1956 when Cold Warriors sought to dust off American lore for a new purpose. Seeing Washington and the Cherry Tree on the face of a German mug emphasized the connections between the two countries just as the Soviets were closing the border and leaving Berlin an isolated island.

But, Dr. Paton's mug never received any widespread expert approval. It made a nice story, but not much more. Was the whole thing a collector's trick to gin up the price of an insignificant stoneware tankard? Was it the fancy of a few true believers who just hated seeing the nation's stories derided so publicly? Probably it was some combination of the two. But it did not work. The mug did not convince many that the Cherry Tree story was true, nor did its reputation make it a national treasure. Instead, over the years, it quietly passed from private collector to private collector until it faded finally from view. It may still be sitting on someone's shelf today, or it may have long since shattered into a hundred pieces. No one can say for sure.

Ferry Farm's excavations unearthed a small set of ceramic fragments, though, that would have made the true believers of the bicentennial rejoice. They came from a few different places on the site, as opposed to being a single object broken, dropped, and buried. They were fragments of a punch bowl fashioned in a lead-glazed earthenware that the 1760s collectors and scholars alike call Creamware, in tribute to its yellowish white tint. It was a widely popular ceramic, stealing the market from most of its rivals and becoming almost ubiquitous wherever English goods were sold. It came in a host of forms, but unlike many of its more ornate predecessors, its stylists preferred the minimal—clean lines, sparse edge adornments, large surfaces of smooth cream-colored plate all mark the style. Its open surfaces allowed all manner of decoration, as well. The most affordable variants had patterns stenciled onto the plate or bowl before application of the final glaze. The most costly pieces were delicate, hand-painted, one-of-a-kind masterpieces brushed onto the glaze by master craftsmen.

Creamware came in every form imaginable, from sauceboats to dinner plates to punch bowls, and of course, tea sets. All an eighteenth-century buyer had to do was look in a pattern book, or handle some tiny doll-houselike sample pieces, and put in an order. For Virginians, that order could take months to arrive, packed in sawdust-filled barrels in the hold of a ship from England. The sets might have survived or been shattered in transit—the anticipation must have been excruciating, especially if the set was in some way special.

Sometime in the 1760s someone ordered a specially ornamented punch bowl for Mary Washington. The order is not in any surviving account books, but the bowl made it to Ferry Farm. Not too long after it got there it somehow cracked—usually a death sentence for table ceramics. But the bowl was special enough to Mary that she paid a craftsman to repair the cracks with a special glue paste. It was not as good a drinks vessel as when it was new, but it could still hold pride of place on a shelf or a mantle. In time though, it suffered the fate of most fragile ceramics—short use life, breakage, and discarding.

The bowl was in most respects fairly typical in its form—it was about the size of half a cantaloupe and shaped more or less the same way, tapering down to a ringlike Chinese-style foot rim at the base. But, as with Dr. Paton's Stralsund tankard, it was mainly the ornamentation of the ceramic that caught the eye.

The surviving pieces were covered with small hand-painted bundles of cherries. The images were grouped in little clusters with stems leading up to leaves—stylized to be sure, but not beyond recognition. Because we only have fragments, we cannot see the whole pattern, but the color red, the way they clump, and the little dimples on their sides make them cherries, as opposed to apples or some other fruit.

They are painted onto the glaze, rather than being stenciled on prior to glazing and firing. Their fine reds and greens would not have survived the kiln's heat as would have specially made stencil inks. Instead, an artisan painted the design on the surface after it was fired. This meant that the colors could be full, but that came at the expense of durability—overpainted ceramic designs fell victim to every knife or spoon scratch.

But despite the design's vulnerability, consumers were willing to spend a pretty penny to have these specially adorned ceramics. On top of that, these cherries were not very common design elements—none quite like them seem to have been found on American sites, and only a few have survived above ground. That means that the set was an expensive and therefore, presumably, intentional purchase. Mary had a cherry-ornamented punch bowl because she or someone else very much wanted her to have one.

What are we to make of a set of rare and expensive cherry-adorned fragments emerging from a landscape later so famously associated with the best-known cherry story of them all? Do we have to have what Arthur Merritt called a "remarkably tolerant digestive apparatus" to see it as a coincidence, or is there some meaning here?[7]

We can begin with what it almost certainly does not mean—and that is that the Cherry Tree Story is true. It is easy to imagine what old-time true believers like George Allan England or Robert Siegrist might have made of such a find. Here would be proof positive. Mary had the bowl made to commemorate her son's ultimate fidelity, or perhaps the bowl itself was the source of the story. J. B. Colbert would have laid the fragments in a place of honor and had visitors pay to have a close viewing. The Youth for Christ pastors would have placed them front and center in the old Colbert house museum and Sidney King would have painted Mary serving George some punch from the very same set. The painting would have hung over the display, or maybe the whole thing could have been set up in the "Truth Temple."

For people who wanted the Cherry Tree to be true, or at least wanted to make use of the sentiments it conveyed, the Creamware would be invaluable. For skeptics, the bowl would be just another Surveyor's Office-quality fraud—more Weemsian nonsense. There is no reason to expect that the Creamware would have been any more persuasive than was the tankard. It might be able to claim a direct and irrefutable link to the Washington family, but that does get us much closer to understanding what it might be saying.

And that is the problem. The tankard was a creative, albeit probably innocent fraud—one of many cropping up over the years. But the Creamware cherries are real archaeological finds. They came from real layers on a real site, and were really part of Washington family life on the site—a site that would later become famous (sometimes infamous) for a cherry story. That may simply be a coincidence, and if it is, it is a noteworthy one. So much of living with a site entails turning its bits over and over, day in and day out. Sometimes that means spending days staring at piles of old site photos to figure out what came before what. Other times it means sitting in archives struggling to read challenging handwriting. And of course there is always the site itself, with its incessant demands for maintenance and protection from the elements, and the challenge of making sense of its artifacts. Perhaps it was living with the Cherry Tree for so long—reading every version of it I could find, seeing it turn up over and over in letters and newspapers—that made this handful of ceramics seem to matter. But I found that it made me want to rethink just how I understood this story that so affected this landscape.

During the July 2008 media events, Dave and I divided up aspects of the story so as to keep things moving smoothly through a wave of what promised to be rather similar interviews. In the division, I got the Cherry

Tree. We knew that the story would come up again and again—how could it not. And indeed, we made a conscious choice to not try and silence the most famous story the land produced. It was a full and legitimate part of the place's history in and of itself, and so it made sense to talk about it. George Allan England was half right when he claimed that time and retelling had made it so the Cherry Tree "crystallized" into fact. It might not be fact, but its retellings and their effect on the landscape had crystallized the old tree into history.

So, in a host of interviews, I took great pleasure in paraphrasing England by saying that (and here I quote myself) "if George Washington did indeed chop down the Cherry Tree, as generations of Americans have believed, this is where it happened."[8] I liked that line. It was sufficiently circumspect, safely devoid of a claim that the story was truth, well within the tradition of Ferry Farm's larger story, and completely true. That line, in one form or another, was picked up and repeated literally hundreds of times as the story wended its way through newspapers and Web sites.

The news stories all made full use of the Cherry Tree, as we expected. Headlines said archaeologists found Washington's home, but no hatchet, and TV reporters reminded their viewers of the story they all knew, and that all knew was not true.

By and large, the coverage was wonderful—just the right mix of serious and nostalgic. I received e-mails and letters from people who were thrilled about the find and wanted to share how much the Cherry Tree Story meant to them. A few people told me they had insights into what the Washington home looked like—one man even sent me a photograph of a painting his mother had done years ago, others sent digital copies of old lithographs they had sitting around. Of course each of these were variants of the Currier and Ives lithograph of Wakefield, which had been a fixture of calendars for decades. The old drawing was still working its magic, convincing the well-intentioned that this had been the old

Washington home. These were all friendly attempts to touch something Washington, to share what Americans had known for generations. How could one mind such letters?

There were negative reactions, too, though. One fellow history professor wrote a flabbergasted note in which he was indignant that I suggested that the old story was true. Weems was a proven liar he fumed. Was I not aware of this or that essay on the topic that proved it once and for all? Of course I was, and as I wrote back, I did not understand myself as having said Weems was in fact right, only that Ferry Farm was long known as the setting for the story—a fact we would have been foolish to try and hide. In 1990 when an earlier reconstruction plan emerged, the Fredericksburg paper carried a letter to the editor warning against Ferry Farm's plans to rebuild the Washington home. The letter cited Washington's Birthplace and recalled the troubles reconstruction had meant for Wakefield. The author urged that locals see the birthplace confusion as a cautionary tale. Right after the 2008 announcement, an almost identical letter from a different but similar expert source appeared. The cautionary tale, the irresponsibility of repeating long disproven lies, and so on—it was Charles Arthur Hoppin and his contempt for Weemsian flotsam and jetsam all over again. Anyone familiar with Ferry Farm's history could only have grinned at this—we certainly did.

But the larger message was clear: The Cherry Tree was still a bit of a head turner, for better or worse. It still had its power to enthrall or infuriate. It was as high stakes a tale as ever it was.

When we found the intricate Masonic pipe, there were those who wanted it to belong to Washington himself. The dates simply did not work—it was a bit too late and Washington's presence on the site too spotty in those years for it to have been his. In conversation with a member of the general public, I presented the problems with the case while praising the pipe as the wonderful find it is, offering us an open door to discussing old-time smoking habits, Washington's own Masonic career in Fredericksburg, and the role of his fellow Masons as sometime owners of

Ferry Farm. After a moment's reflection, the person leaned in and said as if revealing a bit too much secret knowledge, "well, I believe it was Washington's anyway."

Likewise, an amber-colored carnelian bead we found opened a very different discussion. This semiprecious gem was mined in India, and shaped into bead form in Africa where it held special value. The one we unearthed was one of very few found in the Americas—others had been buried with their enslaved African owners as grave goods. The carving that made this bead strongly suggested that it was, perhaps like its owner, an African import. But it is hard to push the bead too much further. Did its possible owner see it as an African holdover? Was it associated with some sort of traditional authority? Was it just a mere curio or keepsake? Was it carried overseas in African hands or worn on African necks, or was it a purchased or purloined trinket of some sailor? Hard to tell—the bead itself is tantalizingly mute, even though its presence speaks loudly and invites a discussion about the ways that enslaved Africans came to America.

So, how much harder would it be to make an unusual cherry design on a punch bowl speak directly to a story usually dated to well after its manufacture? And how much more risky and contentious to suggest that this handful of fragments spoke to this most famous of American tales?

Instead, let's focus on the land, the Washingtons, and the ignored parts of the story, as opposed to the specifics that still elicit such hand-wringing. Even though it is framed as a tale of an ideal son and the healing powers of honesty, at its core the Cherry Tree Story is also a tale of loss; the same is true of its equine cousin, the Sorrel Colt Tale. In both, the Washingtons suffer a loss—a tree in one, a horse in the other. In both cases the lost objects are favorites as well. The focus on the moralistic side of the tale has long obscured that there really is a truth hidden in these twin stories. That truth is loss.

Ferry Farm was not a great place for George. Here, he lost first his sister, and then later, more significantly, his father. Here, his chance at an easy slide into gentry life slipped away, and was regained only through hard effort. The land itself slipped away as well, as Lawrence sold off the farmed acres, and confusion from that sale colored George's thinking even as he sold the place thirty years later. Even the enslaved African population added loss to loss with Harry's killing of Tame, and then the state stepped in with Harry's execution. Finally, Lawrence's death sealed George's future in the land—a separation he helped set in motion by selling off the northern tract. In the end, Washington cut all of his ties with Ferry Farm, and with Fredericksburg as well. He returned to visit his mother and sister, but those visits were far from frequent.

Washington's whole experience of Ferry Farm was one long string of losses, one long chronicle of setbacks and hurdles. It is true that each loss, each stumble, each frustration inched him closer to becoming the man he became, but that was far from clear at the time. In hindsight, it is easy to see how the blazes of loss gradually marked a path that led Washington to the heights he achieved. But for a young man eager to make his name, what comfort was there? Had it been all sunshine and light, had Ferry Farm indeed been crowned with Weems's fruit-heavy trees and happily buzzing bees, then Washington would have grown to become an Anthony Strother or perhaps even a Fielding Lewis. Well set, comfortable, established, happy even, but nothing more, nothing larger. Specialists and scholars would know his name, but few others would.

Instead, Ferry Farm and its litany of loss hardened the domesticated gentry lad into a man who threw himself into the woods and rarely looked back to the place he left behind. Its parade of loss made him a man who could hear bullets whiz by and be unfazed—an officer who could ride before his own men and knock aside their muskets to keep them from firing. Perhaps after enduring Ferry Farm's five deaths, its noise and cramped surroundings, its pickpockets, and the constant plans of greater men to impinge on what little his family could retain, he just felt lucky to get out alive.

Ferry Farm's patchwork of small parcels, always for sale or being eyed by a possible buyer, taught Washington to see land as property—to see acres as various sized bits to be gathered, traded, and consolidated. It taught him to accumulate as he did his whole adult life—but in the end, Ferry Farm was the only farmable Virginia parcel he sold off.[9] The small size of Ferry Farm after Lawrence's sale to Strother helped him set his eye westward where the parcels were bigger and the horizons less hemmed in by other's people's successes. And as he turned his back on the old place, he did so with a survey that made special note of his family's first loss on the land—the death of Mildred, recalled always by her little walled-in grave near the house.

The truth that the Cherry Tree Story has held close to its chest all of these years was that it maintained the connection between the Washingtons, Ferry Farm, and loss. That little triangle, always lurking but long overlooked within the story, tells a very powerful truth about George Washington and his boyhood home.

In Washington's day, the Rappahannock was about one half wider at Ferry Farm than it is today. The old bay in the river that Washington knew, that Chapman painted, and that was once filled with wrecked ships is no longer there. It was filled in with mica-rich riverbed dirt, dumped into the shallows when the Army Corps of Engineers dredged the Rappahannock in the last years of the nineteenth century. They set poles and boards into the mud (they are still there to be seen), and piled the upended slop onto the shore side of their water wall, making Ferry Farm's riverfront a much bigger chunk of land than it had been. In Colbert's day it was a second little pasture—it even had some small frame buildings on it until the great flood of 1942 washed them all away.

This all means that the river is now far narrower and far straighter than it was meant to be. You can walk out on that half natural, half man-made floodplain and find the exact line where the old shore ends and the dredged fill begins. The place where the ferry once landed is buried; the little strip of waterside where enslaved Africans first touched free soil was covered over by the institutional descendants of the army engineers who made the bridge that linked one bank to the other.

At that point the soil changes. Before the line, the dirt is rich, hard-packed alluvial soil; over the line, it is dusty and loose—you can feel it move under your feet. Before the line, the dirt produces lush grasses—after, the grasses' roots hold the dirt together.

The old freshwater creek that kept house after house in place is still there—nestled in a stand of trees that love the water there as much as did Mary Washington and countless other Ferry Farm residents. The expanded shoreline, though, has affected the creek as well. In its heyday as a water supply, it ran down the slope and fed right into the river. All one had to do was catch it before it mixed with the brackish river. Today, it has a whole long man-made flat that it has to meander through before it meets the Rappahannock. That means the water gets to settle into sulfurous stagnant pools where exposed rocks take on discoloring mineral deposits and the water's surfaces glisten with an unappealing oily sheen. A sign calls attention to the fact that this was the main water supply, but no sign calls attention to how the land has changed since those days. Visitors see those fetid, smelly pools and understandably conclude that things must have been terrible for the Washingtons if they had to drink that swill, or at a minimum, their bodies must have functioned completely differently from our own. Thanks to this error, a common need for water actually divides past people from present ones in visitors' minds.

There is a small, poison ivy–lined path that leads down to new edge of the water. By the time you get there and look down at the river's brown water, you would now be standing about a third of the way across George's river—a bit past the guardhouse on the 1862 canal boat bridge. In the 1750s, to attain this view of Fredericksburg you would be hearing the water slap on the bottom of the ferry. During the Civil War you would have had to have step-stoned your way out here on the staves of ruined ships or walked out on a rubbery feeling pontoon bridge.

And even so, the view is not the same. The main difference is the trees. Their presence has come full circle. In John Smith's day they were thick on the ground and from then on, one tree at a time, the covering got thinner and thinner. Clark and Strother cut them to farm the land and make buildings. Mann and Teasdale cut them to sell them. The Civil War soldiers cut them for fires and shelter. After that they were almost gone, and not many were left to cut. A Civil War photograph taken from the river's town side, looking back at Ferry Farm, shows it to be all but bald. A thatch of scrubby trees cluster (as always) along the creek, but apart from that, the ground is as treeless as a Kansas cornfield.

But after WWII, as suburban culture replaced agriculture and the river became the back of town and not its gateway, the trees slowly reasserted themselves. The 1942 flood cleared the muddy flats and the river islands of the various factories and electrical stations that lined them. Downtown Fredericksburg was filled with mud and sludge. A huge riverside oil tank caught fire and was carried downriver, blazing all the way. Ferry Farm's lower acres were washed clean and a small tenant's house halfway up the slope floated off. Not wanting to see those losses again, owners and rebuilders moved to higher ground and left the floodplain land to the trees. Soon trees had filled in every old wharf, unused farm field, and riverfront slope. They blocked the old views and shut out whatever breezes might have broken the humidity. On top of that, these were (and are) hybrid forests made up of as many invasive species as local ones. So, as the river's newly narrowed banks regreened, they created something totally new and without local precedent. The once wide and clear Rappahannock became a narrow green tunnel.

Standing at the new river edge—at Ferry Farm's small break in that tunnel—you can see bits of the old and bits of the new all mixed together. Fully modernized eighteenth-century homes and 1830s brick buildings all sit arrayed across the river. Most of these have changed little on the outside, since they were repeatedly photographed during the Civil War.

A large and neatly manicured floodplain stretches out beneath the homes. That green lawn makes a perfect landing spot for a stone.

On one particular summer day I, and a group of students and Ferry Farm staff, amble onto our side of the river's edge for an annual ritual. It is the middle of the day, the sun is high, and the opposite bank of the river is quiet—no kids playing games or old folks walking their dogs. No fishermen sit on their barstool-like seats mounted on low sleek boats right in our line of sight. To all appearances, we have the river to ourselves. That is a good thing—we don't want anyone to get hurt.

There is some laughing and chatter—the dusty crew is glad to have a break from digging. Most of the assembly, though, are kicking up stones, weighing them in their hands, and inspecting them for aerodynamics. This one is too flat, that one too heavy. It is crucial to find just the right stone, just the right mix of hand fit and vaultability. Each person will only get a few throws, so the balance of rock to hand is essential to making a good try. These are all rocks that would not have been available to Washington when he allegedly tried this feat—they were all buried in the river-bed then.

Likewise, that "huge fellow from Michigan" who made his toss on a far darker and rather grimmer day in 1862 did not have the assortment of river-worn cobbles we have at hand.[10] When former Washington Senators' pitcher Walter Johnson took a toss in 1932, it was as an arranged stunt by Fredericksburg's tourism-hungry patriots. Sol Bloom himself upped the stakes, betting that Johnson had not the arm that the Great Washington had (even at the age of eleven, according to the story). On top of that, Bloom noted that even though the river was far narrower, he still had more faith in Little George than he had in the "Big Train," as the rather formidable Johnson was nicknamed by sportswriters—and by probably a few terrified batters as well.

The plan then was for Johnson to use a silver dollar—chosen in deference to George Washington Parke Custis from whom we learned the story—even though Washington's dollar would have been a coin of Spanish minting commonly called the dollar. Johnson claimed that he practiced his throws at his Maryland home by banging coin after coin against the barn door until the wood began to splinter and he felt he had the range.

On February 22, a crowd of over one thousand gathered to see the Big Train cross the Rappahannock. On the other side, another three thousand waited anxiously, perhaps hoping to catch a much-desired Depression-era dollar. The weather was cold and icy as watchers stamped their feet and blew into their hands to keep warm. Undeterred, Johnson stripped down to his bare arms—still powerful, even though his salad days were behind him.

After a few preliminary warm-ups, he was ready to throw. The first toss plopped into the water just as Bloom had said it would. The second, though, made it to the far bank, as did the third—the one that was officially the one for the record books. Johnson had shown that a practiced professional pitcher could hurl a coin a distance just under three hundred feet—nearly a whole baseball field. And even though the event made a good photo op, most newspaper coverage thought the whole thing rather silly and based on a rather "Weemsian" family fable to boot.

That might have been too quick a dismissal, though. Washington's physical strength was noted in his own day, and on more than one occasion he was said to have shown off his abilities by throwing a stone some crowd-impressing distance. One veteran recalled "the General's" arm outdistancing those of a small squad of Continental Army soldiers passing time in "jerking stones."[11] Painter Charles Willson Peale recalled how one hapless iron bar "lost the power of gravitation" when Washington's "mighty hand" grasped it and threw it at some waiting bowling pins.[12] Parson Weems has Fielding Lewis recalling that his "play-mate" George could throw a stone over the Rappahannock "at the lower ferry of Fredericksburg."[13]

Parke Custis, who penned the Sorrel Colt Story, also claimed that "the power of Washington's arm" was the subject of "several memorable instances." One saw Washington "throwing a stone" from the "stream bed" at the base of Virginia's Natural Bridge and clearing its over 215-feet height. Another had Washington hurl a stone over 300 feet to the top of New Jersey's Palisade cliffs—a feat more plausible, top to bottom, than the way Custis told it. Custis, of course, also told of Washington throwing "a piece of slate, fashioned to about the size and shape of dollar," over the Rappahannock with "an arm so strong" that it "not only spanned the river," but continued its flight "at least thirty yards on the other side."[14] For the mathematically inclined, that could have been a distance of anywhere from a staggering 440 feet (professional baseball fields vary from 390 to 435 feet at the centerfield wall) to an impressive 340 feet. Over years of retelling, a version of the story eventually migrated to Mount Vernon, where the Potomac is over a mile wide. That little move made a difficult but plausible act into something more on a Paul Bunyan scale. Nevertheless, Washington's strength became part of his legend. Even actor Charles Martin, who matched Washington's real-life over-six-foot height, featured cracking a walnut between his fingers as part of his Washington role in Colonial Williamsburg's *The Story of a Patriot*.

George is credited with killing only one cherry tree, but his legend has quite a bit of flinging in it.

The Rappahannock story captured something of Washington's physical strength that many contemporaries either praised, or in some cases ridiculed. But all in all, the story is a great allegory of Washington's Ferry Farm. First off, it centers on the river, the land's defining trait. The river brought the English here. It enabled the town, the roads, and the ferry. Its ancient floods made the land fertile and its frontage made it valuable. Even Washington used the vista the river afforded to market the land. The land and the river have always been knotted together.

When Washington threw his coin or stone, he had to turn his back to the land. In reality, he did just that. He faced west, crossed the river, and claimed a fortune that quickly had him outgrow these small cramped acres. If anything, the coins came to him from across the river.

All of these echoes are in the air as the small group of us gather at the

water's edge to play one of Washington memory's most venerated games—
the stone throw.

I try first. My effort is hard to describe. Not "pathetic," that is too
strong—"wasted" may be a better word. I put everything I have into it, a
few lead-up steps and all, but I release way too early and send my little
stone way too high into the air to have any real chance of making the far
bank. It falls in midriver with a satisfying, enveloping "ploop," while the
assembled offer a sympathetic, if slightly condescending, "awww" as a
consolation. Even Walter Johnson had bungled his first toss. I smile and
go back to my starting point again, pretending that it does not feel like I
have torn all the ligaments in my shoulder.

A few skipping steps and I let fly my second stone. The timing on this
throw is much better—I release it at the right moment and the stone's
arch has a very reassuring low bow to it. But that is as far as my Big Train
comparison goes—and the middle of the river is as far as this second
throw goes. There not being much reason to try again, I declare myself
defeated and step to the sidelines with the spectators.

Dave is next. He looks very determined and powerful as he steps into
the throw. But even so, he does not make it to the other bank—even
though he clearly beat my first try (maybe not my second). He tries once
or twice more, but like me, he never reaches the far shore, despite excellent showings.

We all cheer on a few more tries by various crew members—some of
whom get very close—but each throw ends with a splash. Finally, one of
my graduate students steps up. He is a solid guy with a baseball background, both as a player and a coach. He has a serene, confident smile as
he sets his feet and moves forward. As he begins his throw, his whole
body leans back and his throwing hand almost touches the ground behind him. He becomes a human trebuchet—this is someone who knows
how to throw.

The rock flies skyward and I lose sight of it.

We wait. But this time there is no splash. Instead, we all can see the rock bounce on the grass on the far side and, as a sportscaster might say, the crowd goes wild.

On the face of it, our little game was what corporations might call a "team building exercise": a shared experience that brings everyone closer together. We built culture and enacted it by participating in a ritual that tied people to place and story and to previous seasons of excavators and students who made the same ritual. We also created a nice little fully sanctioned break from the workday. Wins all around.

But scrape the surface a bit, and something deeper emerges. Ours is a country without a national religion—a rarity when it was founded by men who understood the risks in resting a government on something as fleeting and fragile as human agreements. We have no divinely rooted sovereign to embody the nation and we have no single set of ancestors to venerate. Instead, we have figures like Washington and we have the places he inhabited and the stories of what he did there.

Throwing rocks across the Rappahannock on a summer's day is just one of many ways to touch something of Washington and feel part of the polity he helped create. Playing at being Washington and matching his alleged throwing ability, ultimately, is a small part of an American secular religion that allows us all to connect with an often elusive, often confusing national past.

Parson Weems's Cherry Tree has also survived because it always played such a central role in that faith. Its values of honesty and paternal love mattered more than the truth of the story. And so Americans held onto it, even as they acted like careful arborists and pruned it from the genre of history only to replant it as myth—an act that did not kill the tale, but rather helped ensure its long life in new soil.

At Ferry Farm, Washington has always lived in the space between the real and the unreal. From the life his father and mother might have planned for him to the one he really led, or as the historical figure floating somewhere between his life and his legend, Ferry Farm's George has always been colored in many shades. People have made of him what they had to—as indeed, he did. How many rocks made it across the river in the years since Washington's day? How many arms strained to match the Great Washington's? What was it that they hoped to gain from their own throws—was it emulation, admiration, or just a plea for a blessing? Was it for sport or piety? Were they enacting myth or history—how could we tell the difference?

Acknowledgments

There are so many people I want to thank for their contributions, support, and inspiration as I researched and wrote this book. I would list them all but they are too numerous. I wish to mention some by name though, and to all others I extend my heartfelt thanks. First on the list have to be the close to two hundred University of South Florida Ferry Farm Historical Archaeological Field School students, field interns, and volunteers who made the dig a reality. Their work, their eagerness to learn, and their boundless enthusiasm for Ferry Farm and its story were an endless joy. A few stand out for various reasons and for what we might call service above and beyond the call of duty. These include, but are not limited to, James Trueman, Brad Jackson, Giselle Portuondo, Alena Pirok, Jean Louise Lammie, Mechelle Morgan, Jarred Wilson, and Neel Amin. I have to say as well how proud I have been to work with a fine set of graduate teaching assistants who know all too well the burden they shouldered so ably. Thanks to Nunzio Carrubba, Justin Castells, Jackie Barber, and Rebekah Eaton. Very special thanks to Jill Ficarotta and Michelle Davison for taking on other challenges so well and getting things done. Managing the field school over the years has meant relying on the help and cooperation of the University of Mary Washington. Special thanks to Susan Knick and Kari Gent.

Special thanks as well are due to the many archaeological staff and volunteers at Ferry Farm and the George Washington Foundation, including Kate Ruedrich Jackson, Heidi Kroft, Shelby Gunderman Castells, Brad Hatch, and Melanie Marquis.

Special thanks are also due to Dale Brown, John Copely, Joyce Darr, and especially Travis Walker, who has performed yeoman service ferreting out records, and Alma Withers, for all she has done for us. Laura Galke has been a fabulous colleague and sometime conference panel partner. Although she came late to Ferry Farm, Mara Katkins stepped in just in the nick of time to keep me from making a big error. Paul Nasca has known the layers and features of Ferry Farm perhaps better than anyone. His skilled hand and exacting eye shaped the excavation year by year, always for the better.

The entire Ferry Farm project has been lovingly funded and supported by the George Washington Foundation. Its board of directors has had the generosity and vision to ensure that world-class archaeology and museum presentation carry on year after year. The foundation's president, William Garner, has been a tireless supporter of research and preservation at Ferry Farm and in Fredericksburg. He has also been singularly supportive of this book and I thank him so much for that. Others there who have made things happen over the years include Paula Raudenbush, Carol Underhill, Matt Webster, Greg Stoner, Paula Felder. Very special thanks to Mark Wenger for his expertise, to Les Barker for making all the inferences visible, and to Jeff Howard and his wonderful staff. Additional thanks to John Hennessy, Lucy Lawliss, Rijk Morawe, and Logan Metesh of the National Park Service.

Several generous foundations have helped make this project and my own writing possible. Among others, the Mary Morton Parson's Foundation and the Dominion Foundation both offered generous support. Thanks to the Homeland Foundation for the John Gadsby Chapman painting of Ferry Farm. In 2008 the National Geographic Society stepped in not only with grant money but with media expertise that helped make our announcement of findings a huge success. Amanda Hobbs and Barbara Moffet of NGS were invaluable. I also thank Diane Rehm for hosting us on the air during those exciting weeks. The Virginia Foundation for the Humanities made this book real in two ways, first through a summer fellowship during which the ideas for it crystalized, second through a long-term fellowship during which I spent days in the UVA library making PDFs and then long nights hiding out and writing early drafts of chapters. While there I benefited greatly from the support and advice of William Freehling as well as the aid and guidance of Ann Spencer and Nancy Damon. This book is truly a VFH product.

My marvelous agent, Rachel Sussman, hammered this book into shape. I thank her for her remarkable ability to say "this is great—just write it all again differently" and somehow make it happen. I can't thank St. Martin's Press enough. Michael Flamini's unflagging enthusiasm and Vicki Lame's careful guidance have made this process nothing but a pleasure.

I have in the Department of History of the University of South Florida as great a group of colleagues as anyone could want. Special thank-yous go to Giovanna Benadusi, Barbara Berglund, David Johnson, Brian Connolly, Julia Langford, Frances Ramos, Steven Prince, Julia Irwin, Jolie Dyl, Bob Ingalls, and Scott Ickes. Judy Drawdy, Jennifer Dukes Knight, and Theresa Lewis deserve special note for keeping everything running. During this project I worked with two departmental chairs, William Murray and Fraser Ottanelli. No department has had better leadership. Their support and encouragement were boundless. I keep them both near and dear. USF Department of Anthropology colleagues also deserve special thanks. These include Elizabeth Bird, Nancy White, Brent Weisman, and Thomas Pluckhahn. Special thanks as well to Dean Eric Eisenberg, Provost Ralph Wilcox, and President Judy Genshaft, all of whom have been great friends of Ferry Farm and our work there.

Along the way one turns to countless professional friends and colleagues who offer some good advice here, some inspiration there, some encouragement when things seem bleakest, and some distraction, vital information, or writing advice when most needed. They offer critical reads of chapters or more, they suffer long e-mails, phone calls, or conference dinners going over and over the tiniest of details; they help hone, and shape, and refine. On so many levels books are really collaborative endeavors. A short list in no particular order of friends and colleagues who have contributed in ways great and small, near and distant, includes Daniel Ingram, Anthony DeStefanis, Bernard K. Means, John C. Coombs, Elizabeth Kelly Gray, Jon Kukla, James L. Axtell, Daniel Peck, Warren Billings, François Furstenburg, Scott Casper, Thad Tate, Dennis Pogue, Esther White, Julia King, Barbara Little, Martha Zierden, Mary Beaudry, Marley R. Brown III, Ann Yentsch, Douglas Owsley, Emmy Munroe, Eric Gable, Alan Outlaw, Robert Blair St George, James O'Neil Spady, Wendy Gonaver, Bill Dudley, Rabbi Uriel Rivkin, Rabbi Lazar Rivkin, Rabbi Menachem Mendel Schneerson, D'vorki Rivkin, Yosi Appel, Yakov Kuzmenok, Eyup Izler, and Nurcan Izler.

The people of the City of Fredericksburg and its environs deserve special note as well. It was they who came together to make Ferry Farm something special. The leadership of Cessie Howell and Bill Beck were vital at just the right time. The memories of people such as Norma Polly helped keep stories alive. The tireless and scrupulous reporting by Clint Schemmer has kept the area informed for years about matters of significance to historical preservation in general and Ferry Farm in particular. Local readers are lucky to have him. Thanks as well to Billy Withers, Phill Solo, Devorah Lynn, Wayne Gootee, Sarah Anne Bachman.

I am a city kid at heart and tend to do best when there is activity around me. For that reason, I have developed the habit of writing in coffee shops. Night after night I sit with my Macbook and write in my corner and drink hot chocolate. In Fredericksburg, that special corner is in the renowned Hyperion Espresso and I thank Dan Peterson and Anna Burgos for the loan of it. In Tampa, I generally claim the window table at the Starbucks on Fowler Avenue, where I have been ably looked after by Sean Malone, Chelsea Borden, Manuel Perez, Hailey Rose, Kristi Seline, Charlene Byssaintthe, Ali Shrum, and Needra Miller, among others. They are all wonderful. I share these odd writing habits with Susan Boettcher and I am deeply grateful for her being there for chat and camaraderie, and for helping monitor the comings and goings in the coffee shop and in the larger cosmos.

I also want to thank my parents, Jerome and Natalie, as well as my brother, Matthew, my sister, Carla, and my brother-in-law, David, for always being family. The same goes for my family by marriage, Bill and Loomis, Stephanie, Jim and Lucy, Leslie and Greg, Julie and Tim, and all the young ones.

To Sarah who reads every word and knows every thought, I don't want to say a word here. Let's just smile at each other like we did in Joe and Tory's attic. And then let's kiss again next to the tire.

My son, Rami, the little boy in my life, in my book. The rain came down on us as we climbed up into the cloud. We followed the switchbacks and tried not to slip. As you always do, you went ahead of me and I followed. You like the uphills better than I do. There were cottonmouths at the rock overlook—at least that is what the guys at the foot of the slope told us. I was worried that you might get too curious when you got there. When I got there though, you had passed safely and I stopped to drink. I looked up the hill, peering over the next switchbacks as they zigged and zagged away from me. There you were. You did not look down—you were too determined. You looked so strong and so confident, so up to the task, so in your element. You were magnificent. You write a book by plugging away at it every single day—taking small steps day in and day out—just the way you climb a mountain or hike hundreds of miles of trails. The best things are all a matter of discipline. There is no secret magic. You just plug away at things and they get done. Always remember that life is a very narrow, winding mountain-side path—the trick is to not be afraid.

And then there are Dave and Amy. For all that they have done over twenty years of support, mentorship, and above all, friendship, there are not enough thanks. Of course this book is for you both—how could it be otherwise?

Notes

❧

Introduction: "Welcome to Ferry Farm"

1. There were many newspaper stories emerging from the day's events. A great photo was on the cover of the *Richmond Times-Dispatch*. See, Lawrence Latane III, "Washington's Home Uncovered at Ferry Farm," *Richmond Times-Dispatch*, July 3, 2008. Web edition. See also David Zax, "Washington's Boyhood Home," *Smithsonian* (September 2008).

1. From Unburned Woods to "Clear and Distinct Views"

1. *Virginia Gazette*, October 1772, in George H. S. King, "Washington's Boyhood Home," *William and Mary Quarterly* Second Series, 17:2 (April 1937), 275. King reprinted other useful Ferry Farm documents including other land sale ads and inventories.
2. The literature on Virginia's earliest English history is large and varied. My vision is shaped powerfully by Kern Ordahl Kupperman, *The Jamestown Project* (Cambridge: Belknap, 2009); James Horn, *A Land as God Made It: Jamestown and the Birth of America* (New York: Basic Books, 2006); William Kelso, *Jamestown, the Buried Truth* (Charlottesville: University of Virginia Press, 2008); Frederick Gleach, *Powhatan's World and Colonial Virginia: A Conflict of Cultures* (Lincoln: University of Nebraska Press, 2000); Alfred Cave, *Lethal Encounters: Englishmen and Indians in Colonial Virginia* (New York: Praeger, 2011); Stephen Potter, *Commoners, Tribute, and Chiefs: The Development of Algonquian Culture in the Potomac Valley* (Charlottesville: University of Virginia Press, 1993); Helen Rountree, *The Powhatan Indians of Virginia: Their Traditional Culture*

(Norman: University of Oklahoma Press, 1989); Camilla Townsend, *Pocahontas and the Powhatan Dilemma* (New York: Hill and Wang, 2004).

3. John Smith, *The Complete Works of Captain John Smith (1580–1631) in Three Volumes*, Philip L. Barbour, ed. (Chapel Hill: University of North Carolina Press, 1986), 2:174–175.

4. Smith, *Complete Works*, 2:174.

5. Ibid., 2:175.

6. Ibid., 2:175.

7. Ibid., 2:175.

8. Ibid., 2:176.

9. Susan Myra Kingsbury, ed., *Records of the Virginia Company of London, Five Volumes* (Washington, D.C.: United States Government Printing Office, 1906–1935), 3:107.

10. Some of the most important works on the settlement of Virginia and its growth as a tobacco growing, land-hungry, and slave-owning society include: Edmund Morgan, *American Slavery, American Freedom: The Ordeal of Colonial Virginia* (New York: W. W. Norton, 1975); James Horn, *Adapting to a New World: English Society in the Seventeenth-Century Chesapeake* (Chapel Hill: University of North Carolina Press, 1994); Kathleen Brown, *Good Wives, Nasty Wenches, and Anxious Patriarchs: Gender, Race, and Power in Colonial Virginia* (Chapel Hill: University of North Carolina Press, 1996); T. H. Breen and Stephen Innes, *Mine Own Ground: Race and Freedom on Virginia's Eastern Shore, 1640–1676* (New York: Oxford University Press, 1980); John Coombs and Douglas Bradford, eds., *Early Modern Virginia: Reconsidering the Old Dominion* (Charlottesville, University of Virginia Press, 2011); Lorena Walsh, *Motives of Honor, Pleasure, and Profit: Plantation Management in the Colonial Chesapeake, 1607–1763* (Chapel Hill: University of North Carolina Press, 2010). Lois Green Carr, Philip D. Morgan, and Jean B. Russo, eds., *Colonial Chesapeake Society* (Chapel Hill: University of North Carolina Press, 1991); Darrett and Anita Rutman, *A Place in Time: Middlesex County, Virginia, 1650–1750* (New York: W. W. Norton, 1986).

11. Nell Marion Nugent, *Cavaliers and Pioneers: Abstracts of Virginia Land Patents and Grants, 1623–1666* (Baltimore: Genealogical Publishing Company, 1963), 313.

12. Ibid., 1:410.

13. William Cronon, *Changes in the Land: Indians, Colonists, and the Ecology of New England* (New York: Hill and Wang, 2003); Timothy Silver, *A New Face on the Countryside: Indians, Colonists, and Slaves in South Atlantic Forests, 1500–1800* (New York: Cambridge University Press, 1990); Carolyn Merchant, *Ecological Revolutions: Nature, Gender, and Science in New England* (Chapel Hill: University of North Carolina Press, 1989).

14. Nugent, *Cavaliers and Pioneers*, 1:548–549, 557.

15. Ibid., 1:557–558.

16. Ibid., 1:558, 567, 557, 558.

17. Ibid., 1:558, 548.

18. Ibid., 1:557, 567.

19. Warren Billings, ed., *The Papers of Sir William Berkeley* (Charlottesville: University of Virginia Press, 2007), 338.

20. W. G. Stannard, "Abstracts of Virginia Land Patents," *Virginia Magazine of History and Biography* 3:1 (July 1895), 62.

21. George Atwell, *The Faithfull Surveyor* (London, 1658). There is a large number of these manuals and they stayed in use for many decades after their first printing. Much of the material is mathematical, but the introductions to these books are troves of early modern wisdom.

22. William Byrd, *The Prose Works of William Byrd of Westover*, Louis B. Wright, ed. (New York: Belknap Press, 1966), 395.

23. George Washington, *The Writings of George Washington*, 39 volumes, John C. Fitzpatrick, ed. (Washington D.C.: United States Government Printing Office, 1937–1944), 1:7.

24. John Lederer, *The Discoveries of John Lederer* (London: Samuel Heyrick, 1672), 21.

25. Ibid., 21.

26. Ibid., 22.

27. Clarence Walworth Alvord and Lee Bidgood, eds., *The First Explorations of the Trans-Allegheny Region by the Virginians, 1650–1674* (Cleveland: Clearfield Press, 1912), 163. For more on this sort of travel see, Philip Levy, *Fellow Travelers: Indians and Europeans Contesting the Early American Trail* (Gainesville: University Press of Florida, 2007).

28. Alvord and Bidgood, *The First Explorations*, 163.

29. Warren Billings, *Sir William Berkeley and the Forging of Virginia* (Baton Rouge: Louisiana State University Press, 2004), 200.

30. Billings, *Papers of Sir William Berkeley*, 284.

31. Bacon's Rebellion has long been a centerpiece of Virginia history. In addition to Billings—who has much to teach on this and related topics—for more on this multi-dimensioned crisis see, Morgan, *American Slavery, American Freedom*, Wilcomb Washburn, *The Governor and the Rebel: A History of Bacon's Rebellion in Virginia* (New York: W. W. Norton, 1972); Stephen Webb, *1676: The End of American Independence* (Syracuse: Syracuse University Press, 1995), Brent Tarter, "Bacon's Rebellion, the Grievances of the People, and the Political Culture of Seventeenth-Century Virginia," *Virginia Magazine of History and Biography* 119:1 (2011): 2–41; James Rice, *Tales from a Revolution: Bacon's Rebellion and the Transformation of Early America* (New York: Oxford University Press, 2012).

2. The Washingtons Make a Home at the Falls

1. What we know of Clark comes from very few sources. The main one is his will, Richmond County Will Book 5:40, Warsaw, Virginia. The second is a photograph of his Ferry Farm land deed in the Ferry Farm collection. Understanding his world therefore relies on years of regional historical and archaeological study. Lois Green Carr, Russell Menard, and Lorena Walsh, *Robert Cole's World: Agriculture and Society in Early*

Maryland (Chapel Hill: University of North Carolina Press, 1991); Cary Carson, Norman F. Barka, William M. Kelso, Gary Wheeler Stone, and Dell Upton, "Impermanent Architecture in the Southern American Colonies," *Winterthur Portfolio* 16 (1981): 135–96; Matthew Johnson, *Housing Culture: Traditional English Architecture in an English Landscape* (Washington, D.C.: Smithsonian Institution Press, 1993); Matthew Johnson, *English Houses 1300–1800: Vernacular Architecture, Social Life* (New York: Longman, 2010).

2.   All towns have their historians. For two of early Fredericksburg's see: Oscar Darter, *Colonial Fredericksburg and Neighborhood in Perspective* (New York: Twayne Publishers, 1957), and Paula Felder, *Forgotten Companions: The First Settlers of Spotsylvania County and Fredericksburgh Town* (Fredericksburg: The American History Company, 2000).

3.   This era was the beginning of what scholars call the Golden Age of Virginia. See: Rhys Isaac, *The Transformation of Virginia: 1740–1790* (Chapel Hill: University of North Carolina Press, 1999); Warren M. Billings, John E. Selby, and Thad W. Tate, *Colonial Virginia: A History* (Millwood, NY: KTO Press, 1986).

4.   Douglas Southall Freeman, *George Washington: A Biography* (New York: Scribner, 1948–1957), 1:41. George Washington's life is one of the most studied ever. Most of the work focuses on his adult achievements, leaving the silences of the childhood years more or less in place. Many masterful authors and wonderful scholars have stepped up to attach their name to Washington's. Here are some of the ones I have referred to most often in understanding Washington's life. Freeman's multivolume biography is still the best and most thorough and I have used it in this chapter. Amongst more recent work, the most important and influential are James Thomas Flexner's multivolume biography, particularly for this study the first volume, *George Washington: The Forge of Experience* (Boston: Little, Brown, 1965); Paul K. Longmore, *The Invention of George Washington* (Berkeley: University of California Press, 1988); Joseph Ellis, *His Excellency: George Washington* (New York: Knopf, 2004); John Ferling, *The First of Men: A Life of George Washington* (Knoxville: University of Tennessee Press, 1988); John Ferling, *The Ascent of George Washington* (New York: Bloomsbury, 2010). Jack Warren has produced one of the best researched childhood histories in "The Childhood of George Washington," *The Northern Neck of Virginia Historical Magazine* 49:1 (1999), 5785–5809. Although in an older essay, Samuel Eliot Morison's work has been of some lingering influence, particularly in regard to Washington's relationship with his mother, see: "The Young Man Washington," *George Washington: A Profile*, James Morton Smith, ed. (New York: Hill and Wang, 1969), 42–43. See also François Furstenberg, *In the Name of the Father: Washington's Legacy, Slavery, and the Making of a Nation* (New York: Penguin Press, 2006); Henry Wiencek, *An Imperfect God: George Washington, His Slaves, and the Creation of America* (New York: Farrar, Straus, and Giroux, 2003); Edward Lengel, *Inventing George Washington: America's Founder in Myth and Memory* (New York: Hill and Wang, 2011). See as well: Ron Chernow, *Washington: A Life* (New York: Penguin,

2010), for the most popular current biography. See as well Barry Schwartz, *George Washington: The Making of an American Symbol* (Ithaca: Cornell University Press, 1987), and Karal Ann Marling, *George Washington Slept Here: Colonial Revivals and American Culture, 1876–1986* (Cambridge: Harvard University Press, 1988).

5. Jacob M. Price, *Tobacco in the Atlantic: The Chesapeake, London and Glasgow, 1675–1775* (New York: Variorum, 1996); Allan Kuikoff, *Tobacco and Slaves: The Development of Southern Cultures in the Chesapeake, 1680–1800* (Chapel Hill: University of North Carolina Press, 1986); Warren Billings, John Selby, and Thad W. Tate, *Colonial Virginia* (Millwood, NY: KTO, 1990); T. H. Breen, *Tobacco Culture: The Mentality of the Great Tidewater Planters on the Eve of the Revolution* (Princeton: Princeton University Press, 2001).

6. *Virginia Gazette*, April 21, 1738, in King, "Washington's Boyhood Home," 266.

7. John Mack Faragher, *Daniel Boone: The Life and Legend of an American Pioneer* (New York: Henry Holt, 1992), 326.

8. This understanding of the Washington home comes mainly from our excavations. Reports of each year's work are on file at Ferry Farm and with the Commonwealth of Virginia. These technical reports live up to their names and are rather specialized documents. My goal here is to distill rather than to enumerate. David Muraca, Paul Nasca, and Philip Levy, *Report on the Excavation of the Washington Farm: The 2002 and 2003 Field Seasons*, The George Washington Foundation, Fredericksburg, Va. State Site No: 44ST174, 2011; Idem., *Report on the Excavation of the Washington Farm: The 2004 and 2005 Field Seasons*, The George Washington Foundation, Fredericksburg, Va. State Site No: 44ST174 2010; Idem., *Report on the Excavations at the Washington Farm: The 2006 and 2007 Field Seasons*, The George Washington Foundation, Fredericksburg, Va. State Site No. 44ST174 2010.

9. Understanding the enslaved side of a plantation's landscape is a very different task than learning the values and activities of the master family. Benchmarks on this project include: Philip Morgan, *Slave Counterpoint: Black Culture in the Eighteenth-Century Chesapeake and Lowcountry* (Chapel Hill: University of North Carolina Press, 1998); Max Edelson, *Plantation Enterprise in South Carolina* (Cambridge: Harvard University Press, 2011); Peter Wood, *Black Majority: Negroes in Colonial South Carolina from 1760 Through the Stono Rebellion* (New York: W. W. Norton, 1996); Theresa Singleton, *"I, Too, Am America": Archaeological Studeis of African-American Life* (Charlottesville: University of Virginia Press, 1999); John Michael Vlach, *Back of the Big House: The Architecture of Plantation Slavery* (Chapel Hill: University of North Carolina Press, 1993); Morgan, *American Slavery, American Freedom*; Daniel Blake Smith, *Inside the Great House: Planter Family Life in Eighteenth-Century Society* (Ithaca, NY: Cornell University Press, 1986); Mechal Sobel, *The World They Made Together: Black and White Values in Eighteenth-Century Virginia* (Princeton: Princeton University Press, 1989); Anthony Parent, *Foul Means: The Formation of a Slave Society in Virginia, 1660–1740* (Chapel Hill: University of North Carolina Press, 2006). My vision of Ferry

Farm's social and physical landscape is based on the site's archaeology as well as Augustine Washington's will and probate inventory.

3. George Washington, Master of Ferry Farm

1. David Humphreys, *Life of General Washington*, Rosemarie Zagarri, ed. (Athens: University of Georgia Press, 2006).
2. Augustine Washington's Will, 1743, King George County Wills, King George County, Virginia, Book 1, 138. Hereafter cited as AW Will. Understanding the changing shape and ownerships of colonial-era farmland is famously challenging. Even the most skilled expert's work is often little more than best guesses given the vagaries of land records. The story is always in need of some refinement, but I have relied somewhat on the work of Thena Jones, "Reconstructing the Washington Farm and Catlett Patent," 1993, and an unpublished report housed in the Virginiana Room of Fredericksburg's branch of the Central Rappahannock Regional Public Library.
3. Horace Edwin Hayden, *Virginia Genealogies: A Genealogy of the Glassell Family* (Wilkes-Barre, PA, 1891), 77.
4. Peter Henriques, "Major Lawrence Washington versus the Reverend Charles Green: A Case Study of the Squire and the Parson," *Virginia Magazine of History and Biography* 100:2 (April 1992), 250.
5. Moncure Daniel Conway, *Barons of the Potomac and the Rappahannock* (New York: The Grolier Club, 1892), 240.
6. Ibid., 240.
7. Ibid., 240.
8. Hayden, *Virginia Genealogies*, 77.
9. Ibid., 77–78.
10. George Washington, *The Papers of George Washington, Colonial Series,* W. W. Abbot, ed. (Charlottesville: University of Virginia Press, 1983–1995), 1:5. Hereafter cited as PGW.
11. AW Will.
12. George Washington, *The Diaries of George Washington, Volume 1, 1748–1765*, Donald Jackson, ed. (Charlottesville: University Press of Virginian, 1976), 9–23.
13. PGW 1:47; Freeman, *Washington*, 1:235–236 (document photograph insert).
14. PGW 1:6.
15. Laura Galke, "The Mother of the Father of Our Country: Mary Ball Washington's Genteel Domestic Habits, *Northeast Historical Archaeology* 39 (2009): 29–43. Cary Carson, Ronald Hoffman, Peter J. Albert, eds., *Of Consuming Intrests: The Style of Life in the Eighteenth Century* (Charlottesville: University Press of Virginia, 1994).
16. Freeman, *Washington*, 1:48–49.
17. Ibid., 1:48–49.
18. Voyages, The Trans-Atlantic Slave Trade Database, http://www.slavevoyages.org/tast/resources/slaves.faces.
19. Archaeologist Jerome Handler has found the only other carnelian beads in the Ameri-

cas. See his online newsletter for "An African-Type Healer/Diviner and His Grave Goods: A Burial from a Plantation Slave Cemetery in Barbados, West Indies," 1995, http://www.diaspora.uiuc.edu/newsletter.html.

20. King George County Order Book, King George County Wills, King George County, Virginia, Book 1, 670.

21. Ibid.

22. PGW 1:26.

23. King George County Order Book, King George County Wills, King George County, Virginia, Book 3:373.

4. Washington's Parting Survey and the Parson's Pen

1. PGW 1:6.

2. Ibid., 1:38.

3. In Freeman, *Washington*, 1:263.

4. AW Will.

5. PGW 1:232–233.

6. Ibid., 6:421.

7. Ibid., 7:308.

8. Ibid., 7:308.

9. Ibid., 7:308.

10. Ibid., 7:308.

11. Ibid., 7:308.

12. George Washington, *The Diaries of George Washington, Volume 3, 1771–1775, 1780–1781,* Donald Jackson, ed. (Charlottesville: University Press of Virginian, 1976), 33.

13. Ibid., 33.

14. All quotations from the survey come from "13 Sept 1771 Ferry Farm Survey Notes," Research Files, Ferry Farm, George Washington Foundation, Fredericksburg, Virginia. During the 1930s some adventurous souls tried to draw out on paper an approximation of Ferry Farm's boundaries based on these survey notes. The document has been widely seen, but is really little more than a good guess.

15. PGW 10:2.

16. Ibid., 10:10.

17. Ibid., 10:9.

18. *Virginia Gazette* ad, in King, "Washington's Boyhood Home," 275.

19. Ibid., 275.

20. PGW 10:10.

21. Ibid., 10:27.

22. John W. Reps, *Tidewater Towns: City Planning in Colonial Virginia and Maryland* (Charlottesville: University of Virginia Press, 1972), 202, Fig. 133.

23. Ebenezer Hazard, "The Journal of Ebenezer Hazard in Virginia 1777," Fred Shelley, ed., *Virginia Magazine of History and Biography* 62:4 (October 1954): 417.

24. Ibid., 417.

25. Ibid., 419.

26. Ibid., 419.

27. Ibid., 419.

28. *Mason Locke Weems,* oil on canvas, c. 1810, Unidentified artist, National Portrait Gallery, Smithsonian Institution; gift of the Weems family.

29. Weems has had an array of scholars. Harold Kellock, *Parson Weems of the Cherry-Tree* (New York: The Century Company, 1928); Marcus Cunliffe's introduction to his edited edition of Mason Locke Weems, *Life of Washington* (Cambridge: Harvard University Press, 1967), is excellent as is Peter Onuf's introductory essay in M. L. Weems, *The Life of Washington* (Armonk, NY: M. E. Sharp Press, 1996); François Furstenberg, "Mason Locke Weems: Spreading the American Gospel," *In the Name of the Father: Washington's Legacy, Slavery, and the Making of a Nation* (New York: Penguin Press, 2006), 105–145. See also, Scott Casper, *Constructing American Lives: Biography and Culture in Nineteenth-Century America* (Chapel Hill: University of North Carolina Press, 1999), 19–77. Edward Lengel echoes the current consensus on Weems in *Inventing George Washington: America's Founder, in Myth and Memory (*New York: Harper-Collins, 2011), 18–26. The most enduring and thorough biography of Weems remains Lewis Leary, *The Book-Peddling Parson* (Chapel Hill, NC: Algonquin Press, 1984). See also: Skeel, ed., *Mason Locke Weems.*

30. Mason Locke Weems, *Mason Locke Weems: His Works and Ways in Three Volumes*, Emily Ellsworth Ford Skeel, ed. (New York, 1929), 2:126. Hereafter cited as *Weems Letters.*

31. Ibid., 2:126.

32. Ibid., 2:126.

33. Ibid., 2:126.

34. Ibid., 2:127.

35. Weems, *Life of Washington*, 17.

36. Ibid., 15.

37. Ibid., 15.

38. Ibid., 6.

39. Ibid., 19.

40. Ibid., 8, 12.

41. Ibid., 45–46.

42. Ibid., 8.

43. Ibid., 10.

44. Ibid., 13.

45. Ibid., 13.

46. Ibid., 12, 9.

47. Ibid., 9–10.

48. Mason Locke Weems, *Mason Locke Weems: His Works and Ways*, 2:126.

49. Ibid., 1:25.

5. Memory Encamps on a Field of Clover

1. John Gadsby Chapman, *The American Drawing-Book: A Manual for the Amateur* (New York: J. S. Redfield, Clinton Hall, 1847), 2. The subsequent images I discuss are all in the Ferry Farm image collection, Fredericksburg, Virginia. The Chapman painting itself is owned by the Homeland Foundation, Amenia, New York.

2. Much of what we know about this period comes from the extended court cases involving Mann's and Teasdale's businesses. The records were collected from Stafford County Court and Fredericksburg Circuit Court by Travis Walker and were transcribed by Jill Ficarrotta. Copies of the documents all reside at Ferry Farm, Fredericksburg, Virginia, Mann and Teasdale File.

3. George Washington Parke Custis, *Recollections and Private Memoirs of Washington* (New York: Derry & Jackson, 1860), 132–34.

4. Susan Riviere Hetzel, *The Building of a Monument* (Lancaster, PA: Wickersham Company, 1903), 6.

5. "The Mother of Washington," *Rhode Island American and Gazette*, 2:87 (May 13, 1831).

6. "To the Editors of the Enquirer," *Richmond Enquirer*, 28:3 (May 17, 1831), 3.

7. "Presbyterians in American History," *New York Observer and Chronicle*, March 30, 1876, 54.

8. Weems, *Weems Letters*, 1:126; Lengel, *Inventing George Washington*, 89–90.

9. "To the Editors of the Enquirer," *Richmond Enquirer*, 28:3 (May 17, 1831), 3.

10. Hetzel, *The Building of a Monument*, 7.

11. http://files.usgwarchives.net/va/fredericksburg/cemeteries/gordon.txt; "The Death and Burial of Mary Washington, *The New York Evangelist,* Volume 7 (April 16, 1836), 16.

12. Hetzel, *The Building of a Monument*, 10–12.

13. Ibid., 12.

14. Charles Dickens, *American Notes for General Circulation* (London: Chapman and Hall, 1842), 12.

15. "Fredericksburg and Alexandria Railroad," *Public Arena*, August 11, 1835, 2.

16. Benson Lossing, *Pictorial Field Book of the American Revolution in Two Volumes* (New York: Harper and Brothers, 1851), 1:2, 1:219–220. Harold Mahan, *Benson J. Lossing and Historical Writing in the United States, 1830–1890* (Westport, CT: Greenwood, 1996).

17. http://trove.nla.gov.au/work/23849180?q&l-format=Map%2FAerial+photograph&l-decade=185&c=map.

18. George William Bagby, "Editor's Table," *Southern Literary Messenger* 32:21 (April 1861), 321.

19. Ferry Farm Civil War Files (FFCWF), 7 WI File. Ferry Farm Fredericksburg, Virginia. May 1, 1862. As part of understanding the land's history, Staff Archaeologist Paul Nasca collected documents relating to the Civil War regiments that encamped at the site. These principally came from three sources: regional historical societies, current commemorative groups for each of the regiments, and some National Park Service Files. The bulk of this material is composed of letters to local papers written home by soldiers at the

front. At Ferry Farm these published letters are organized principally in folders labeled by the regiment to which they apply. Some of these letters are signed with full names, others with only initials. Some have dates, others do not. All of this is an effect of the nature of the various collections. My following citations use the file name followed by the best available date and author information. The most prolific regiments were the 6th Wisconsin Volunteer Infantry, the 7th Wisconsin Volunteer Infantry, and the 6th Wisconsin Volunteer Infantry. Nasca has done wonderful work on Ferry Farm's Civil War years.

20. FFCWF, 6 WI, May 21, 1862.

21. FFCWF, 6 WI, J. Weirich, July 20, 1862.

22. FFCWF, File 2, Correspondence of the Herald, May 13, 1862. If Fredericksburg is known for one thing, it is the 1862 Civil War battle that bears its name. For more on that episode in the town's story see: Francis Augustin O'Reilly, *The Fredericksburg Campaign: Winter War on the Rappahannock* (Baton Rouge: Louisiana State University Press, 2006); George Rable, *Fredericksburg! Fredericksburg!* (Chapel Hill: University of North Carolina Press, 2001).

23. FFCWF, 6 WI, May 21, 1862.

24. FFCWF, 7 WI, "SD," April 6, 1862.

25. FFCWF, 6 WI, Luke Parsons, June 23, 1862.

26. FFCWF, 7 WI, "T.R.C.", May 12, 1862.

27. FFCWF, 6 WI, Luke Parsons, 1862.

28. FFCWF, 7 WI, "W.D.W.," May 4, 1862.

29. FFCWF, 7 WI, May 19, 1862.

30. FFCWF, File 2, "Letter from the Seventh Wis. Reg.," May 15, 1862.

31. FFCW, 7 WI, May 19, 1862.

32. FFCWF, 7 WI, p. 7.

33. FFCWF, 7 WI, "W.D.W," April 28, 1862.

34. FFCWF, 7 WI, Isaac Cooper, May 15, 1862.

35. FFCWF, File 2, "Letter from McDowell's Division," May 13, 1862.

36. Jane Hollenbeck Conner, *Lincoln in Stafford* (Stafford, VA: Parker Publishing, 2006), 13.

37. FFCWF, File 3, "Opposite Fredericksburg, May 13, 1862; Mason Locke Weems, *The Life of Washington*, Marcus Cunliffe, ed. (Cambridge: Harvard University Press, 1967), 3.

38. FFCWF, File 2, "Correspondence of the Herald, May 13, 1862"; File 2, Horace Currier, May 18, 1862.

39. John H. W. Stuckenberg, *I'm Surrounded by Methodists: The Diary of John H. W. Stuckenberg Chaplain of the 145th Pennsylvania Volunteer Infantry*, David Hedrick and Gordon Barry Davis Jr, eds. (Gettysburg, PA: Thomas Publications, 1995), 55.

40. FFCWF, File 2, "Correspondence of the Herald," May 13, 1862; FFCWF, File 2, "Letters of the Seventh Wisconsin," May 15, 1862, FFCWF, File 2, "Civil War Letters"; FFCWF, George Brayton, Sunday May 11, 1862; S. Millett Thompson, *A Diary Covering Three Years and a Day* (Boston: Houghton Mifflin, 1888), 39.

41. S. Millett Thompson, *A Diary Covering Three Years and a Day* (Boston: Houghton Mifflin, 1888), 94.

42. Ibid., 68.

43. FFCWF, File 4, p. 7.

44. FFCWF, File 3, "from the Second Wis. Regiment," May 26, 1862.

45. FFCWF, File 3, "Camp Opposite Fredericksburg," May 21, 1862.

46. FFCWF, File 3, May 19, 1862.

47. FFCWF, File 3, "from the Second Wis. Regiment," May 26, 1862.

6. Mary Washington's Grave and the "Terrible Advertisement"

1. "A Card," *Free Lance,* Fredericksburg, VA, 3-12-1889. The *Free Lance* hereafter cited as FL.

2. Jane Hewett, ed., *The Roster of Confederate Soldiers, 1861–1865,* reprint (Wilmington, NC: Broadfoot Publishing, 1996).

3. Sue Gordon, ed., *WPA Virginia Historical Inventory*, 3 volumes (Fredericksburg, VA, 1937), 2:160–162.

4. The full body of court case documents that make up the bulk of this chapter's evidence are collected in the Fredericksburg Circuit Court Archive Annex in Fredericksburg, Virginia. The papers are organized by author and by case as well, making them something of an organizational challenge and difficult to cite. I have collected copies of all of the relevant papers and placed them in the Ferry Farm archive in four files. Some documents are long and paginated depositions or transcriptions, while others are single sheets either added to case files or admitted as evidence. My citations reflect that order and document naming. As best as records allow, I have used recognizable document names and their own page numbers. Where such are unavailable or unclear, I have fallen back on the Ferry Farm file numbers. The copied files at Ferry Farm are labeled as the Mary Washington Monument Case files (MWM). The rest of the material are hereafter cited as Fredericksburg Circuit Court Records (FCCR) Colbert and Kirtley vs. Shepherd (CK v S). MWM Case File 2 p52. FCCR CK v S.

5. FCCR CK v S, Court Transcript, 16.

6. FCCR CK v S, Transcript Second Iteration, 7.

7. FCCR CK v S, Record 13.

8. FCCR CK v S, Court Transcript, 18.

9. Ibid.

10. FCCR CK v S, March 1891, Review, 4.

11. FCCR CK v S, Court Transcript, 21.

12. FCCR CK v S, Court Transcript, 18.

13. "Much Ado About Nothing," *The Fredericksburg Star*, March 2, 1889, 2.

14. FCCR CK v S, Court Records, File 3.

15. "Mary Washington's Grave," *Free Lance*, March 5, 1889, 1.

16. Charles W. Calhoun, *Minority Victory: Gilded Age Politics and the Front Porch Campaign of 1888* (Laurence: University of Kansas, 2008).

17. *Washington Post*, April 30, 1889, 4.

18. Ibid., 4
19. *Free Lance,* March 5, 1889, 1.
20. Ibid.
21. Ibid.
22. FCCR CK v S, Court Transcript, 12.
23. "Mary Washington's Monument to Be Sold at Public Auction—Oh! The Shame of It," *Free Lance*, March 1, 1889, clipping in FCCR CK v S.
24. "A Card," *The Fredericksburg Star*, March 9, 1889, clipping in FCCR CK v S, "Exhibit 5."
25. " A Card to the Pubic," *Free Lance*, March 12, 1889, clipping in FCCR CK v S.
26. Ibid.
27. Ibid.
28. Ibid.
29. *The Fredericksburg Star*, January 11, 1890, 3.
30. *The Fredericksburg Star*, January 18, 1890, 3.
31. Ibid.
32. Ibid.
33. Ibid.
34. Ibid.
35. Ibid.
36. Ibid.
37. Ibid.
38. "There May Be a Duel," *The World*, January 20, 1890, in FFCR CK v S, newspaper clippings.
39. *The Fredericksburg Star*, January 25, 1890, 3.
40. Ibid.
41. Ibid.
42. *The Fredericksburg Star*, January 22, 1890, 3.
43. Ibid.
44. *The Fredericksburg Star*, January 25, 1890, 3.
45. FCCR CK v S, Record B.
46. "Colbert and Kirtley vs. Shepherd," *Report of Cases Decided in the Supreme Court of Appeals of Virginia*, 89: 52, 1893, 416–417.
47. Ibid., 250.
48. Hetzel, *The Building of a Monument*, 25.
49. http://books.google.com/books?id=vZ8dAQAAIAAJ&pg=PA1202&lpg=PA1202&dq =dredging+the+rappahannock&source=bl&ots=aCsENQ8B0c&sig=8ML5nRBX4y 8FF5-UVQwGU-sqxNY&hl=en&ei=8SbLTpPbONSDtgev28iZAQ&sa=X&oi=book _result&ct=result&resnum=5&ved=0CDQQ6AEwBA#v=onepage&q=dredging %20the%20rappahannock&f=false
50. "The Monument to Mary Washington," *Harper's Bazaar* 27 (May 19, 1894), 399.
51. Hetzel, *The Building of a Monument*, 58–59.
52. *The Fredericksburg Star*, April 24, 1890, 3.

7. The Farmer and the Bicentennial

1. *Free Lance,* September 7, 1909, 6.
2. *Fredericksburg Daily Star*, September 7, 1903, 3.
3. "Colbert to England," *Gressitt v. Colbert*, Stafford County Courthouse, Stafford, Virginia, Gressitt v. Colbert Case File. This decadelong set of lawsuits created a large and confused record. The whole pile of documents is in a drawer at the Stafford County Courthouse. My reconstruction of Colbert's farm and business comes from the evidence in these files and in some court cases in the Fredericksburg Circuit Court.
4. These photographs are all donations to the Ferry Farm collection. A few are collected in scrapbooks, most have been digitized. Norma Polley also donated a set of photographs from the 1980s and 1970s. Apart from her, the donors are unknown. The photographs and postcards I discuss are all in this collection.
5. Joseph Dillaway Sawyer, *Washington*, volume 1 (New York: Macmillan, 1927), 78–79.
6. "George Washington Surveying Office," Report, Drafting, and Photographs, 1935, Historic American Building Survey, Library of Congress Prints and Photographs Division, Washington, D.C.
7. *The Washington Post*, May 10, 1925, 4. England has not only his own literature, but a small literature about him. See: Philip Levy, "'The Most Exotic of Our Cities': Race, Place, Writing, and George Allan England's Key West," *Florida Historical Quarterly* (April 2011), 431–461, and Mark Pittinger, "Imagining Genocide in the Progressive Era: The Socialist Science Fiction of George Allan England," *American Studies* 35:1 (1994): 91–108. James Lindgren, *Preserving the Old Dominion: Historical Preservation and Virginia Traditionalism* (Charlottesville: University of Virginia Press, 1993).
8. *Portland Sunday Herald*, 1925. A faded photocopy of this article hides in the records of the Kenmore Association in Fredericksburg, Virginia. The paper seems to have only existed for a year and I have not been able to locate a proper copy. As the lone photocopy lacks the full date and page number, I cite it as above.
9. His papers appear lost, but there were some choice biographical details in some interviews and of course in his obituary. "George A. England, Explorer, 59, Dead," *New York Times,* June 28, 1936, N 8. Stranger though is a typewritten unpublished essay entitled "George Allan England—Writer, Linguist, and Sportsman," September 16, 1981, which resides in the Collections of the Woodstock Historical Society, Woodstock, Maine. I thank Larry McBride there for sharing the essay with me.
10. Sol Bloom, *The Autobiography of Sol Bloom* (New York: G. P. Putnam's Sons, 1948), 215.
11. Ibid., 136–137.
12. George Allan England, "Plea for Preservation," *The Washington Post,* November 1, 1925, E2.
13. George Allan England, "Washington's Old Home Farm," *Daughters of the American Revolution Magazine* 59:12 (December, 1925), 737.
14. George Allan England, "Plea for Preservation," *The Washington Post*, November 1, 1925, E2.

15. George Allan England, "Washington's Old Home Farm," *Daughters of the American Revolution Magazine* 59:12 (December, 1925), 738.

16. Ibid., 740.

17. Ibid., 742.

18. Ibid., 742.

19. George Allan England, "Washington's Home," *The New York Times*, January 2, 1926, 12.

20. Ibid., 12.

21. *Colbert v. Gressitt*, "Depositions," Stafford County Courthouse, Stafford, Virginia. My reconstruction of this deal relies on the lawsuits that happened when it all fell apart. The records for all of this are in the large file called "Colbert v. Gressitt," Stafford County Courthouse, Stafford County, Virginia.

22. James Lindgren, *Preserving the Old Dominion*.

23. Seth Bruggeman, *Here George Washington Was Born: Memory, Material Culture, and the Public History of a National Monument* (Athens: University of Georgia Press, 2008).

24. "Sol Bloom to John C. Fitzpatrick, June 2, 1930," Henry Woodhouse Collection, Library of Congress, Washington, D.C.

25. "Jonce McGurk to Charles Arthur Hoppin," Correspondence, February 10, 1932, Hoppin, Box 1 Folder 6, WA Papers, George Washington Birthplace National Monument, Westmoreland, Virginia.

26. "F. Dumont Smith to Charles Arthur Hoppin," Correspondence, August 1, 1932, Hoppin, Box 1 Folder 10, WA Papers, George Washington Birthplace National Monument, Westmoreland, Virginia.

27. "Jonce McGurk to Charles Arthur Hoppin," Correspondence, February 10, 1932, Hoppin, Box 1 Folder 6, WA Papers, George Washington Birthplace National Monument, Westmoreland, Virginia.

28. "F. Dumont Smith to Charles Arthur Hoppin," Correspondence, August 1, 1932, Hoppin, Box 1 Folder 10, WA Papers, George Washington Birthplace National Monument, Westmoreland, Virginia.

29. "Charles Arthur Hoppin to Mrs. H. L. Rust," Correspondence, April 5, 1928, Hoppin, Box 1 Folder 3, WA Papers, George Washington Birthplace National Monument, Westmoreland, Virginia.

30. Charles Arthur Hoppin, "The House in Which George Washington Was Born," *Tyler's Quarterly Historial and Genealogical Magazine* 8:2 (October 1926), 75.

31. Ibid.

32. "Hoppin to Rust," April 5, 1928, Wakefield National Memorial Association, "Ferry Farm, 1928–1940," Box 2, Folder 3. Thanks to Seth Bruggeman for the Hoppin deafness anecdote.

33. "Hoppin to E. L. McClain Estate," Jan. 25, 1938, WA Papers, Correspondence, 1921–1938, Box 4, Folder 10.

34. Colbert to England, May 25, 1929, *Gressitt v. Colbert,* Stafford County Courthouse, Stafford County, Virginia.

35. *Free Lance-Star*, January 6, 1931, 1.

36. Ibid., 1.

37. Ibid., 6.

38. Sol Bloom, *The Autobiography of Sol Bloom* (New York: G. P. Putnam's Sons, 1948), 217.

39. "James B. Colbert Dies Suddenly," *Free Lance-Star,* April 27, 1931, 1.

8. From Weems to Walmart

1. "Washington's Home as Boy Will Be Put Up at Auction," *The New York Times*, February 3, 1940, 12.

2. "Washington's Early Home Sold as Public Ignores Auction, *Sunday Star*, Washington, D.C., February 4, 1940. Ferry Farm Clippings File.

3. Ibid.

4. "George Only 'Barked' Tree But Did Chop Pea Sticks," *The Washington Post*, February 23, 1946, 4.

5. "Colbert Estate," *Colbert v. Gressit*, Case Files, Stafford County Court, Stafford, Virginia.

6. "Group Organized to Restore Boyhood Home of Washington," *The Washington Post*, February 14, 1946, 7.

7. *The Washington Post,* June 6, 1958, a17.

8. "Information and Work Plan for the George Washington Boys' Home (GWBH)," Archives of the Billy Graham Center, Wheaton, Illinois (ABGC), George Washington Boys' Home Files, unpaginated report. These files are archived at the BGC, but a large copied portion of them are also filed at Ferry Farm thanks to a generous gift from Paul Millikin who worked on the 1960s project. As with such archives, most of the papers are reports, brochures, letters, and loosely sourced newspaper clippings lacking any overarching organizational system. Millikin also provided Ferry Farm with a trove of photographs and brochures from the boys' home as well as his own memories of the project and backers like Sidney King. My citations in this chapter try to capture as best as possible a usable traceable title for each cited document.

9. "Work Plan for GWBH," ABGC.

10. "Home Family Has Grown to 10," *Free Lance-Star*, February 16, 1968, 7.

11. "Work Plan for GWBH," ABGC.

12. William Lakeman, "Rezoning Sought for GWBH," *Free Lance-Star,* May 23, 1969, 12.

13. Paige Williams, "Stafford County Trying to Buy Washington's Boyhood Home," *The Washington Post*, August 11, 1988, 12.

14. Jonathan Yardley, "Preservationists Are Barking Up the Wrong Cherry Tree," *The Washington Post*, March 18, 1996, D02. Q5.

15. Samuel P. and Irma Warren Deeds, Deed Books, 1970 to 1991, Stafford County Courthouse, Stafford, Virginia.

16. Alice Digilio, "Public Gets Washington Boyhood Farmplot on Rappahannock with House Foundation Given to Stafford," *The Washington Post,* January 3, 1990, d.05.

17. "Couple's Gift and a Public Gain, *Free Lance-Star*, January 5, 1990, 14; Ted Byrd, "Ferry Farm Deal Cemented," *Free Lance-Star,* March 21, 1990, 18.

18.	"Couple's Gift a Public Gain, *Free Lance-Star,* January 5, 1990, 14; Jim Clardy, "Arlington Couple Gives In, Donates Washington Boyhood Site," *Washington Times,* January 3, 1990, B2.

19.	Ted Byrd, "Ferry Farm Deal Cemented," *Free Lance-Star,* March 21, 1990, 1.

20.	Ibid., 1–4.

21.	My principal sources for information about Siegrist are his own files at Ferry Farm, Fredericksburg, Virginia, and discussions with people who knew him at the time. Alan Outlaw was hired by Siegrist to conduct Ferry Farm's excavations and offered a wonderful glimpse of the man over lunch at an academic conference. Also, Norma Polley was a member of local D.A.R. and was active in Ferry Farm's preservation. She shared many vivid memories of Siegrist and also had a photo album including images of the Colbert house right after it burned down. Some of Polley's stories have been transcribed at Ferry Farm.

22.	Maria Carrillo, "Stafford Given Part of Ferry Farm, Negotiates for Rest," *Free Lance-Star*, January 3, 1990, 14.

23.	"Man with a Vision," *Town and Country, Free Lance-Star,* October 9, 1999, 9–11.

24.	"Siegrist to Schlafly," February 18, 1992. Ferry Farm Stafford Folders. "Outgoing Correspondence, 1992–1993."

25.	Ibid.

26.	Keith Epps and Jim Hall, "Ferry Farm House Burns," *Free Lance-Star,* September 26, 1994, 1.

27.	Jim Hall, "Protecting the Past," *Free Lance-Star,* April 1, 1995, B 5.

28.	*The Washington Post*, February 25, 1995, F18.

29.	"History of Wal-Mart Ferry Farm Deal Traced," *Stafford County Sun*, August 28/29, 1996, A13.

30.	Ibid., A13.

31.	Michael Wallace, *Mickey Mouse History and Other Essays on American Memory* (Philadelphia: Temple University Press, 1996).

32.	Michael Janofsky, "Protesters Fight a Plan for Washington's Home," *The New York Times*, March 13, 1996, A 12.

33.	"What's Buried at Ferry Farm, *Free Lance-Star*, March 2, 1996, A 10.

34.	"History of Wal-Mart Ferry Farm Deal Traced," *Stafford County Sun*, August 26, 1996, A13.

35.	"Is Ferry Farm a 'Pipe Dream'"? *Free Lance-Star,* March 4, 1996, A 6.

36.	Maryann Haggerty, "First in War, First in Peace—Next in Wal-Mart," *The Washington Post*, March 7, 1996, A1.

37.	Ibid.

38.	Christine Neuberger, "Wal-Mart Sticking to Plan as Decision Is Delayed," *Richmond Times- Dispatch,* March 12, 1996, B3.

39.	Rusty Dennen, "Wal-Mart Battle Over Ferry Farm Site Recalled," *Free Lance-Star,* July 5, 2008. Digital article reposted online at Fredericksburg.com.

40.	Michael Janofsky, "Protesters Fight Plan for Washington's Home," *New York Times,* March 13, 1996, A 12.

41. "History of Wal-Mart Ferry Farm Deal Traced," *Stafford County Sun*, August 28/29, 1996, A13.

9. The Land Tells Its Story

1. We have many wonderful examples to look to when building an approach to the field and how to make sense of findings. Some of the best historical archaeological scholarship includes: James Deetz, *In Small Things Forgotten: An Archaeology of Early American Life* (New York: Anchor Press/Doubleday, 1977); James Deetz, *Flowerdew Hundred: The Archaeology of a Virginia Plantation, 1619–1864* (Charlottesville: University of Virginia, 1993); Mary C. Beaudry, *Findings: The Material Culture of Needlework and Sewing* (New Haven and London: Yale University Press, 2007); Stephen A. Mrozowski, Grace H. Ziesing, and Mary C. Beaudry, *Living on the Boott: Historical Archaeology at the Boott Mills Boardinghouses, Lowell, Massachusetts* (Amherst: University of Massachusetts Press, 1996); Anne Elizabeth Yentsch, *A Chesapeake Family and Their Slaves: A Study in Historical Archaeology* (Cambridge: Cambridge University Press, 1994); Rebecca Yamin and Karen Beschere Metheny, *Landscape Archaeology: Reading Interpreting American Historical Landscapes* (Knoxville: University of Tennessee Press, 1996); Matthew Johnson, *An Archaeology of Capitalism* (Hoboken, NJ: Wiley-Blackwell, 1996); Barbara J. Little, *Historical Archaeology: Why the Past Matters* (Walnut Creek, CA: Left Coast Press, 2007); Barbara J. Heath and Jack Gary, *Jefferson's Popular Forest: Unearthing a Virginia Plantation* (Gainesville: University of Florida Press, 2012); Julia A. King, *Archaeology, Narrative, and the Politics of the Past: The View from Southern Maryland* (Knoxville: University of Tennessee Press, 2012); Leeland Ferguson, *Uncommon Ground: Archeology and Early African America, 1650–1800* (Washington, D.C.: Smithsonian Books, 2004); Rebecca Yamin, *Digging in the City of Brotherly Love: Stories from Philadelphia Archaeology* (New Haven and London: Yale University Press, 2008); Stephen A. Mrozowski, *The Archaeology of Class in Urban America* (Cambridge: Cambridge University Press, 2012); Susan Kern, *The Jeffersons at Shadwell* (New Haven and London: Yale University Press, 2012); Dan Hicks and Mary C. Beaudry, eds., *The Cambridge Companion to Historical Archaeology* (Cambridge: Cambridge University Press, 2006). The following narrative, however, is based on my own memories, discussions, and of course the many site reports prepared by David Muraca, Paul Nasca, and myself.

2. Jack Warren, "The Childhood of George Washington," *The Northern Neck of Virginia Historical Magazine* 49:1 (1999): 5790–5791; "Robert Douglas to George Washington," May 25, 1795, George Washington Papers, Library of Congress; Conway, *Barons of the Potomac and Rappahannock*, 68–69; Humphries, *Life of General Washington*.

3. "Information and Direction to Such Persons as Are Inclined to America, More Especially Those Related to the Province of Pennsylvania," Original printing 1682, author unknown, *The Pennsylvania Magazine of History and Biography* 4:3 (1880), 335. See

also: Carson et al., "Impermanent Architecture in the Southern American Colonies," and Johnson, *English Houses 1300–1800.*

10. The Truth About the Cherry Tree

1. Arthur H. Merritt, "Did Parson Weems Really Invent the Cherry Tree?" *New-York Historical Society Quarterly* 40:3 (July 1956), 258.
2. Ibid., 260.
3. Ibid., 261.
4. Henry Cabot Lodge, *George Washington, in Two Volumes* (Boston: Houghton Mifflin, 1899) 1:10–11.
5. Merritt, "Did Parson Weems Really Invent the Cherry Tree?," 261.
6. Joseph Rodman, "The Hatchet and the Cherry Tree," *The Critic,* February 1904, 44, 2.
7. Merritt, "Did Parson Weems Really Invent the Cherry Tree?," 261.
8. http://www.gostaffordva.com/George-Washingtons-Boyhood-Home.cfm.
9. Warren, "The Childhood of George Washington," 5785–5809.
10. S. Millett Thompson, *A Diary Covering Three Years and a Day* (Boston: Houghton Mifflin, 1888), 68.
11. Alexander Milliner, printed digitally at Americanrevolution.org, http://www.american revolution.org/last%20men/lastmen4.html.
12. Charles Willson Peale, recounting an incident of 1772, as quoted in *Recollections and Private Memoirs of Washington,* Benson J. Lossing, ed. (New York: Derby and Jackson, 1860), 483.
13. Weems, *Life of Washington,* 17.
14. George Washington Parke Custis, *Reflections and Private Memoirs of Washington* (New York: Derby and Jackson, 1860), 482.

Index

❧

mL   3-13